About the authors:

Of the past decade, Karen and Terry Whitehill have spent almost three full years exploring European roads by foot and by bicycle, covering more than 20,000 self-propelled miles in the process. When they first set foot on European soil in 1984, they were travel "rookies" with little experience or knowledge in the field of European adventuring. A year of "learning by doing" yielded the first edition of *Europe by Bike*. In between European jaunts, their trips to California's Sierra Nevada mountains produced two guidebooks, *Best Short Hikes in California's Northern Sierra* and *Best Short Hikes in California's Southern Sierra*, for The Mountaineers. Daughter Sierra Jo, born in 1989, followed them for 6000 miles in a bright green bicycle trailer on their recent trip to update *Europe by Bike* and write *France by Bike*. When the Whitehills are not traveling, they reside in Portland, Oregon.

■ ■ ■

The MOUNTAINEERS, founded in 1906, is a nonprofit outdoor activity and conservation club, whose mission is "to explore, study, preserve, and enjoy the natural beauty of the outdoors...." Based in Seattle, Washington, the club is now the third-largest such organization in the United States, with 15,000 members and five branches throughout Washington State.

The Mountaineers sponsors both classes and year-round outdoor activities in the Pacific Northwest, which include hiking, mountain climbing, ski-touring, snowshoeing, bicycling, camping, kayaking and canoeing, nature study, sailing, and adventure travel. The club's conservation division supports environmental causes through educational activities, sponsoring legislation, and presenting informational programs. All club activities are led by skilled, experienced volunteers, who are dedicated to promoting safe and responsible enjoyment and preservation of the outdoors.

The Mountaineers Books, an active, nonprofit publishing program of the club, produces guidebooks, instructional texts, historical works, natural history guides, and works on environmental conservation. All books produced by The Mountaineers are aimed at fulfilling the club's mission.

If you would like to participate in these organized outdoor activities or the club's programs, consider a membership in The Mountaineers. For information and an application, write or call The Mountaineers, Club Headquarters, 300 Third Avenue West, Seattle, Washington 98119; (206) 284-6310.

Send or call for our catalog of more than 300 outdoor books:
The Mountaineers Books
1001 SW Klickitat Way, Suite 201
Seattle, WA 98134
1-800-553-4453

Other books you may enjoy from The Mountaineers:

Europe by Bike, 2nd Edition: 18 Tours Geared for Discovery, Whitehill. Detailed, point-to-point information on bicycling in England, Sweden, Denmark, Belgium, Holland, Germany, France, Austria, Greece, Italy, Spain, and Portugal.

England by Bike: 18 Tours Geared for Discovery, Woodland. Day trips and longer tours to all corners of England, with three trips into Wales. Written by a native Briton for American cyclists. Pre-trip and access information, finding accommodations, road habits, and more.

Germany by Bike: 20 Tours Geared for Discovery, Slavinski. Tours through Germany's quiet countryside range from 76 to 281 miles in length. Includes tips on finding campsites, food, and lodging.

New Zealand by Bike, 2nd Edition, Ringer. Guide to North and South Islands includes how-to- and where-to information for 14 tours, plus trip planning, accommodations, and more.

Bicycling the Atlantic Coast: A Complete Route Guide, Florida to Maine, Aitkenhead. The only complete touring guide to the East Coast. Covers road conditions, where to buy provisions, camping, and points of interest, plus daily mileage logs and maps.

Bicycling the Pacific Coast, 3rd Edition: A Complete Road Guide, Canada to Mexico, Kirkendall & V. Spring. Classic touring guide covers road conditions, availability of provisions, accessible campgrounds, and points of interest. Detailed daily mileage logs, elevation profiles, and maps.

Bicycling the Backroads Series. Details, maps, and mileage logs for numerous tours. Series includes *Bicycling the Backroads Around Puget Sound, 4th Edition,* Woods. *Bicycling the Backroads of Northwest Washington, 4th Edition,* Woods. *Bicycling the Backroads of Southwest Washington, 3rd Edition,* Woods. *Bicycling the Backroads of Northwest Oregon, 2nd Edition,* Jones & Henderson.

Available from your local book or outdoor store, or from The Mountaineers Books, 1001 SW Klickitat Way, Suite 201, Seattle, WA 98134. Or call for a catalog of over 300 outdoor books: 1-800-553-4453.

FRANCE
BY BIKE
14 TOURS GEARED FOR DISCOVERY

FRANCE
BY BIKE
14 TOURS GEARED FOR DISCOVERY

Karen and Terry Whitehill

THE MOUNTAINEERS

For Rocky Roi Whitehill—our most treasured souvenir of France

© 1993 by Karen and Terry Whitehill

First edition: first printing 1993, second printing 1995, third printing 1997, fourth printing 1999

Published by The Mountaineers
1001 SW Klickitat Way, Suite 201, Seattle, Washington 98134

Published simultaneously in Great Britain by Cordee, 3a DeMontfort Street, Leicester, England, LE1 7HD

Manufactured in the United States of America

Edited by Heath Silberfeld
Maps by Newell Cartographics
All photographs by the authors
Cover design by Watson Graphics
Book design by Bridget Culligan Design
Book layout by Ann Amberg

Cover photograph: Châteauneuf, France
Frontispiece: The rounded towers and spire-topped church of Semur-en-Auxois invite exploration.

Library of Congress Cataloging in Publication Data
Whitehill, Karen.
    France by bike: 14 tours geared for discovery / Karen and Terry Whitehill.
        p.   cm.
    Includes index.
    ISBN 0-89886-316-3
    1, Bicycle touring--France--Guidebooks. 2. France--Guidebooks.
I. Whitehill, Terry, 1954–   . II. Title.
GV1046.F8W47   1993
796.6'4'0944--dc20   92-43043
                                                   CIP

Printed on recycled paper with soy-based inks

CONTENTS

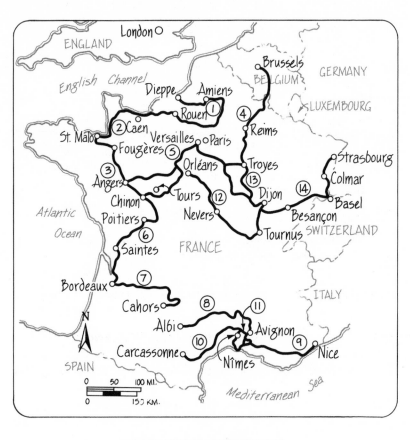

The view from a hotel room on Tournus's main square

PREFACE

As authors of two previous books about our travels on the roads and pathways of Europe, we were faced with a difficult decision as we anticipated returning to Europe with our bicycles in 1991. We knew we would spend a great deal of time retracing old routes and checking out new ones for the pages of a second edition of our first book, *Europe by Bike—18 Tours Geared for Discovery*. But our publisher, The Mountaineers, had also asked us to complete research on a new volume, a one-country European cycling guide. But which country? That was largely up to us.

In the two years and 15,000 miles' worth of Europe we'd experienced so far, we had lots of favorite places—the exquisitely beautiful hillsides of Greece, the lush vineyards of northern Italy, the history-rich roadways of Spanish Galicia. We had lots of favorite foods—the buttery *croissants* of France, the warm *böreks* of Turkey, the *pytt i panna* we'd sampled in Sweden. And we had lots of friends, too—an adopted grandmother in Germany, an athletic family in England, assorted cyclists and hikers, farmers and engineers, grape growers and computer experts, scattered over fifteen European countries.

But where did we want to spend several months pedaling and writing this time around? What country did we want to know better than any country in Europe? And what country did we want our two-year-old daughter Sierra to camp in, eat in, play in, and—most importantly—safely ride the roads in her bright green bike trailer for the many months and thousands of miles ahead of us? The answer wasn't difficult to find: France.

In our opinion, there is no better country in Europe for cycling than France. The small roads of France are a cyclist's dream—smooth pavement, lovely surroundings, and very little traffic. Maps are excellent and route finding is easy, so there's no reason to grit it out on busy roads for hours at a time. Instead, one can escape France's truck-plagued major thoroughfares to find curving, quiet riverside roads or straight-arrow lanes through rolling fields, where only tractor drivers pause to wave and groups of barn-bound cows cause brief delays.

French food is delicious and affordable, and French bakeries are unsurpassed. Hotels here span a wide range of luxuries and costs, fitting the needs of almost every traveler, and the campground system is among the best in Europe. Besides being well fed and well housed, the visitor to France will be satiated by a wealth of tourist sights, ranging from soaring Gothic cathedrals to fairy-tale *châteaux* to treasure-packed museums. Natural scenery is varied and spectacular, as well.

Perhaps best of all, the French people, despite the bad reputation fostered by rude Parisian waiters, gruff subway clerks, and grim big-

Bicycles—in every shape and form—are French transportation at its best.

city businessmen, are delightfully hospitable and surprisingly friendly everywhere you go. And there is no better way to *go* in France than to go by bike.

A NOTE ABOUT SAFETY

The authors have provided important tips on bicycle safety in the introduction to this book. In addition, they and the publisher have taken all reasonable measures to ensure the accuracy of the route descriptions contained herein. Even so, bicycling entails certain unavoidable risks, and routes may have changed after this book was written. Current political conditions also may add to the risks of travel in Europe in ways that this book cannot predict. For these reasons, the descriptions in this book are not guarantees that a particular trip will be safe for you or your party. When you take a trip, you assume responsibility for your own safety. Keeping informed about current road conditions, weather changes, and political developments, and utilizing your common sense, are keys to a safe, enjoyable tour.

The Mountaineers

PART I

FRANCE BY BIKE

France offers its visitors a visual feast—from every angle.

WHY CHOOSE FRANCE?

France and bicycles—the two words just seem to go together, don't they? And anyone who has done much bicycle touring in this beautiful, varied, and uncrowded country will tell you, "France and bicycles are a perfect match!" French roads are among the best in Europe. The secondary road system is excellent, with well-maintained surfaces, light traffic, courteous drivers, and surprisingly direct routes. While planning our tours here, we often found that our "sacrifice" in using the small French roads instead of the major ones actually resulted in fewer kilometers to pedal rather than more.

Sure, the French drivers routinely travel at suicidal speeds, and you'll be shocked by the "rockets" that catapult past you during your first days on French roads. But you'll also be delighted by the consistent, careful courtesy extended to cyclists here.

We especially love to tell the story of the time we were forced to ride a few kilometers on a traffic-heavy main road. Trucks were flying past us at a steady rate, and oncoming cars sometimes made it a tight squeeze. Yet, despite the narrow shoulder, all of the drivers that passed us somehow allowed an ample distance between their bumpers and our bikes—so ample, in fact, that one truck driver simply straddled the center line and shoved a group of approaching cars right off the pavement on our behalf. Were they angry? You bet! They all shook their fists at each other as they rattled past—then they gave us cheerful shrugs and smiles in their rearview mirrors as they sped away!

Cycling in France will open doors for you that other tourists never find. The French are sports-minded people. They excel in rock climbing, kayaking, hiking, and cycling. And they have a natural affection for travelers who choose to see their vast and varied country in a sporting way—not from the window of a blurred and speeding train, not from the seat of a stuffy tour bus, not from behind the wheel of a rented Renault—but from a bicycle.

A cyclist is exposed to the rain, pummeled by the wind, warmed by the sun. A cyclist is vulnerable. He is not a user, not a consumer—a cyclist is an experiencer. And a cyclist has chosen to experience France in a way that is infinitely revered by the French people—from the seat of a bicycle. As such, a cyclist is open to experience the unassuming friendliness and spontaneous love of life that make the French people a delight.

In the years we've spent exploring France, we've been invited into the homes of dairy farmers, computer programmers, teachers, and grape growers. We've been given directions, stuffed with homemade *crêpes*, provided with beds, had our chains lubricated, our water bottles filled, and our bicycles repaired—the list goes on and on. We've

The French people are delightfully friendly and helpful.

even had days in France when we tried our hardest *not* to meet people, and we still met them.

We'll never forget the night we spent—or tried to spend—near a soccer field in a tiny town in Normandy. We'd pedaled 40 miles into the wind that day, and we were totally exhausted. We put up our tent in a city park and crawled inside it to collapse. That's when seven French schoolchildren showed up to admire our bicycles. Thirty minutes later, despite our protests, despite our weariness, and despite our escalating embarrassment, we had packed up our tent, loaded our bikes, and followed a blaring moped escort through the streets of town. One boy's parents met us with smiles and open arms at their front door. The mother filled a bathtub. The father showed us our beds. We "talked" with hand signals and a pocket dictionary until well after 11:00 P.M. In short, *vive la France!*

PLANNING YOUR TRIP

Begin with a good general book on travel in France. *Let's Go: France* (Harvard Student Agencies) and *The Real Guide: France* by Kate Baillie and Tim Salmon (Prentice-Hall) are excellent choices. They provide general information on getting to Europe, in addition to specific details on France. If you've never visited Europe before, glance through *Europe Through the Back Door* (John Muir Press) by Rick Steves, too. Although these books are essentially designed for train travelers, they will provide you with more of the information pertinent to general European travel than we can present in this book. Just to get you started, though, here's a brief summary of the most important things to do.

PASSPORTS AND VISAS. If you don't have a passport for international travel, you should apply for one at least two or three months in advance of your departure date. At peak times, the application process can take several weeks. Go to a passport agency or U.S. Post Office. Once you get your passport, photocopy the pages that show the date and place of issue, passport number, and your name. Leave one photocopy at home with someone you can contact from Europe, and take one copy with you, stored separately from your passport. This will help ensure a quick replacement if the passport is lost or stolen.

At the current time, no visa is required for American, Canadian, or British citizens entering France. Check with the passport office or with your travel agent to be sure.

OTHER DOCUMENTS. If you're a full-time student, be sure to check into obtaining an International Student Identification Card (ISIC) for your trip. This card could entitle you to major savings on your plane flight to Europe, as well as discounts on museum admissions, transportation, and many other things you'll be spending money for once you're there. You'll need to show proof of student status, age, and nationality to get the card, and you'll be asked to provide a passport-type photo and a small fee. Check at a Council Travel office or write to the Council on International Educational Exchange, 205 East 42nd Street, New York, New York 10017.

Another document that will come in handy if you're planning to camp as you cycle is an International Camping Carnet. Although French campgrounds vary in regard to the amount and type of identification they require, with registration policies ranging from a first name and a smile to a passport and fifteen minutes of paperwork, the camping carnet is a widely accepted document. We found our carnet to be an excellent piece of identification to hand over at both camping offices and hotels when we didn't want to part with our passports—for instance, when we needed them for banking or mail pickup during the day. The International Camping Carnet is also good for slight discounts in some French campgrounds.

If you want to buy the carnet before you go, you'll need to purchase it through Family Campers and RVers, 4804 Transit Road, Building No. 2, Depew, New York 14043. The cost of about $35 includes membership, with associated privileges (organization magazine and equipment discounts). The financial outlay and paperwork involved in obtaining the carnet is probably only worth it if you'll be in France (or Europe) several weeks or months.

HEALTH INSURANCE. If you're taking a brief vacation from work or school to travel in France, you'll probably have health insurance already. But if you're giving up "normal" life (as we did on our first time over), with goodbyes to job, apartment, car, and related insurance policies, you may want to give serious thought to investing in special medical insurance for travelers.

Ask your travel agent about a policy that covers medical and hospital expenses, medical evacuations, repatriation of remains, baggage, and trip cancellation. He or she may be able to clue you in to a good deal.

Also, write to the International Association for Medical Assistance to Travelers, 417 Center Street, Lewiston, New York 14092, or 40 Regal Road, Guelph, Ontario, Canada N1K1B5. A free membership (donations are eagerly accepted) in this nonprofit organization will provide you with the names of English-speaking physicians throughout France, and in more than 400 cities throughout the world. Associated doctors have agreed to serve English-speaking patients at fair prices.

Fortunately, we've had to call on European doctors only infrequently during the almost three years we've spent traveling here—an infection in southern France, a tumble (with resultant stitches) in Holland, a skin problem in Germany—and we've found medical treatment to be fast, efficient, and reasonable. However, medical costs are probably not part of your anticipated traveling budget, and you may not receive treatment without putting cash up front. Take a look at the Money section, under "What to Take,"to find out about different ways of obtaining emergency cash abroad.

One note of advice—before you head for France, be sure you've had a tetanus booster within the past seven years. It's unpleasant enough to endure a puncture wound, a nasty cut, or several unplanned stitches while you're on a trip. Why add the discomfort of an inoculation, too?

HOSTELS. Because it's most convenient and least expensive to obtain a hostel card in your home country, we've placed our hostel information in this "advance planning" section of the book. If you're thinking of using hostels as one of your accommodations options in France, you'll need to get an International Youth Hostel Federation card before you go.

As a married couple with a toddler in tow, we did our best to avoid the segregated lodgings and noisy surroundings common to most hostels, but there were a few times when, stuck without a campground or an affordable hotel, we wished we'd had a card. Even if you plan to camp almost exclusively (as we did), many French hostels will allow cardholders to set up their tents on the grounds—often for a much-reduced fee. And on occasion you may prefer the hostel's location over that of a city's campground.

Check your city telephone directory under "American Youth Hostels" to find a local office where you can purchase your card, or write to American Youth Hostels, 733 15th Street NW, Suite 840, Washington, D.C. 20005; the Canadian Hostelling Association, 400-205 Catherine Street, Ottawa, Ontario, Canada K2P 1C3; or the Youth Hostels Association, Treveleyan House, 8 St. Stephens Hill, St. Albans AL1 2DY, Great Britain.

There are more than 200 official hostels in France. A hostel is called an *auberge de jeunesse* there, and these budget lodgings usually cost much less than a hotel room. However, if you're traveling with a companion and don't mind doubling up in cheap hotels, you'll find the price difference shrinks considerably. There is really no overall rule about French hostels—some are wonderful, some are real stinkers. Talk to other travelers or check out the facilities before you pay. These are simple survival tactics you'll soon master, especially if you hope to sleep affordably, comfortably, and well.

RESEARCH. Another worthwhile task to spend time and postage on before you begin your trip is to write in advance to the French National Tourist Office, 444 Madison Avenue, 16th Floor, New York, New York 10022. Don't forget to mention that you'll be cycling, camping (if you are), and visiting Paris (if you are). If you've already planned your tour, list the larger cities you'll be visiting. With any luck, the tourist office may be able to send you free city maps.

Once in France, be sure to make use of the local tourist offices to collect English-language literature. Offices in France are called *Office de Tourisme* or *Syndicat d'Initiative*. We found them to be invaluable sources of information on a wide variety of subjects. "Where's the nearest bicycle shop? Is there a laundromat nearby? How do we find the campground?" The list goes on and on.

Often, regional offices are stocked with informative English-language pamphlets and excellent city maps. Always try to think ahead—any city maps you can obtain in advance will be a blessing later, as there's nothing worse than riding into a large city without an adequate map. If you do get to a tourist office in a big city and still don't have a map of town, one sure way to get a free map is to ask directions to the city campground. Nine times out of ten, your benefactor will whip out a wonderful map that extends all the way to the suburbs, scribble all over it (usually in red) while noting details of the route to the campground, and hand it over with a smile.

The regional campground listings (usually in booklet form) provided by French tourist offices are extremely helpful, too. Again, try to anticipate a week ahead of time where you'll be, and request a region's listing before or as you enter it. You may need a French tutor or a pocket dictionary to help you with translation the first time around (although some listings are printed in English and German, too), but many campground features are depicted with symbols.

Look for a road number or name to clue you in to the campground's location. A listed feature (e.g., on a river or near a swimming pool) may also help you find the place. It's best to have an idea where the campground is before you pedal into a city, as you may end up pedaling right back out the way you came in order to find it. French campground listings may or may not provide information on prices, but you'll find the majority of campgrounds rated from one to four stars, with the four-star facilities being most expensive.

One note of warning—the listed opening and closing dates for specific sites are not always accurate. If the weather is unseasonably wet or cold in September or May, for example, a caretaker at a little municipal campground may simply decide to close early or open late. Don't fight it—it's the French way! The good news is, we've camped at almost as many "closed" municipal campgrounds as open ones. As long as there's no fence to exclude you, and you seek permission from a neighbor (if you can), you probably won't have any trouble. Pick up your own garbage, resign yourself to a showerless night, and use the bathroom facilities in the village, if you can. Of course, you camp "unofficially" at your own risk. Our experience has been that most people simply walk by and smile. This, too, is the French way.

As with the campground listings, most French tourist offices offer detailed accommodations guides, too. Since hotels are classed from one to four stars in France, it should be relatively easy to select hotels in your price and comfort range before you begin to shop around. If you simply hate to hunt, make use of the accommodations services provided by many of the tourist offices in French cities. You'll need to pay a slight fee for the service, but it saves a lot of time and energy. (Be sure to have the person booking your room inform the hotelkeeper that you need a place for your bike.)

Undoubtedly, you'll want to learn more about the history, culture,

French maps are easy to use and affordable (baguettes *are, too!*).

and sights of France than this book can tell you, so get to know the travel shelves of your local bookstore or library before you go. Every minute you spend familiarizing yourself with the places you'll be visiting will enhance your appreciation for and understanding of the things you see. After nearly three years of traveling in Europe, we're firm believers in the benefits of knowing about places *before* we go, and in the joys of continuing to learn about them *while* we're there.

You'll probably want to carry at least one favorite travel guide with you on your trip. We've noted the titles of region-specific guidebooks with the tours in Part II. For overall coverage of France, the *Let's Go* and *Real Guide* (both mentioned earlier, both specific to France) are informative and helpful, especially to budget travelers who'll be scrambling for rooms, laundromats, inexpensive restaurants, and the like. These two volumes concentrate primarily on the more well-known tourist spots, however, and suffer from a paucity of information on the towns and villages in between.

An extensive, if somewhat dry and undeniably hefty, reference source for France is the Rand McNally *Blue Guide France*. You'll thumb through the index in back a hundred times if you pedal many miles here, and you'll be amazed at how many times you actually find the tiny town you're seeking. It's such a treat to know that the castle you're cycling past is "a notable Renaissance château in a spacious park," for example, and to discover that the church in the last town "is an admirable specimen of Romanesque architecture." Kind of helps you plan your day. . . .

Other guidebook options include *2 to 22 Days in France* by Rick Steves and Steve Smith, and Fodor's *Affordable France*. Our personal favorites for France are the Michelin series *Green Guides*. There is one overall guide, entitled *Green Guide France*, that is packed with useful information, but buy the regional volumes if you really want to do it right. These books are great for planning, and they're wonderful once you're there. They provide adequate city maps for the larger towns, and they're rich in information on regional history, cuisine, culture, and architecture. Perhaps best of all, they rate the sights on a zero- to three-star scale that's particularly helpful when you simply cannot see it all. (We'll warn you, though, if the Michelin guide gives something three stars for scenic beauty, you can be pretty sure you're about to work your tail off pedaling up a monster hill.)

Currently, ten of Michelin's twenty-four regional guides are offered in English. We've listed the English-language *Green Guides* applicable to each tour with the specific tour introductions in Part II.

MAPS. Rather than spend an incredible amount of money buying detailed maps of France at home, use the free map provided by the French National Tourist Office to help you with your planning and/or to do rough figuring of routes, times, and distances. Or purchase the excellent Michelin Map No. 989, covering the entire country at 1:1,000,000 scale, utilize it for planning purposes, then buy Michelin's 1:200,000 maps (or even more detailed ones) once you arrive in France. Maps are considerably less expensive in France than in the United States, so you'll save lots of money by waiting, if you're buying very many.

Again, if you'll be covering only a small area on your trip, you may want to go ahead and order your maps in advance to save you shopping time and "now where is that bookstore?" hassles. Be sure to take along a good map of the area you'll be arriving in. That way, you'll at least be able to get out of the airport and on your way without difficulty.

Michelin produces two excellent map series for route finding in France, and the 1:200,000 detail will satisfy all your needs. Maps in the Michelin forty-map series are easier to handle, as they're quite a bit smaller than those in the seventeen-map series. The smaller maps must be purchased more frequently, however. Maps in the seventeen-map series have the same scale and features and are fairly cost equivalent, covering larger regions for more *francs*. However, they do produce a plump map case. The best way to make your map decision is to study the Michelin display at a French bookstore to determine how your planned tour is best covered.

You'll also find a seventy-two-map series of France, published by the Institut Géographique National (IGN) at 1:100,000 scale. This added detail will cost you a bit more than the Michelins do, but you may find it a help to route finding. From our experience, however, the Michelin maps show every French road we've ever wanted to cycle, and they're easy to find and to use. Road maps are readily available in bookstores in France. If you're conserving *francs*, they're usually a bit cheaper at monster supermarkets, such as Hypermarché or Mammoth. Be sure to familiarize yourself with the legend of your map. Michelin offers an extensive array of symbols to aid the sight-seeking tourist, indicating châteaux, noteworthy churches, viewpoints, ruins, and so on. Michelin maps also highlight particularly scenic roadways with a paralleling green line. Campers should be forewarned that, although Michelin maps do show campgrounds, they show *only* campgrounds listed in the companion Michelin camping guide. Hundreds of existing campgrounds are *not* shown on the Michelin maps.

MAIL. We completed one more task during our pretrip planning that brought us a day of excitement and joy every three weeks throughout our ride. As we worked out our cycling routes, we compiled a list of cities, addresses, and tentative dates, choosing the best times and places to pick up mail from home. We distributed this list to families and friends, instructing them how to address the letters correctly and warning them to mail at least two weeks in advance of our pickup dates.

For pickup at French post offices via *Poste Restante* (general delivery), use the following address style: WHITEHILL, Terry, c/o *Poste Restante*, City Name, R.P. (*Recette Principale*), Postal Code (if you know it), FRANCE. *Poste Restante* mail should be picked up at the central post office in cities with more than one post office. You will be asked to show your passport as identification and pay a slight per-letter fee. (We've run up quite a bill at French post offices with this system and prefer to use American Express offices when possible.)

For American Express pickups (free if you have American Express travelers' checks), use this address style: WHITEHILL, Terry, Client

Letter Service, American Express, 11 rue Scribe, Paris, FRANCE. Ask for a list of American Express office addresses when you buy your checks (be sure to note that some offices are only affiliates and do not accept mail).

CONDITIONING. One more thing you should begin working on well in advance of your departure date is you! Too many cyclists spend the first weeks of their already short vacations wishing they had replacement sets of muscles and backup cardiovascular systems. Start working on your physical conditioning several months before your trip if you want to get the most enjoyment from those early weeks in the saddle.

Of course, you should have some idea of just how much effort will be demanded of you from reading our tour description for your chosen route. However, any classification of difficulty is necessarily subjective. One thing we've learned from talking to other cyclists using our books—they may think a hill *we* think is a "long and gradual ascent" is the "killer incline of the century." One American rider we shared a few days of cycling with on our most recent trip smilingly confessed that she had cursed us only once during three months of relying on the first edition of *Europe by Bike*. Those curses came on an incline on the Mediterranean coast of Italy—a *big* hill that we called a *little* one. In other words, expect the worst!

If winter weather won't allow you to do much preparatory riding for a spring tour, any strenuous physical activity will help. Try jogging, racquetball, swimming, or rapid walking—anything that gets your heart rate up and your muscles pumping. Of course, cycling is the best way to toughen up the muscles you'll use the most. Try making friends with a stationary bicycle at the local gym. The fact that you haven't been "sitting around" before your trip will help you toughen up the beginning tourer's constant foe—the tender rear end.

If you haven't done cycle touring before, go out on at least one realistic trial run before your trip. If you'll be camping in Europe, it's a good idea to ride and camp at home first. If you're going to stay in hotels or hostels, then simply go out with loaded packs, preferably overnight, to get a feel for handling your suddenly heavy bicycle and to find out what a daily riding regimen is like.

Despite all your efforts to prepare, if this trip is your first, it'll feel like it. Expect to be nervous on the flight, terrified when you roll out of the airport, and absolutely exhausted for the first week. We had 15,000 miles of European roads already behind us when we made our most recent trek to Europe. Yet all that "experience" didn't eliminate our jitters *or* our aching muscles. It will take your body time to adjust—ease up and give your tired legs the rest they need. And instead of concentrating on mileage totals or accomplishing preset goals, simply let yourself enjoy.

BUYING AND OUTFITTING A BIKE

If you'll be buying a new bicycle for your trip, and your knowledge of what to look for is limited, do what we did: Find two or three bike shops with a good selection of touring equipment, acquaint yourself with some knowledgeable employees, and begin asking questions. You'll probably get different opinions on which brand is best from every person you talk to, but if you keep listening, eventually you'll be able to make a good decision based on your specific needs and the information you've collected.

Another good way to find out more about touring bicycles, equipment, and maintenance is to read a general book on the sport of bicycle touring. *The Bicycle Touring Book* by Tim and Glenda Wilhelm or *Living on Two Wheels* by Dennis Coello are both good resources. And take advantage of cycling seminars at your local bicycle or outdoor equipment shop, if you have the opportunity.

Important things to look for in touring bikes are the following:

- A sturdy frame, strong enough to carry heavy loads.
- Correct fit for the rider. It's too big if you can't straddle the frame with both feet flat on the ground and have an inch of clearance between you and the bar.
- Superior-quality wheels and touring tires (we recommend "clinchers" with Kevlar reinforcing) to provide you with a stable and durable ride. Choose from $1\frac{1}{8}$-inch width to $1\frac{3}{8}$-inch width, depending on how much rough-road cycling you intend to do.
- A high-quality, dependable braking system. If you haven't toured before, you'll be surprised at how much longer it takes to stop a loaded bicycle than an unloaded one.
- Gearing that provides from 10 to 21 speeds, with the most important factor being the low-range capability. If you're new to touring, ask a bike shop employee to explain the complexities of gears and sprockets to you. Hills seem much steeper with a loaded bicycle, and you'll need the "granny" gears that a good touring bike offers more often than you might expect.

Mountain bikes have enjoyed increasing popularity in the past decade and, unless you're a long-term tourer, you probably own one. There is no absolute rule that says you must use a touring bike for your trip. In fact, we used a "city-type" bicycle on our most recent European journey, and it performed well enough to pull a toddler and a trailer more than 6,000 miles. As mentioned earlier, the roadways in France are excellent. Even the tiniest lanes are usually paved. However, if you do choose to ride a mountain or "city" bike, be sure to use a street tire rather than a "knobby." And plan to work harder and cover less distance than you would on a touring bike.

If you're like most people, price is an important factor when making your purchase, too. On our first trip, we went for middle-of-the-line touring bikes and equipped them with low-riding front racks and with rear racks. Because we knew we would be traveling together, we selected identical bikes (except for frame size) for ease of maintenance. Although one of those was "retired" for a city bike on our last outing, the other now has almost 20,000 miles on it—and it's still going!

"Extras" we consider to be touring essentials include at least two frame-mounted water bottles (if you use them for juice or pop, expect mold), front and rear fenders, a rearview mirror, and a bell. Other extras you'll need for your bike are toe clips, padded handlebars (or padded riding gloves), and a light source. We avoided night cycling at all costs, so we chose not to mount lights on our bicycles. Instead, we each carried a strong flashlight that could be attached to the handlebars in case of a dire emergency (or an unlit tunnel).

One more item you won't want to neglect is a comfortable bike seat. Get to know it before you go. Some hardcore cyclists might tell you that discomfort is just one of the penalties of the sport, that the seat must be rock hard to ensure freedom of movement, or some other crazy thing. Don't listen to them. You and your bike are going to be spending a lot of hours together. Make sure you're not incompatible before you go. If you just can't get comfortable on any seat, invest in a "cushy" gel cover or a gel seat to put some padding between you and your foe.

You'll need to choose touring bags for your bike, as well. If you'll be staying in hotels or hostels and you're a light packer, you might be able to get along with a handlebar bag and two rear saddlebags. If you're camping out, carrying cooking equipment, or going for the long haul, you'll probably need the works—two front bags, two rear bags, and a handlebar bag.

Important things to look for in touring bags are color (choose bright and visible), quality of construction (durability), ease and security of attachment to racks, and efficiency of closure system (such as zippers and drawstrings). You'll be amazed at how many times you dig into your bags in a single touring day. It's very important to have panniers that are both easy to use and durable. Shop around—bike bag prices range from reasonable to sky high. You'll have to match your budget to your needs when making a personal selection.

We talked to lots of other cyclists who had spent twice as much on their touring bags as we did, and we all agreed on one thing. No matter how expensive the bags, they rarely kept their contents dry in major downpours. All of us relied on plastic grocery sacks or giant plastic garbage bags to protect our belongings in the rain. (If you're considering purchasing panniers overseas, the Germans make some admittedly ugly but delightfully water-tight bags for tourers. They are expensive, though.) Check on the latest developments before you make your purchase. Perhaps some innovative manufacturer in your home country has finally mastered the trick of keeping water out of bags that are repeatedly subjected to driving rainstorms, gallons of road spray, and occasional tidal waves from passing trucks. We'll believe it when we see it!

Select your bags with their purposes in mind—a handlebar bag for valuables, delicate items, and things you want quick access to (camera, sunglasses, chocolate bars), two back bags to carry heavy or bulky items, and low-riding front bags to catch the extras. You'll need to do some experimenting with loading to minimize the wobble and weave. It's particularly important to load the front bags evenly. We were surprised to discover what seemingly insignificant things affected our wobble rates. As a result, we became positively superstitious about packing, driving each other crazy with our quirks and arguing about who got the bottle of vitamins or where an extra package of dry soup should go.

One trick for a pair of riders with identical bags (or for a single rider who has trouble staying organized) is to number bike bags or differentiate them in some way and then pack the same items in the same bag each day. Our packs started out with numbers, then they gained identities from the cloth souvenir patches we sewed on them. These patches, showing cities or tourist sights, also make excellent conversation starters with the local citizens.

Finally, you'll need to put together a maintenance kit for your bicycle, including such items as the following:

- Adjustable wrench—6-inch
- Allen wrenches—only sizes you'll need for your bike
- Brake pads (long-term trip only)
- Cables—one replacement each for gears and brakes (long-term trip only)
- Chain link removal tool (long-term trip only)
- Foldup tire (long-term trip only)
- Freewheel tool (long-term trip only)
- Helmet
- Locks—we carried both a metal shackle and a cable lock
- Locks—for seat and hubs (optional)
- Lubricant
- Phillips and/or regular screwdriver
- Pliers
- Pump and pressure gauge
- Spokes—at least three or four
- Spoke wrench
- Tire irons
- Tubes—so you don't have to patch flats on the road

If you're fortunate enough to tour France and/or Europe at several-thousand-mile whacks, as we are, you may want to mail additional replacement parts (e.g., tires, tubes, brake pads) to a European friend. Although bike shops in France are rich in excellent touring gear, you'll probably have to hunt to find just what you want—and you'll undoubtedly pay more for it than you would in the United States or Canada.

WHAT TO TAKE

The items you'll require as a "normal" European traveler are listed in most general travel books—passport, camping carnet, hostel card, student identity card, and money. We've already dealt with most of them, but following are some things you should know about money, security, and equipment.

MONEY. Travelers' checks are one of the safest and most convenient ways to go. You can purchase your travelers' checks overseas at American Express offices, utilizing an American Express Card for the transaction. Purchasing travelers' checks at home usually involves paying a commission charge, but members of certain organizations and holders of special types of bank accounts can avoid these extra fees. Even if you do have to pay a commission charge, the security of knowing your travelers' checks will be replaced if lost or stolen is well worth the effort and cost of getting them.

Don't forget to keep a record of your check numbers (preferably a photocopy of your receipt) and a list of when and where checks are spent. Leave a list of the numbers at home, and carry one list separately from your checks. Be sure to copy your check company's emergency replacement telephone number into your address book, as well.

If you'll be staying in France for several months, you may want to consider having part of your funds sent over later, but this can be quite an inconvenience—and expense. We chose to live with plump money pouches for a few months instead. In case of emergency, it's a good idea to travel with at least one major credit card (Visa, MasterCard, and American Express are widely accepted). Wiring funds overseas is another way to obtain emergency cash, but it's a costly and time-consuming process.

Be sure to keep at least some American dollars in reserve for emergencies (we carried about $100). It's a lot more painless to spend a $20 bill on an unanticipated holiday than it is to cash a $100 travelers' check at an unfavorable rate. Generally, you'll find the best exchange rates at French banks and post offices (avoid train-station offices and hotel desks). Shop around the first few times, as rates and commission fees do vary from bank to bank. Then settle on a favorite and look for its logo whenever you visit midsize cities.

Most French banks are open from 9:00 A.M. to noon and from 2:00 to 4:30 P.M., Monday through Friday. Expect to spend at least fifteen

Even the best lock can't protect against poor locking techniques.

minutes to half an hour each time you exchange. You'll need to keep track of the calendar to avoid being caught with an empty wallet. For a list of French holidays, refer to the Shopping section under "Survival Skills." If you already have (or can easily obtain) a major American credit card, such as American Express, Visa, or MasterCard, bring it along. These cards are becoming increasingly handy in Europe, and you'll be glad you have one if you lose your travelers' checks or need to pay an unexpected medical bill. Automated Teller Machines (ATMs) are now quite common in France, mainly in midsize and larger cities. Check with your agency to discover how your card can be used in Europe and/or to acquire a European PIN number.

SECURITY. Three essential pieces of personal equipment you'll want to take along on your trip are an under-clothing money pouch, a sturdy bicycle lock, and common sense.

Money pouches come in many styles (shoulder, neck, or belt), but their purpose is always the same—to help you avoid the pickpockets and purse snatchers who prowl the streets of tourist areas, looking for anyone foolish enough to carry an exposed wallet or handbag. For comfort, we stowed our pouches inside our handlebar bags when we were cycling, but we always put them on immediately when we entered a large city or if we left our bikes even for a moment. Don't make the mistake of one California cyclist with whom we talked. He put down his handlebar bag "just for a minute" while waiting for a train. The next time he looked, the bag was gone, complete with passport, travelers' checks, and his visa for a trip to India.

Simple good fortune and the efforts of the guardian angel who has ridden more than 17,000 bumpy miles on our handlebars may be responsible for the fact that we have never had a single item stolen during nearly three full years of European travel. Certainly, we have been forced into vulnerable positions often, simply because of the nature of our transportation and accommodations. But, throughout our travels, we have unfailingly followed some common-sense rules that have helped us to emerge unscathed while those around us have fallen prey to thieves and pickpockets.

- We always wear our money pouches inside our clothing when we are in a large city or mingling with a crowd.
- We always remove our valuables from our bicycles when we leave them unattended, and we try to park our bicycles in a high-traffic area (e.g., beside the tourist office).
- We always lock our bikes securely if we leave them for even a moment in a large city, or for several minutes in a small one.

Much of the crime that victimizes tourists in France takes place in big cities or high-density tourist areas, so be especially careful there. Paris, Marseilles, Toulouse, Bordeaux, and the entire French Riviera are potential trouble spots, but crime can occur anywhere. Vigilance is also a necessary survival tool if you'll be staying in youth hostels or student *foyers*, using trains, or frequenting train stations on your trip. Avoid overnight trains whenever possible, especially in the south of France.

The great thing about bicycle touring is that you'll be in between large cities and big tourist spots more than you'll be in them. We were continually delighted by the honesty of the French people. Despite our disadvantage as linguistically ignorant foreigners and (initially) inexperienced travelers, we encountered very few attempts to overcharge us or to steal from us. Hotel clerks, campground managers, and storekeepers alike treated us with courtesy and respect. Still, it never hurts to be careful.

PLANE TICKETS. Another essential you'll be taking with you to France is your plane ticket. You'll want to shop around for a package that's best for you. Because we were planning to stay in Europe for several months but didn't have a specific return date set on our first trip over, we bought an "open-ended" ticket. This allowed us to select our return date any time within one year after our departure. However, it limited the cities we could choose for our arrival and departure, eventually forcing us into a snowy ride to Brussels to catch a late-March plane flight home.

Long-term cyclists will have more freedom if they buy a one-way ticket to Europe and purchase return flights there, but this option is usually more expensive, and it requires responsible money management. Probably the cheapest ticket setup is to fly in and out of the same city within a 6-month time period. Find a travel agent you trust. Discuss your needs and budget, and decide on an itinerary that's best for you.

One other thing you should keep in mind when you buy your plane ticket is your arrival time in Europe. A midday or morning landing time will help you avoid the frustrations we faced our first time over— a frenzied assembly and loading job in the airport lobby and a twilight sortie into an unfamiliar city on arrival day.

If you're flying into France, you'll probably be landing near Paris. Depending on which tour you've chosen from this volume (or which tour you've designed for yourself), you'll arrive at either Roissy– Charles de Gaulle Airport north of Paris or Orly Airport to the south. Neither is overly convenient for cyclists. (A third option is to fly into Brussels's airport and pedal south with Tour No. 4.)

We've always arrived with our bicycles in Brussels, so we can only provide you with second-hand information on Paris. According to reports, there is a bike path from Orly toward Paris, but it's difficult to find and difficult to stay with (one cyclist told us he ended up on the freeway with his first try). Ask at the information desk in the airport for help finding the path. The cycle route dumps you onto the terrifying Road N7 into Paris before long, and things get more terrifying the farther into the city center you ride. It may also be possible to get your bicycle and gear aboard a city-bound Air France bus (their storage spaces are large enough to handle bikes). These buses run three to four times per hour and arrive in the downtown core.

Entering Paris from Roissy–Charles de Gaulle is a sticky proposition, too. Try getting your bicycle aboard the Roissy Rail commuter train, if you must. Quick departures, steep stairways, crushing crowds, and narrow passageways make handling French rapid-transit systems with a bicycle in tow extremely difficult, if not impossible. We recommend avoiding Paris with your bike, setting up a base camp at a peripheral town such as Versailles or Chantilly, and relying on public transportation to take in the sights of the French capital.

BICYCLES AND RELATED GEAR. What about your bicycle? Should you even try to bring it with you? Yes. Although getting it to France can be a bit of a headache, it's well worth it. Although more than 250 French train stations rent bicycles to tourists, you won't find the quality you want for long-distance pedaling in a train-station lineup. If you plan to mix brief cycling sessions with train hops to various parts of France and/or Europe, however, a rental bike may fit your needs.

Buying a bicycle once you're over involves a heap of hassle and tre-

Use a sturdy box from a bike shop to pack your bicycle for the airplane or a long train journey.

mendous expense. In France, where excellent touring gear is now available, you'll routinely pay twice as much for cycling equipment as you do at home. If you already have a touring-quality bicycle, bring it with you. If you're thinking of buying one for the trip, do it at home.

Most major airlines will accept your bike at no extra charge as one of your two allotted pieces of checked luggage. If you need to take your bike along as a *third* piece of luggage, you may be charged as much as $100 extra. Charter flights may be even stingier with weight and size restrictions. Again, check with your travel agent or carrier. Do keep in mind that intra-European flights have a much lower baggage-weight limit than flights coming from the United States or Canada (about 44 pounds as opposed to 70 pounds). Before you plan any airborne country hopping, check with your travel agent about hidden costs.

Regulations will also vary as to whether your bike must be boxed, bagged, or simply wheeled aboard the plane. The majority of carriers will require you at least to loosen the handlebars, turn them sideways, and remove the pedals so that the bike takes up less space. We recommend a full boxing job to help ensure your bicycle makes it safely to your destination. (If you're uncertain about your boxing skills, Bikecentennial, Inc., offers a handout on packing bicycles for airplanes. It's available by mail from P.O. Box 8308, Missoula, Montana 59807.)

We carefully dismantled our bikes, removing handlebars, pedals, and front wheels. Then we put them inside sturdy bike cartons provided by a local bike shop, padding them with excess baggage such as sleeping bags and clothing. We closed the boxes securely with a strong filament tape, and we wrote names, flight numbers, and destinations on the boxes and all other pieces of luggage.

You'll probably sweat and squirm when you relinquish your bike to a burly baggage handler, and you'll undoubtedly worry about it during the entire flight. We did! But if you're careful in your packing job, the odds are good that you and your bicycle will roll happily out of the airport and onto European soil several hours later.

If you're only visiting France for a few weeks, you may be able to leave your bike carton with a friend, a hotelkeeper, or a passing good Samaritan. If you're staying for much longer, however, dump the box and rustle up a new one when it's time to head for home. You may be able to purchase a box or bag from a carrier (the Dutch airline KLM almost always has them), or simply visit a French bicycle shop and ask for an empty packing carton. Most shops have at least a couple of bike boxes lying around, and they're only too happy to unload some surplus cardboard on a needy tourer.

CLOTHING. Once you have your bicycle and bags, what are you going to carry? This will vary, depending upon the length of your trip. Don't overdo it on clothes, as you'll certainly want to buy souvenirs, and you can put them to use right away if you leave an extra T-shirt or pair of shorts behind.

A good rain jacket is crucial, unless you're only cycling the Riviera in August (and you may even get some warm rain there). Rain pants are limited in their effectiveness for the cyclist, however. They tend to get you wet from the inside if the rain doesn't get you from without. We opted for polypropylene long underwear instead, wearing this under shorts when the weather was wet or cold. Full- or three-quarter-length Lycra tights are another good option. They provide needed warmth, and they dry quickly when the rain finally stops (or when you do). Also, a pair of nice sweatpants is great to have when you enter a city for sightseeing or to look for a room, or when you're setting up your tent in a campground and don't want to freeze before you have a place to change.

We don't use cycling shoes when touring in Europe, mainly because we do so much walking when we're not pedaling. However, if you're accustomed to riding in biking shoes, bring your favorite pair along. Many touring styles are designed for comfortable off-the-bike performance. Toss in a pair of lightweight sandals, too. They're great for airing out fragrant biker's toes, and they come in handy for the often less-than-hygienic European campground showers.

If you'll be doing some cool-weather cycling, invest in a pair of rubberized biking booties to avoid the discomfort of cold and soggy feet. The booties are light and compact, and they help prevent frozen toes when you get off your bike after a cold day. Warm, waterproof gloves are also a necessity in nasty weather.

CAMPING GEAR. The French campground system is among the finest in Europe. Campgrounds are abundant in most areas, although they're more scarce in the rural and less-touristed parts of the country. Municipal campgrounds are excellent bargains here, and they're generally easy to find and well maintained. As mentioned earlier, it's usually quite acceptable to pitch your tent in an unfenced municipal campground out of season as well as in (ask for permission first).

A superbly situated campground at Nevers offers a fantastic vista of the town.

We've paid as little as eight *francs* for a night in a municipal campground in France—that's less than the price of two chocolate *croissants*!

There are no campgrounds in Europe more consistently wonderful for cyclists than the French ones, in our opinion. Many French cities seem to take their most delightful patch of ground, with the most superlative view of the city's cathedral, château, or citadel, and turn it into the municipal campground. Although hot showers are pretty much standard equipment at French campgrounds today (they weren't ten years ago), you'll still encounter lots of pit toilets. It's a good idea to carry a spare roll of toilet paper in your panniers when camping in France. For some reason, BYOTP (bring your own toilet paper) seems to be the accepted policy in many French campgrounds.

One of the best things about camping in France is that you'll meet the Europeans at their best—when they're on vacation, having fun, and eager to talk to others. Camping outside of organized campgrounds is acceptable in France, provided you obtain the landowner's permission. We met a host of fascinating people this way—from dairy farmers to auto workers to housewives. If you do intend to "free camp" on occasion, it's a good idea to carry at least one or maybe two containers for water. We found two-liter pop bottles to be super for this purpose—they're easy to obtain, virtually weightless (at least when empty), and disposable.

Your baggage weight will increase markedly if you're camping, but we found the extra pounds to be worth the payoff in new friendships and reduced costs. In fact, after more than two and a half years on the road, we still prefer the familiar walls of our tent to the constantly changing and often drab surroundings of hotel rooms.

As mentioned earlier, the French tourist offices are great sources of information regarding campsites in the areas you'll be pedaling through. Pick up a free listing for each new area. If you'll be spending quite a bit of time in France, you might find it worthwhile to purchase the French campground guide *Guide Officiel Camping/Caravaning*. It lists hundreds of sites in every corner of France. If you find yourself without a listing, without a guide, and without a clue, here are a few additional tricks for finding French campgrounds. First, look for campground symbols on your map. Second, study the city maps that often grace roadside billboards as you're entering midsize and larger French cities. They usually proclaim *Plan au dos* (map on the back). Third, watch for camping signs along the road. Most French campgrounds are quite well signed.

If you'll be camping while you ride here, you're probably an experienced camper at home. You'll need the same equipment—tent and rainfly, sleeping bag, a lightweight tarp for covering your bike, stove and fuel, matches, cookset, and an all-purpose rope to use as a clothesline. As mentioned earlier, we also carried flashlights and let them double as emergency bike lights. One American cyclist (and light sleeper) we talked to also suggested that would-be campers bring along a set of eye shades (for brightly lit sites) and earplugs (for noisy ones) to help them get to sleep at night. We advocate this practice *only* if you feel good about your surroundings, your bicycle is securely locked, and all of your gear is inside your tent.

Choose your tent carefully. Make sure it's roomy enough to allow you to bring in your bags for security and protection from the weather, tough enough to withstand European downpours, and light enough to allow you to navigate the hills without hiring a sag wagon to carry your gear. A good lightweight sleeping pad is a welcome pleasure for tired muscles at the end of a tough riding day.

You won't be able to build fires in French campgrounds, and you shouldn't plan on any freelance wiener roasts, either. We carried a Gaz cookstove that has done morning coffee duty and evening dinner duty for almost three years without giving us a problem. Unlike white gas, the small blue fuel cartridges the stove uses are sold everywhere in France (the half-size cartridges are more difficult to obtain, however). They grace the shelves of grocery stores and gas stations, are often sold at campgrounds, and are almost always available in hardware stores. Watch for the small blue Camping Gaz signs in store windows as you pedal through towns.

You'll need to be careful about food shopping if you're camping and cooking, as well. Regardless of our day's destination, we tried to always carry one night's emergency rations (a couple of packages of dry soup or something similar) so that if we stumbled on a lovely campspot or got caught between towns, we could sleep and eat without having to ride to a restaurant or store.

MISCELLANEOUS ITEMS. Here's an alphabetical list of other general items we took along:

- Address book—for sending postcards and gathering new friends
- Aspirin
- Camera and film (film is *much* cheaper at home); also a photo log
- First-aid kit
- Gifts for European friends—souvenir pins are popular, or carry items like music cassettes or T-shirts
- Glasses or contacts—second pair for emergency replacement (and your prescription)
- Guidebooks—the more the merrier
- Journal—for recording those memories you don't want to forget
- Maps—for arrival, and any good city maps
- Mirror
- Needle and thread
- Phrasebook or dictionary

- Pictures—family snapshots to share with friends
- Playing cards
- Prescriptions for medicines
- Shampoo and soap
- Sunglasses and sunscreen
- Toilet paper—a must if you're camping, as French campgrounds often neglect this item
- Towel
- Vitamins
- Watch

SURVIVAL SKILLS

At last, after all the planning, the preparation, the purchases, and the planes, you'll arrive. You'll watch as your bike carton comes tumbling down the baggage chute, and you'll claim it with trembling hands. You'll unpack, assemble, repack, and load, then make your way through customs to officially set foot on French soil. Now what? Enjoy!

All the preparation you've done should ensure a pleasurable trip, but here are a few additional tips, gathered from our years of "learning by doing," that will help you avoid the potholes and find the smoothest going as you ride.

SECURITY AGAIN. We've already mentioned the importance of keeping your valuables in an under-clothing money pouch and of locking your bicycle when you leave it unattended. Security is always a concern when you leave your bags and bike to enter the tourist flow on foot—for example, when you're visiting a large city while staying in a hotel or campground. When we stayed in rooms, we always asked the proprietors to provide us with a place to lock our bicycles (off the street) and they generally complied quite graciously. If a hotel manager won't accommodate your bicycle and there are other hotels available, try again.

Our bikes claimed the other bed in a tiny room in Vienna where we celebrated our fourth wedding anniversary; they spent Christmas with us in our room above Las Ramblas in Barcelona; they shared a restaurant/hotel storage room with several bags of pigs' legs in southern Spain; and they hid behind a table in a hotel dining room in Carcassonne.

In campgrounds, we used a tree or post to lean and lock our bikes, then covered them with a lightweight tarp (doubles as a groundsheet for picnics) to protect them from the weather. We zipped our bags and gear into the tent when we left to sightsee, and we took our cameras and other valuables with us. A zipper and a bit of fabric won't do much to deter a thief, so strike up conversations with your campground neighbors before you leave. That way, those around you know what body goes with what tent, and they'll be more likely to keep an eye on things while you're away. (We usually positioned our bag of dirty clothes next to the tent doorway, as an added discouragement for would-be thieves.)

SAFETY AND HEALTH. Besides taking care of your passport, money, and possessions, what are some ways you can take care of yourself while you're traveling?

For riding safety, keep to secondary roads whenever possible. If you follow the tour routes we've described, you'll be on quiet roads most of the time. We made a point of sacrificing short riding days whenever we had to decide between main road "straight shots" and circuitous secondary routes, and we've tried to provide you with small-road options when our routes do stray onto busy thoroughfares. If you do add a few kilometers in your quest for quiet roads, you'll find they're well worth it for the solitude, safety, and scenery they'll provide.

Try to make your helmet a habit. It's easy to remember to reach for the plastic "brain bucket" when you're forced to cycle heavily traveled routes, busy city streets, or dangerous terrain (steep downhills, for example), but the unexpected tumbles on ordinary roads can be every bit as dangerous—more so when your helmet is tucked inside a bike bag instead of cinched beneath your chin. We've tumbled on slick railroad tracks and mischievous curbs, and the falls came without warning and without time to prepare. Knees and hands and pride may take a beating when you topple, but, if you can discipline yourself to lash on your helmet every morning, your skull should survive unscathed.

Another key element of safety is bicycle maintenance. If you get into a daily checkup routine, you'll avoid unnecessary breakdowns and accidents. Check tire pressure, brake pads, cables, spokes, and wheels daily. Make sure your bags are mounted securely when you load your bicycle, too.

One tedious task that will save you time in the long run is a daily "sliver search." Examine your tires regularly for tiny shards of glass imbedded in the tread; dig them out gently with the tip of a pocketknife blade to prevent them from working into the tube and producing those hated flats. Don't forget to lubricate your chain and derailleur at least once a week, more often if you're cycling through rain.

Of course, you'll want to keep your body in good working condition, too. Eat enough food to replace the calories you're burning each day. This won't be a difficult task, especially with the endless selection of French delicacies tempting you from every store window you'll cycle past. But choose your fuel with care. We once met a haggard-looking tourer in Normandy who had just completed a 100-mile day. All he had in his panniers when he hit the campground that night was a hunk of cheese and some stale bread—which does not

Avoid going hungry by learning to recognize French grocery stores and always respect French opening and closing times.

amount to much of a supper for a famished body.

Water is always a concern when you're on the road and exercising hard. Carry enough containers to hold the water you'll need on hot and hilly days. Although bottled water is widely available (and widely consumed) in France, we quenched our thirst with tap water everywhere—without any dire results. Let budget, convenience, individual constitution, and your ability to swallow occasional offerings of rotten-tasting *eau* dictate your choice.

SHOPPING. While we're on the subject of food and drink, we might as well talk about how to get it. First of all, it's essential to leave your American "7-11" mentality behind when you enter France. Once you're away from the 24-hour shopping options in the United States or Canada, you'll find that having plenty of *francs* in your pocket doesn't mean you'll always be able to find a place to spend them.

Shopping hours in France can be troublesome, especially outside of the big cities. The monster supermarkets that inhabit nearly every midsize and larger city in France are usually open from 9:00 A.M. to 8:00 P.M. from Monday through Saturday (with some exceptions). But in rural areas, French shopkeepers adhere to a strict set of opening and closing times that will have your stomach growling in dismay. Watch out for Sunday afternoons and Mondays, in particular. These are sacred times to shopkeepers, and you can often search high and low for sustenance—without luck. Also, the hours between 12:30 and 2:00 or 3:00 P.M. are dedicated to crazily hung *fermé* signs and lots of locked doors.

Larger supermarkets (Intermarché, Mammoth, Géant Casino, etc.) may ignore the traditional lunchtime closure, as well as the equally revered Sunday afternoon and Monday shutdowns. These "megastores" are becoming increasingly prevalent in France, much to the detriment of a delightful element of the French culture—the small, single-owner shops where townsfolk assemble elaborate meals, one element at a time. Admittedly, these giant stores are more convenient and economical for most consumers, but please don't limit yourself to supermarket shopping while you're in France. You'll give up too much in the bargain. (One thing to remember if you do plan to shop at *supermarchés*—you'll usually need a ten-*franc* coin to free a shopping cart. The coin is returned when you return the cart.)

Expect the vast majority of shops, banks, and public monuments to be closed on holidays. Here is a list of French dates to watch out for: January 1, Easter Sunday and Easter Monday, Pentecost, Ascension Day, May 1, May 8, July 14, August 15, November 1, November 11, and December 25. Watch out for the "long weekend," too. The French people (like most Europeans) absolutely adore holidays. If a chance to stretch a weekend into a four-day vacation presents itself with a holiday that falls on a Tuesday or Thursday, many businesses (and their employees) gleefully pack their bags and hang the *fermé* sign.

If you shop for lunch early, shop for dinner by 6:00 P.M., buy for the weekend on Saturday, and keep abreast of holidays, you'll be able to enjoy some of the most delicious food you'll find anywhere in Europe. If you're a cheese and bread lover, France is just short of heaven. If pastries are your weakness, it may be even closer! Hunt down breakfast feasts of buttery *croissants* or *pain au chocolat*; enjoy wonderful picnic lunches of crusty brown *baguettes* and creamy cheese; and make your dinners special with a glass of one of France's scores of outstanding regional wines. We'll give you more detailed regional recommendations on food and drink with the individual tours in Part II.

If you plan to eat your meals in restaurants while you're cycling in France, plan to bring along a wad of money. Eating out is not cheap here. In fact, when compared to the country's economical campgrounds and reasonable hotels, French restaurants are way out of line. Perhaps that's because of France's justifiable reputation for delicious food. More likely it's related to the French people's love of carefully prepared dishes consumed at the pace of a sluggish *escargot* (snail). Whatever the cause, you'll pay plenty for a meal here, even if it's just a burger and fries at McDonald's.

To save a few *francs*, look for a *menu à prix fixe* (fixed-price menu) as opposed to eating *à la carte*. Avoid the fanciest restaurants (inflated prices) and the sidewalk cafés (not much volume for the money). Try to eat in out-of-the-way establishments frequented by local citizens instead. Save your wine tasting for château tours and/or impromptu

Be sure to get the rest you need—you'll enjoy your trip more fully if you do.

picnics stocked from grocery-store shelves. While budget dining in a restaurant, ask for *eau gazeuse* (mineral water) instead of wine.

SLEEPING. Individuals vary in their sleep needs, and you know your own requirements better than anyone. Do keep in mind, however, that lots of physical exertion may transform your once-predictable body from an energetic, six-hour snoozer into a semi-comatose, nine-hours-or-nothing lump. Listen to your system's messages. It's one of the best ways to stay healthy.

We've already discussed camping as a wonderful way to meet your sleeping needs in France (please refer to the Camping Gear section under "What to Take"). Youth hostels are another option (glance back to the Hostels section under "Planning Your Trip"). Like the campground system in France, the hotel system is also a delight. A one-, two-, three-, and four-star rating scheme allows you to select your luxuries (and your approximate price range) in advance, then shop around in the right "neighborhood." One- and two-star hotels vary greatly in their quality, but, with a little hunting, you can usually find something entirely adequate at a comfortable price.

Room prices are usually posted at the front of hotels, either on a window or in the lobby, and also on the doors of individual rooms. You can always check out your room in advance. If you're looking at low-budget hotels, this should be standard practice. Be sure to find out whether you'll be paying for any food or extra services with your room. If you don't rent a room with a shower (*douche*), you may have to pay fifteen *francs* or more to use the one down the hall. And some hotelkeepers require their guests to purchase the French version of breakfast (*petit déjeuner*) with their room rental. This generally consists of rolls, butter and jam, and coffee with milk (*café au lait*). It's delicious, but it can be an unwelcome expense if you're on a budget.

French hotel managers are usually friendly to cyclists, owing to the country's widespread love of bicycling and French citizens' generally easygoing attitude. We've been greeted with kindness and hospitality in hotels all over France. We'll never forget the hotel manager in Carcassonne who rented a room to two drenched, mud-splattered cyclists and one extremely energetic toddler in a very dirty bike trailer, leading us into his cozy establishment with a smile that made a wintry day turn warm.

Besides hostels and hotels, France offers yet another indoor lodging option to the cyclist. The charming *gite d'etape* is a wonderful way for a cyclist to sleep cheaply and experience a slice of French culture at the same time. *Gites d'etape* are specifically targeted for self-propelled travelers—hikers, bikers, backpackers, boaters.

A *gite d'etape* usually consists of somewhat spartan communal lodgings made available in an area popular for outdoor pursuits. Most often, *gites d'etape* are small establishments administered by towns or villages and overseen by townsfolk. Fees are minimal and the atmosphere is relaxed. In off-season, your *gite d'etape* may be empty. But be forewarned: Holidays, weekends, and hot summer days can make for very crowded conditions. Either way, the *gite d'etape* is a good option to keep in mind. You can obtain listings at area tourist offices. To plan longer, less spartan stays, you could contact the Fédération Nationale des Gîtes de France, 59 rue Saint Lazare, 75009 Paris.

LANGUAGE. The thought of surviving in France often strikes fear into the hearts (and tongues) of English-speaking tourists. Take it from us—it's really not so bad. It's true that French is an exceedingly difficult language for English mouths to master. Pronunciation is of paramount importance when speaking French. If you don't say the word just right, you probably won't be understood.

We still blush when we think of the family we met in Laon on our first trip to France. They kept asking us where we were headed next. We kept telling them we were riding to Reims. They didn't have a clue what we were saying. When we finally pointed to the city on a map, they howled for fifteen minutes. City and place names in France sound *absolutely nothing* like they look, so keep a map or a pen and pencil handy if you want to ask directions or discuss geography.

Despite the obstacles to success, please don't give up on speaking French. Yes, you'll find plenty of bilingual citizens here to help you in a pinch, but try to communicate in French *before* you mumble *Parlez-vous anglais?* You're a visitor here, and the locals will appreciate it if you show respect for their language and their culture. Give it a try. If you fall on your face, a helpful (if amused) Frenchman will surely pick you up. Besides, nothing can match the pride you'll feel the first time you walk out of a *pâtisserie* with a bag of three *croissants* (so what, if you really wanted four?), and you handled the entire transaction in French!

What follows is a hodgepodge listing of words and phrases we've found valuable as travelers and cyclists in France.

- *Auberge de jeunesse*—youth hostel
- *Au revoir*—goodbye
- *Baguette*—a carbo loader's dream
- *Bicyclette*—bicycle
- *Billet*—ticket
- *Bon appétit*—good eating
- *Bonjour*—hello
- *Bon nuit*—goodnight
- *Bon soir*—good evening
- *Bon voyage*—have a good trip
- *Boucherie*—butcher shop
- *Boulangerie*—bread shop
- *Café au lait*—coffee with milk
- *Cathédrale*—cathedral
- *Centime*—¹/₁₀₀th of a *franc*
- *Centre ville*—city center
- *Chambre*—room (as in a hotel)
- *Change*—exchange (as in money)
- *Château*—castle or palace
- *Chien méchant*—guard dog (pedal fast!)
- *Clef*—key
- *Combien*—how much?
- *Croissant*—if you need a definition for this one, you shouldn't be in France
- *Defense d'entrer*—no entry
- *Dimanche*—Sunday
- *Douche chaud*—hot shower
- *Droite*—right (directional)
- *Eau*—water
- *Église*—church
- *Étage*—floor (in France, the first floor is the first floor *above* ground level)

Try to master at least a few French phrases. It'll help you to ride safely and legally.

- *Étang*—lake
- *États Unis*—United States
- *Fermé*—closed
- *Fermé la porte*—close the door
- *Fête*—festival
- *Fromage*—cheese
- *Gare*—train station
- *Gauche*—left (directional)
- *Gratuit*—free (no charge)
- *Hôtel de Ville*—town hall
- *Interdit*—forbidden
- *Jeton*—token (purchased for campground showers)
- *Jeudi*—Thursday
- *Lundi*—Monday

- *Mardi*—Tuesday
- *Marie*—small town's town hall
- *McDonald's*—the same in any language
- *Merci*—thank you
- *Mercredi*—Wednesday
- *Messe*—mass (the religious ceremony)
- *Musée*—museum
- *Ouvert*—open
- *Pâques*—Easter (common opening date listed in French camping guides)
- *Pâtisserie*—pastry shop (and/or God's gift to cyclists)
- *Petit déjeuner*—breakfast
- *Plage*—beach
- *Plan au dos*—city map on the back (usually seen on small advertising billboards)
- *Pont*—bridge
- *Poste*—post office (also *Bureau de Poste*)
- *Route barrée*—road blocked (see our route-finding tips)
- *Rue*—street
- *Samedi*—Saturday
- *Sauf bicyclettes*—except for bicycles (usually posted on one-way roads and/or bicycle paths)
- *Sauf riverains*—except for locals (usually posted on small roads with no-entry signs; consider yourself a local)
- *S'il vous plait*—please
- *Son et lumière*—a sound and light show
- *Syndicat d'Initiative*—tourist office
- *Terrain de camping*—campground
- *Timbre*—postage stamp
- *Tourisme*—tourist office
- *Tout droit*—straight ahead (ask directions from any Frenchman and you'll hear this phrase)
- *Toute année*—all year, as in "open all year" (also *T.A.*)
- *Vélo*—bicycle
- *Vendredi*—Friday
- *Vieille ville*—old town
- *W.C.*—water closet (i.e., toilet)

Try to learn to speak (or at least understand) the numbers between one and twenty in French. You'll be much better off in smaller shops if you do. Unlike the supermarkets, where you can help yourself to items off the shelf and "cheat" by discovering what you owe from the cash-register readout, small shops require you to utilize your verbal skills. At least learn to say *une baguette, s'il vous plait* (one loaf of bread, please)—with this skill and a few *francs* in your pocket, you'll never starve in France.

OTHER COMMUNICATIONS. Public telephones in France can be a challenge, too. Modernization has brought the onset of the *télécarte*, a plastic card that replaces the coins all booths used to require. Although you'll still find some public phone booths in villages and rural areas that rely on coins (five *francs*, one *franc*, and one-half *franc*, as a rule), most now require *télécartes*. These "phone cards" may be purchased at post offices and *tabacs* (small tobacco shops). Look for the *télécarte* sign in the window. Once you have your *télécarte* in hand, find a booth and feed it in. A display tells how many *unités* you have to work with, and you'll watch your money "tick away" as you talk.

To save money on phone calls, dial direct and try to call during off hours. Rates vary considerably, depending on day and time. You can try to decipher the rate charts that are usually posted in public telephone booths, but it isn't easy. As a general rule, it's best to chat in the evening, early morning, or on Sunday. To place direct international calls, dial 19, then the country code (1 for the United States and Canada), then the area code and phone number. Most of the public phone booths in France will accept incoming calls, so you can save your money (and spend someone else's) by calling home and having the other party call you back.

To make long-distance calls within France, simply dial the number you want (if you're calling from the Paris area, precede the number with 16, then 1). If you find all of this confusing, you're not alone. You may find it easiest to make long-distance calls from the telephones available at most post offices. Ask the clerk to assign you to a booth, do your talking, then pay at the counter before you leave.

For nonverbal communication, you can turn to the French postal system. Purchase stamps (*timbres*) at post offices or *tabacs*. Mail can be sent via air (*par avion*) or by surface (*par terre* or *par eau*). Surface mail takes one to three months to reach North America, but it's a wonderfully inexpensive option for unloading unwanted clothing or gear and/or sending back gifts or souvenirs. Wrap things *very* securely before you mail—packages do take a beating when they leap the ocean. And make sure your surface-mail parcels weigh less than 2 kilograms (about 4½ pounds), if you can. This accomplishes three things: It reduces paperwork, it speeds passage, and it earns you the lowest postage rates.

TRAINS. Transporting bicycles on trains isn't impossible in France, but it isn't easy, either. And your troubles will multiply in direct proportion to the distance you wish to travel. Short local trains often allow cyclists to load their own bicycles and ride with them (restrictions usually occur during high-use periods). On printed SNCF (Société Nationale des Chemins de Fer) train schedules, look for a tiny bicycle logo accompanying specific local runs. This will clue you in to bike-friendly lines.

On long-distance or international trains, you'll probably have to send your bike a few days in advance. Go to the baggage acceptance area at the train station (usually identified by a graphic of a suitcase and a scale), smile a lot, and bring along a French-speaking friend, if you have one. You'll need to show your passenger ticket, then pay a slight fee for your bicycle.

To prepare your bicycle for a long train trip, we recommend removing all luggage, lights, and computer paraphernalia, taping down cables, and perhaps even unfastening your derailleur and taping it to the frame (to prevent it from getting caught on something and ripped off your bicycle). If you're really serious about protecting your mount, you might even box it. You may be able to obtain a carton from the baggage clerk. Box your bicycle in the same way it was boxed for air travel. Pay the baggage fee, hang on to your receipt, and whisper a prayer (if you'd only heard the horror stories we have).

ROUTE FINDING. One important rule to remember as a bicycle tourer is this: "Pride goeth before a wrong turn." We learned this lesson the hard way, after too many dead ends and extra miles. When you're confused, ask for help. The French people will be delighted to come to your rescue. They won't ridicule your ignorance or laugh at your despair. So what, if the husband and wife you question argue for fifteen minutes before agreeing on which road to point you toward? So what, if every other Frenchman you ask for directions will shrug and mumble, *"Tout droit"* (straight ahead).

In most cases, the people you seek out will know a lot more about the area than you do, and their friendly aid will save you from a host of wrong turns. And occasionally these roadside conversations will result in dinner invitations, collective picnics, refreshments at local cafés, and delightful new friendships, too.

Your main information sources as you ride will be the maps fastened atop your handlebar bag, the tours you're tracing from Part II of this book, and the road signs you'll constantly be seeking. Make a point of getting acquainted with the shapes and colors of the French signs. They follow definite patterns, and knowing them can help you with your route-finding chores. Generally, signs indicating motorway routes are green or blue, and signs for primary roads are black on white. Signs for secondary roads (the ones you want) are usually smaller, also with black type on a white background.

When you're cycling out of a French village on an unsigned road (or leaving a French city on a signed one, for that matter), you'll often be able to tell if you're traveling in the right direction by utilizing a very simple route-finding tip. Many streets in France take the name of the town they're headed toward. For example, the street leaving Reims toward Épernay might be called the "rue de Épernay," and the thoroughfare leaving Chantilly toward Paris might be called the "route de

Paris." If the street is named for a town you didn't intend to visit, you might want to reassess your direction or your route.

Another thing to remember when you're doing urban cycling is that most road signs are directed toward trucks and automobiles, not bicycles. Don't let yourself be routed onto hectic ring roads with the long-distance traffic. You *want* to ride through city centers, not breathe truck exhaust on encircling motorways. Never follow signs directed toward *Poids lourds* (heavy weights—as in, heavy weights inside of even heavier trucks!) and remember that road signs for the big city 100 kilometers away are probably not the ones you want to follow (even if you are headed in that direction). Look for signs for the first village out of town instead.

You will encounter some confusing French words on road signs, too. For instance, a sign reading *Vers RN6* means that this road will take you to Road 6 (not that it goes to a town called Vers). And signs for *Toutes directions* and *Autres directions* (generally seen at busy intersections in large cities) translate roughly as "all routes" and "other routes"—in other words, if you're going anywhere, this is the way to get there.

Think of yourself as a detective with several sets of clues to piece together. Use them all, and you'll arrive at your destination with a minimum of difficulty. We've also included a page of international road signs you'll encounter frequently in France, with explanations from a cyclist's point of view.

To help with the daily task of route finding, we suggest you take a few minutes each morning to study your map, your guidebook, and the tour you're following from Part II of this volume. Use a yellow highlighter to draw the day's intended route on your map. This will help you make quick decisions at junctions, and you can refer to our detailed route descriptions whenever you're stumped.

We've used kilometers as the distance unit in all tours, as this is what you'll see on French road signs and on your maps. That way, you'll be operating in the correct "language." A simple formula for kilometer-to-mile conversion is 8 km = 5 mi. So, an 80-km day amounts to a 50-miler, the basic distance we aimed for as we planned our cycling days. When there's a lot to see or tough terrain to ride through, you'll shorten your rides accordingly. No single distance is "right" or "respectable." Find the pace that works for you, and go from there.

In an effort to make your route finding a bit easier as you use the tours in Part II, we've utilized bold type for certain key words—a **right** or **left turn**, an especially **steep hill**, a **bridge** or a set of **train tracks**, a **campground**, or a new road (e.g., turn **right** on **Road D36**).

Another style you'll find in our tour descriptions is the use of the terms "left bank" and "right bank" when referring to riverside cycling.

A river's left or right bank is determined when facing *with* the current. So, if you were floating down the middle of the Loire River from Orléans to Angers, the left bank would be on your left and the right bank would be on your right. Conversely, if you were paddling against the current, you would find the right bank on your left and the left bank on your right.

French roadways do have a few idiosyncracies we'd like to warn you about. First of all, you should be aware of the French rule known as *priorite au droite* (priority on the right). This is significantly different from the American concept of "right of way," simply because there is no consideration of relative road size when the rule is put to the test. In other words, a car entering a larger roadway from a smaller one has priority (and should be yielded to) if there is no stop sign. This rule is generally only applied in built-up urban areas, however.

One French driver we rode with claimed this "undeniable right" with fierce aggressiveness, plunging into traffic and cursing all who failed to yield. As a vulnerable cyclist, you certainly won't claim any rights, real or imagined, in the face of a flying hunk of steel. But you should be prepared to yield those rights on request. Simply put, don't ever assume a car on your right will stop if the driver doesn't have a stop sign.

With any luck at all, you'll find this sign applies only to motorized travelers.

If you do much cycling in France, you'll eventually encounter a road marked by a no-entry sign (red circle with a red horizontal line) and the words *Sauf riverains* (except for locals—in this case, locals living on a waterfront road). This means it's a small roadway not intended for through traffic or tourists. Consider yourself neither and pedal on through. Similarly, the term *Sauf bicyclettes* (except for bicycles) is often printed on no-entry signs, as well. Sometimes this means you'll be entering a one-way street with auto traffic coming at you. So be careful!

In your days of cycling in France, you may also run into roads signed with temporary markers such as *Route barrée* (route blocked), *Déviation* (detour), or something along those lines. React to these warning signs as you wish, but our personal riding philosophy is this: "Don't believe it for a minute." We've cycled past more road-closed and detour signs than you can shake a tire pump at, and we've only had to turn back once (when a bridge was out and the creek was too deep to wade).

Most of the time, if you pedal onward you'll find only a group of workmen roughing up the pavement, smoothing out the pavement, laying down new pavement, or sipping coffee on the pavement. Perhaps you'll see evidence of a roadslide (French road crews usually get around to fixing these sometime within the next calendar year). Whatever the barrier, as a narrow, mobile cyclist, you'll almost always be able to get past it. And a little boldness will often save you a long detour. Whenever we have had difficulty getting past a *route barrée*, the on-site workmen have smilingly shepherded us through. (One cyclist we spoke to told of having his bicycle handed from workman to workman to get it across a bridge that was under repair.) Indeed, one of the best things about *déviation* and *route-barrée* signs is that most of the cars will heed them—and that means delightfully quiet roads for you!

Another tip for happy cycling in France is to know *when* to cycle. We've tried to recommend the optimum cycling months for individual routes, basing our choices on a combination of weather and tourist flow. But some general rules apply to optimum cycling hours. The French people are not particularly early risers, so the earlier you start riding, the better off you'll be. Saturday, Sunday, and holiday cycling is usually very pleasant, unless you're in a popular recreation area. On Sunday afternoons, French roads can be unnervingly deserted, as most of the locals are inside. Sundays in France are reserved for eating and drinking, from shortly after noon until early evening.

As there are optimum times *to* cycle, there are also optimum times *not to* cycle. If you are near a large or midsize city, you may want to avoid riding during the three weekday "rush hours" in France. More accurately, these are brief commuting flurries when traffic is generally at its worst. Two of the high-traffic periods occur at the expected times, between 8:00 and 9:00 A.M. as people go to work, and then again around 5:00 and 6:00 P.M. when the homeward trickle begins.

The third heavy-traffic period is uniquely French. As one of our office-bound French friends explained to us, "*No one* brings a sack lunch to work here." As a result, right around noon, French workers head out for lunch in force, driving to restaurants or commuting back home. Because the French like to eat at a leisurely pace and because this is often the day's largest and most time-consuming meal (and perhaps because they're starving after working half a day on the standard breakfast of a roll and a cup of milk-laced coffee), everyone is in a major hurry to get to lunch. You'll find the usually mellow and courteous French drivers to be a little testy during this particular rush, so guard your rear.

TRAVELING WITH A CHILD, TRAVELING AS A CHILD

Perhaps one of the primary reasons we chose France as the subject of this specialized cycling guide is the fact that we knew that we would be bringing our two-year-old daughter Sierra along. Anyone who is a cyclist knows that on-the-road safety is a constant concern for a bike rider. Automobiles have a distinct advantage over bikes—in weight, in speed, and in indestructibility. We cyclists persevere with one eye on the road ahead and one eye on the cars behind. And anyone who is a parent knows that his or her child is one of the most precious things that life can offer.

All of this is a rather roundabout way of saying that we chose France because we love it, because we love our child, and because we wanted to cycle the safest roads that we could find in Europe.

If you're hesitating about a trip to France because you have a child, don't hesitate another moment. Invest in a good bike trailer and a good helmet. Resign yourself to a lot of additional baggage and a lot fewer miles. Practice patience and flexibility. Then simply settle into your saddle and enjoy. If your trip turns out like ours did, you'll have a fantastic time.

Europeans adore children. Our daughter stopped crowds wherever we went. We'll never forget the afternoon we rolled into Reims. We leaned our bicycles and trailer against a bench in a small park adjacent to the city's magnificent cathedral, then we sat down to study our French guidebook. A few moments later, a tour bus pulled up. Thirty elderly people piled out. Did they head straight for Reims's fabulous cathedral, the coronation place of French kings for more than 1,300 years? No way. They completely ignored their fuming tour guide, formed an orderly line, and headed straight for Sierra and her trailer.

That kind of thing happened in every French city we visited. The

One of the best things about cycle touring is that it brings out the child in all of us.

fun didn't stop when we were cycling French roadways, either. We had drivers pull their cars over to the shoulder almost every day, pausing to watch us pass, rolling down their windows to shout a greeting, even climbing out of their seats to catch us with a camera or camcorder as we pedaled by. It was almost comical. It was certainly delightful. We began to call ourselves the only mobile three-star Michelin site in France.

Sure, traveling with a young child means you'll cover fewer miles and make more potty stops each day. It also means you'll spend more time in parks and gardens than you do in museums or châteaux. But we guarantee you one thing—it certainly means you'll make more friends. And, perhaps best of all, it means you'll share the joys of cycle touring as a family.

Bring your child or *become* like a child. Cycle touring is great for either task. As a cycle tourist, you'll have time to play, time to savor the sun, time to feel your muscles gain strength and skill. And you'll experience life as a child does—you'll experience life to its fullest.

You'll delight in the sound of cows chewing grass beside the road. You'll smile at old women riding even older bicycles. (And you'll groan as they pass you like you're standing still.) You'll gaze in awe at magnificent buildings and incredible examples of human creativity. Perhaps you'll even weep—as hills humble you and headwinds halt you and unforgettable vistas break you with their beauty.

Whatever you do, and however you do it, we think you'll always be glad you came to France to ride a bicycle.

INTERNATIONAL ROAD SIGNS

Circular Signs—Give Orders

White bar on red background. No entry for vehicles. (One-way traffic coming at you!)

Red ring around motorcycle and automobile. No motor vehicles. (OK for nonmotorized you!)

Red ring around bicycle. No cycling. (Tunnel, freeway, busy road, or bike-eating dog ahead!)

White bicycle on blue background. Pedal cyclists only. (Sometimes obligatory. Follow local custom.)

Rectangular Signs—Give Information

Black letter "i" on blue field. Tourist information. (Where am i?)

White bar with red tip on blue. No through road. (This sign can lie—check it out if you feel adven-turesome.)

Triangular Signs—Give Warnings

Black bump in red border. Uneven road. (Look out for potholes!)

Black gate in red border. Railroad crossing with barrier. (Slow down for tracks or trains!)

Black train in red border. Unguarded crossing. (Slow down for tracks and look for trains!)

Parallel lines bending closer. Road narrows. (So long, shoulder!)

Black hill in red border. Steep downhill. (Yahoo!)

Black hill in red border. Steep uphill. (Could be a "pusher"!)

PART II

14 TOURS GEARED FOR DISCOVERY

There is no better way to experieince France than from the seat of a bicycle.

TOUR NO. 1

A CATHEDRAL CRUISE
Dieppe to Rouen

Distance:	429 kilometers (267 miles)
Estimated time:	7 riding days
Best time to go:	June through September
Terrain:	Gentle hills; lots of quiet secondary roads
Maps:	Michelin Nos. 52, 55, and 56
Connecting tour:	Tour No. 2

This tour from Dieppe to Rouen will take you past a handful of northern France's most outstanding cathedrals. In between the region's captivating cities and their remarkable religious architecture, you'll be treated to mile after mile of quiet pedaling through scenic agricultural land. A visit to the lovely château at Chantilly will add some impressive secular architecture to your ride. Appropriately, the ride ends in Rouen, "the city of a hundred spires," and you'll be able to finish your cycling with a visit to Rouen's host of fine churches.

CONNECTIONS. The busy port city of Dieppe is the starting point for this tour. As such, this ride is a natural choice for a cyclist arriving from Great Britain. However, if you're not planning to visit or cycle in England while in Europe, you might still choose this route for your time in France. Simply hop aboard the tour in Chantilly (a brief train trip from Paris) and close the loop with the one-day ride between Rouen and Dieppe.

If you have more time for cycling in France than this tour requires, consider combining the ride to Rouen with our Tour No. 2 Rouen to St. Malo, and spend some days exploring the treasures of Normandy and Brittany along the way.

INFORMATION. One *Green Guide* for Normandy (*Normandy Seine Valley*) and another for the *Île-de-France* offer lots of reading material for this tour. You might want to do some background reading on World War I, as well, because the area you'll be pedaling through saw heavy fighting during the war years. Check in at tourist offices along the route, particularly in the larger towns like Amiens, Noyon, and Rouen, to pick up English-language pamphlets.

Campgrounds are generally plentiful in the region, especially near the Atlantic ports, along the Seine Valley, and in the vicinity of Paris. A few long cycling days through the agricultural expanses in the north may leave you wishing for more frequent campsites, though. Campers should be sure to request the regional camping guides when they visit tourist offices in Dieppe, Amiens, and Compiègne. Almost every mid-size town offers at least one hotel.

Dieppe is famous for its mackerel, and this can serve as your introduction to the seafood-centered cuisine of Normandy. Meats served in the *Normande* tradition come bathed in rich cream sauce. Cheese is yet another Normandy delight, and you'll want to be sure to sample a wedge of Camembert somewhere along the way. Normandy cider (*cidre*) is offered as either *brut* (hard—with alcohol) or *doux* (sweet—with little or no alcohol). It's a delicious treat at the end of a long day.

In Amiens, try the leek tart (*flamiche*) of Picardy. For something a little sweeter, explore the joys of *tuiles amiénoises*, wonderfully decadent chocolate-nut macaroons. And, when you finish your cycling in Rouen (and don't have to worry about staying light on your feet any longer), feast on duck *pâté* or *sole normande*.

Dieppe to Poix-de-Picardie: 80 kilometers

Daily ferries arrive in Dieppe from Newhaven, England, and you'll notice a high percentage of British tourists in the city. Dieppe's super-

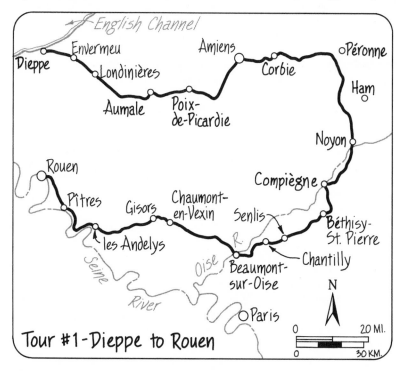

Tour #1—Dieppe to Rouen

markets are packed with English-speaking tourists, most of them greedily stocking their shopping baskets with French wines and cheeses. Despite the heavy influx of British visitors, Dieppe retains its French character, from its lively pedestrian streets lined with aromatic *pâtisseries* to its busy cafés packed with coffee-sipping locals. Pause in the city at least long enough to absorb its unique English–French ambiance, then pedal southeast toward the farms and fields of Picardy.

If you arrive in Dieppe via the Sealink ferry from Britain, cycle the seaside **boulevard Maréchal Foch** to the **rue de Sygogne**. To find the city's inexpensive **Camping St. Nicolas**, swing right off the rue de Sygogne, and climb steeply with the **rue du Faubourg de la Barre**. The campground is about 2 km from the city center. If you're headed for Dieppe's **tourist office**, go **left** off the rue de Sygogne and dive into the city center. The tourist office is on the **boulevard Général de Gaulle**, in an annex of the *Hôtel de Ville*.

Ask the office staff for literature on the city and the surrounding region. Dieppe offers a rather inconvenient **youth hostel** and several hotels, if you're in need of indoor accommodations. Those arriving in Dieppe via train from Paris or other points in France will find the tourist office a short walk northwest of the station.

To begin your ride from Dieppe, head **east** from the **Église St. Jacques**. Cross the **port/canal** on the **Quai du Carenage**, and continue uphill on the **main road** as you climb away from the city center. Veer **right** onto **Road D920** toward **Envermeu**, and enjoy easy cycling as you ride a remarkably quiet road through gently rolling hills. Look for Envermeu's slate-roofed church with a gargoyle-guarded choir, then continue with the river valley to **Londinères**, where you'll swing **right** onto **Road D1314** for **Neufchâtel-en-Bray**.

Endure increased traffic for 4½ km as you pedal to **Clais**, then veer **left** for **Smermesnil** on **Road D14**. Keep to the **right** for **Fesques** to continue with the quiet **Road D36**. You'll stay along the **Eaulne River** as you pedal past Fesques, cycling through serene farmland with only scattered cars to break your reverie. Cross **Road N28** and ride on to **Road N29**, continuing **straight across** for **Mortemer** *centre*. Veer **left** just after to gain **Road D7** for **Auvilliers**.

Face your first **stiff climb** of the day as you **recross N29** and struggle uphill on a tiny road, angling right along the hillside. Cows, corn, and classic vistas will mark your ride to **Auvilliers**, then you'll gain easier cycling as you stay with D7 through **le Caule** and on to **Ste. Beuve**. In Ste. Beuve, veer **right** onto **Road C2** for **Mesnil-David**. Marvel at the joys of tiny French roadways as you keep **right** at the **unsigned Y**, then pedal on past silent fields with only an occasional car for company.

In **Mesnil-David**, go **right** again, then veer **left** just after to get on

Road C1. This unassuming thoroughfare will take you to the howling **Road N29**, where you'll turn **left** for **Illois**. Endure a mercifully brief stretch of suicidal cycling on N29, then dive **right** in **Illois** and put an end to your suffering. First zig left and then zag right to stay with **Road D282** toward **Villers**. Pedal to a junction with **Road D8**, and go **left** here to cruise into **Aumale**.

Cross **N29** to gain the town **center**, and pause to enjoy Aumale's attractive collection of buildings, its restored 16th-century church, and its pleasant town square. Aumale suffered great devastation during World War II, like many of the towns you'll visit in this part of France. If you're late in your cycling day or running low on energy, Aumale offers a **campground** and a few hotels as lodging options. There's a well-signed **tourist office** in the old core of the city.

Leave Aumale with the totally awful **N29** toward **Amiens**. Climb a **long hill** away from the city. You can dive off to the right for Digeon after about 2 km, and zigzag on quiet roads to gain Road D98, or endure N29 a little longer and swing off to the **right** (after the junction with Road D1015 toward Grandvilliers), and join **D98** toward **Marlers** and **Meigneux**.

Enjoy easy cycling through Marlers and Meigneux, then continue **straight** to **Eplessier**. Work your way through a handful of **junctions** in Eplessier, consulting your map for guidance, and cycle past Eplessier's handsome **church** to gain the road descending into **Poix-de-Picardie**. This pleasant midsize city offers good shopping, a few hotels, and a deluxe, centrally located **campground** (near the main square). An attractive hillside church may tempt you into an after-dinner walk if you spend the evening in the city.

Poix-de-Picardie to Amiens: 35 kilometers

Leave Poix with **Road D920** signed for **Conty**. You'll have pleasant cycling through gentle terrain as you follow the river valley past farms and cows and cornfields. Pedal through the little town of **Conty**, where the gargoyles on the church will threaten to spit on you as you glide beneath them, then veer **left** onto **Road D8** for **Loeuilly** and **Amiens**. Follow the valley of the Selle River northward.

Traffic is fairly mellow and the cycling is effortless for the 14 km to **Saleux**, then things pick up as you near Amiens. Pass the city's large **university** complex (on the left), and turn **left** at the junction just past the university to gain the **rue Jean Moulin** toward Amiens's center. Then you enjoy a **gradual descent** into the vast city, with views of the cathedral tower in the distance. You'll hit a growling **main intersection** as you enter the heart of Amiens. Go **right** here for the **Gare SNCF** (train station), then veer **left** shortly after for the **cathedral**.

Pedal cautiously through the busy city streets (or get off and walk) to arrive at Amiens's awesome cathedral. When viewed from a distance, the building seems to crown a hill. In truth, it's simply immense. The intricate stone carvings on the west front deserve long study, and they're best viewed when the late-afternoon sun caresses the staring faces of the scores of sculptured figures. Seek out the **tourist office** on the cathedral plaza (or the one at the train station) to gather information on the church, the city, and accommodations.

Unfortunately, the wonderfully situated campground and youth hostel Amiens once boasted both succumbed to bulldozers in 1991. You'll probably need to get a hotel room if you want convenient lodgings. Stow your bicycle and gear, then spend an afternoon at the cathedral, savoring its more than 4,000 Gothic sculptures and marveling at the 700-year-old building. If you visit Amiens between April and October, you may want to purchase tickets to a *son et lumière* performance, too.

Once you've paid homage to Amiens's fantastic cathedral, descend to the banks of the Somme River for a stroll through the picturesque Quartier St. Leu (great views of the cathedral). Or give your legs a break and pay a visit to a local *crêperie* for a sample of the regional specialty—*ficelle picarde* (a stuffed *crêpe*).

Amiens to Noyon: 98 kilometers

The ride from Amiens to Noyon is fairly flat, relatively boring, and admittedly long. We broke our riding day at Ham (and wished we hadn't), putting up our tent in one of the bleakest campgrounds in France. You'll have hotel and camping options in Corbie, Péronne, and Ham, if you find the day too lengthy. We recommend you get an early start from Amiens and try for Noyon.

From Amiens's **cathedral**, descend to the banks of the **Somme River** and cycle along the **south bank**, passing the signed turnoff for *Les Hortillonages* (the market gardens) and continuing for **Camon** on the **rue de Verdun**. You'll **cross the Somme** into **Camon**, then take the **small road** signed for **Lamotte** to pedal on beside the river. At the far end of Lamotte, ignore the first, signed left turn and take the **second left turn** (this one is unsigned) to **climb** away from the river. Follow this small road paralleling Road D1 to ride toward **Daours**.

Go **straight** at the **stop sign** before Daours, then pedal on to **join D1** into the city. From Daours, stay with **D1** to **Corbie**. You'll pass many Commonwealth graves in this area of France, including an Australian National War Memorial just south of Corbie. This region was host to severe fighting during World War I, and the pivotal Battle of Amiens was waged on August 8, 1918 near the town of Villers-

A condemned soul screams from the cathedral in Noyon.

Bretonneux, which is located about 4 km south of Corbie.

Corbie was once the home of a powerful Benedictine abbey (founded in 657), and the little city has two churches that are offshoots of the order's presence here. A pleasant municipal **campground** may tempt you to linger in Corbie. The site is well signed from D1.

To continue your ride, leave Corbie with **Road D233** beside the **Somme** (swing right off D1 as you pedal through town). Enjoy quiet, scenic cycling as you continue straight with this road (now **Road D42E**) through **Vaux-sur-Somme** and on to **Sailly-le-Sec** and **Sailly-Laurette**. From Sailly-Laurette, swing **right** on **Road D42** for **Lamotte-Warfusée**. **Cross the Somme** and climb away from the river, then make a **left** turn for **Cerisy** onto **Road D71**.

More silent cycling follows as you stay with D71 through Cerisy and **Morcourt** and pedal on toward **Méricourt-sur-Somme**. World War I graves dot the landscape, reminding passersby that these peaceful fields were once the site of bloody battles. Ride through a handful of small towns en route to **Dompierre-Becquincourt**, where a host of white crosses mark more Commonwealth graves. Continue past Dompierre-Becquincourt, pedaling D71 to a junction with **Road D1**.

Go **right** here for **Péronne**, cross above the **freeway**, then angle **right** onto **Road D148** for **Flaucourt** and **Villers-Carbonnel**. You'll **cross Road N17** and **Road N29** in Villers, and continue **straight** through the city on **Road D35** signed for **Nesle**. When the road angles sharply to the right at the far end of Villers (the road sign calls out Licourt and Nesle), continue **straight** onto a tiny **unsigned road**. **Descend quickly** to gain **Road D62** and head south (**right**) along the banks of the **Somme Canal**.

Easy cycling follows as you **parallel the canal** past a handful of small towns. A clue to the region's battle-scarred past can be seen in the host of post-World War I, rebuilt churches. In **Pargny**, swing **right** toward **Nesle**, and join **Road D15** afterward. Continue into Nesle, **crossing Road D930** along the way, and stay with **D15** as you pedal south through **Cressy** and **Ercheau**. Leave Ercheau with **Road D154** (becomes **Road D545**) toward **Campagne**.

Cross the **Canal du Nord** to enter Campagne, and proceed with **Road D103** toward **Bussy**. Stay with D103 to **Genvry** and keep to the **right** as you ride through town. At the far end of Genvry, swing **left** to follow **Road D558** toward **Noyon**. You'll see the towers of Noyon's 12th-century cathedral piercing the sky as you wind into the city. Hit the main road (**Road D934**) on the edge of the city center, and go **left** to reach the cathedral.

Noyon's cathedral is one of the earliest Gothic structures in France. Even so, it's a mishmash of styles, with Romanesque holdouts hidden in its wonderful interior. Study the cathedral's delightful exterior carvings, then wander inside to admire its wealth of arches. The adjacent library contains thousands of priceless books. You'll need to make arrangements with the tourist office well in advance to view them, however.

Seek help with lodgings at Noyon's **tourist information office** in the place de l'Hôtel de Ville. The city offers a handful of hotels and a **campground** to the south. If you're interested in church history, be sure to pay a visit to the birthplace (now a small museum) of the Protestant reformer John Calvin. It's in the center of Noyon, not far from the cathedral.

Noyon to Compiègne: 28 kilometers

Leave Noyon with the frightening **Road N32** toward **Compiègne**, but go **left** onto **Road D145** signed for **Pont-l'Evêque** and the **Clairiére de l'Armistice**. **Cross the canal** and the **Oise River**,

Broken arches pen poems into the sky at the Abbaye Notre-Dame d'Ourscamp.

then turn **right** onto **Road D165** for **Bailly** and the **Clairière de l'Armistice**. When D165 angles left, continue **straight** on the smaller **Road D599** toward **Ourscamps**.

Swing **left** with signs for **Carlepont** just before recrossing the Oise River. Look for the entrance to the **Abbaye Notre-Dame d'Ourscamp** on the left. This vast ruined abbey is well worth a visit, and you'll be able to view the remains of a medieval infirmary, as well as the 12th-century church. We wandered the grounds for free on a sunny Sunday afternoon, but you may be asked to pay a slight fee for your visit.

From the abbey, continue pedaling through the pleasant **Forêt d'Ourscamps** and **rejoin D165** (go **right**) soon after. Cycle onward with signs for **Compiègne**, riding through **Bailly** and **St. Léger-aux-Bois**, and enjoying the shade of the oak and beech trees that line the route. Hit an intersection with **Road D130** about 2 km beyond St. Léger and turn **right**. Then grab the **first paved road to the left** (unsigned when we were there) to climb, then descend through the **Forêt de Laigue** and arrive at the banks of the **Aisne River**.

Cross Road D81, then **cross the river**, continuing **straight** to reach the **Armistice Clearing**. It was here on November 11, 1918, that World War I officially came to a close. In a small museum, you can visit a replica of the railway car where the peace treaty was signed. The surrounding forest and its hiking trails draw as many visitors as the historic site, and you'll pass lots of knapsack-toting French as you pedal onward with **Road D546** toward **Compiègne**.

Arrive at a **roundabout** where **Road N31** and **Road D130** intersect, and go **straight** with N31 toward Compiègne's **center**. To find the city's **Palais National** and **campground**, veer **left** on the **rue President Clemenceau** and follow this street to pick up signs for the **Palais** and **camping**.

Compiègne's **tourist office** is on the place de l'Hôtel de Ville in the center of town. Ask here for help with indoor accommodations (beds can be hard to come by in the summer months, when hikers and horse racers arrive in force). There's a convenient **youth hostel** in town, or try out Compiègne's excellent municipal **campground**. It's next to the hippodrome, about 2 km from the center.

Don't neglect a visit to the Palais National, once the second home of the Emperor Napoleon. Although the building's exterior is rather plain and stern, it's surrounded by lovely gardens and parks, and it houses a pair of excellent museums. Wander Compiègne's compact center and join the tourist flow on its busy streets. The hopping place de l'Hôtel de Ville is a good place to get started.

If you find yourself enjoying Compiègne enough to want to linger an extra day, consider making the 30-km roundtrip ride from Compiègne to the Château de Pierrefonds, a wonderfully restored medieval fortress with picture-perfect turrets. Much of your ride to the château can be routed on delightful small roads (it's a signed cycle route), and you'll discover the charms of the Forêt de Compiègne along the way.

Compiègne to Chantilly: 50 kilometers

From Compiègne's **Palais National**, continue away from the city center on the **avenue Royale**. Pass the city **campground** and arrive at a **roundabout**. Go **right** here with signs for **Paris**, and pedal the **avenue Napoleon** to a second **roundabout**. Take the **paved road** (no road sign) heading **south** into the Forêt de Compiègne. Continue **straight** with this shaded route through several subsequent roundabouts, and enjoy wonderfully peaceful cycling beneath thick trees.

Stay with the paved route as it angles off to the **left, cross Road D85**, and **climb steadily** for a time. You'll reach a **signed intersection** 11 km from your starting point. Go **right** here for **Champlieu** and leave the forest behind. You'll cycle past some lonely Roman ruins scattered on a hilltop, then cruise downhill to **Béthisy–St. Martin** and **Road D123**. Go **right** on D123 to cycle into **Béthisy–St. Pierre**, then make **two lefts** with signs for **Néry** to gain **Road D98** and more quiet cycling.

Climb past Néry and reach a junction with **Road D554**, where you'll veer **right** toward **la Borde**. **Cross over a new road**, then turn **left** for **Raray**. Easy pedaling on a quiet roadway leads to Raray. **Join Road D26** to ride through this small village overwhelmed by an attractive château, and continue on with signs for **Ognon**. **Pass over the freeway** and follow D26 to Ognon, where another fine château awaits.

In Ognon, veer **left** on **Road D120**, then swing **right** just after for **Chamant**. A tiny road will lead you into the jaws of the roaring **Road D932A**. Dive **left** here to pedal the final few hectic kilometers into **Senlis**. Follow signs for the **center** to find the cobbled streets of Senlis's quaint old core. You may want to get off and push when you hit the cobblestones, especially if you're heavily loaded.

Head for Senlis's wonderful 12th-century cathedral, rich in Romanesque carvings. The skillfully rendered figures on the front portal rival those at Chartres. Senlis's **tourist office** is opposite the cathedral's front. Pick up a map of town and head for the Church of St. Frambourg, or visit the hunting museum in the Château Royal, a hunting lodge for French kings. Senlis's undeniable charm adds to its popularity. Unfortunately, its proximity to Paris adds to its crowds. Even so, the little city is well worth a leisurely stop.

From Senlis, head **south** on **Road N17** toward **Paris**, but escape to the **right** on the edge of town at a sign for the **Quartier Brichebay**.

Cycle past the city **hospital**, and swing to the **left** onto the **rue Brichebay**. Continue with this small road past scores of fancy homes, and pedal through the villages of **Avilly–St. Léonard** and **Avilly**. Signs for **Chantilly** lead onward into the **Forêt Chantilly** with **Road D138**. (If you're on a mountain bike, you might want to try angling right onto the walking/cycling route GR 11 that leads directly to Chantilly Château.)

Reach **Road D924A** and go **right**. Chantilly Château appears out of the clearing ahead like a lovely apparition, floating on a sea of blue water and emerald green grass. Just to see this gorgeous palace from afar is enough of a treat, and the adjacent racecourse and 18th-century stables are delightfully ostentatious. If you're a horse lover, you may want to spring for a visit to the horse museum housed in the stables and skip the hefty entry fee for the château (the reality of the palace's interior can't match the dreams woven outside its shimmering walls).

To reach Chantilly's center and begin your hunt for a room (or to continue for the **campgrounds** at Gouvieux or St. Leu), go **left** at the junction just **before the road swings right** toward the château. Get onto a **small, unsigned road** leading past Chantilly's racecourse, and arrive at the frightening **Road N16**. Chantilly's **train station** is just across the busy thoroughfare. (If you're cycling this tour as a loop, you might begin and end here with the short train ride to Paris.)

Go **right** on N16 to pedal into Chantilly's **center**. One note of warning—Chantilly is host to two of France's most famous horse races in June. If you arrive in this little city along with thousands of racing fans, don't expect to find much in the way of accommodations. Seek out the **tourist office** at 23, avenue du Maréchal Joffre, to get advice on sights, hotels, and/or campgrounds in the vicinity.

Chantilly to Gisors: 63 kilometers

From Chantilly's **train station**, head **south** on **N16**. Cross **under the train tracks**, then take the **first right turn** (a *very* sharp right turn) onto the **rue Victor Hugo**. The turn is signed for **Gouvieux**. Climb away from the main road and swing **left** onto the **chemin des Aigles**. You'll pass a host of deluxe stables and expensive houses as you pedal on. Hit a **T** intersection and go **right**, then veer **left** on the **rue de Chantilly** to ride toward the center of Gouvieux.

If you're looking for Gouvieux's **campground**, you'll need to stop and ask directions in the little city. We were lucky enough to find a friendly policeman with a city map. Even so, we had a hard time finding the place. To continue from Gouvieux, pedal through town on **Road D909**, following signs for **Boran** and **Pontoise**. About 2 km from Gouvieux's center, arrive at a **roundabout** where D909 and

Chantilly Château is more than a dream for the architecture-loving cyclist.

Road D924 intersect. Stay with **D909** for **Lys** and the **Abbaye de Royaumont**, and continue with this busy road to reach a **left turn** signed for **Baillon** and the **Abbaye de Royaumont**.

If you'd like to visit the impressive remains of this Cistercian abbey founded in 1228, swing left to enter the grounds. Otherwise, veer **right** onto the **unsigned road** just opposite the abbey turnoff (a war memorial marks the intersection), and ride to **Road D922**. Turn **right** here to cycle past **Asnières-sur-Oise** and on to **Beaumont-sur-Oise**. Steady traffic mars this portion of the day's ride.

Follow signs for Beaumont's **center** to view the city core with its 10th-century citadel and medieval church. This busy little city was in the midst of a massive roadwork project when we pedaled through in 1991, so you'll need to rely on road signs and your map to find the road for **Persan** and **Chambly**. Descend to **cross the Oise River**, then fight your way through Persan's urban sprawl of mega-stores and mega-congestion. Pedal on for **Chambly**.

Swing **left** into Chambly's **center** to view its remarkable parish church, believed to have been founded by Saint Louis, then leave the little city with the road signed for **Bornel** (Road D923). Stay with

D923 to **cross over the N1 freeway**, and breathe a sigh of relief as you leave the hectic Beaumont/Persan area behind. Pedal past rippling wheatfields and nodding late-summer sunflowers, negotiating gentle hills past **Belle-Église** and **Bornel**. In **Esches**, veer **left** onto the small road signed for **Sandricourt**.

Cross the train tracks and climb through cultivated fields to **join Road D105** and enter **Sandricourt**. Then continue with D105 to **Amblainville**. Signs for **Chaumont-en-Vexin** and **Gisors** lead on with D105. Traffic is light and terrain is mellow, but a fierce west wind can make the going tough through here. Pass scattered small towns and dozens of farms before **joining Road D923** and pedaling on for **Chaumont**. Chaumont-en-Vexin is an attractive town with an inviting Gothic church perched on a tree-covered hilltop.

Swing to the **left** through town to ride beneath the church, then follow **Road D923** toward **Gisors**. You'll cross another **main road** just outside of Chaumont, then continue **straight** with D923 toward **Trie-Château**. Pick up increased traffic as you merge with **Road D981** and enter Trie-Château. This is a delightful little city. A sprawling green park lies beside the remnants of a 17th-century château, and the Romanesque church has a wonderful carved façade.

Continue out of Trie-Château with D981 for **Gisors**. Traffic is awful but you'll soon be into town. Head for the center of this charming mid-size city. Attractive half-timbered buildings, a handsome Gothic church, placid canals, and a ruined 12th-century castle combine to make Gisors a treat. Seek out the **tourist office** beside the *Hôtel de Ville,* and ask for a list of the hotels and sights in town.

If you're hoping to camp, the nearest **campground** is at Dangu, 8 km out on the unpleasant Road D181. The campsites occupy a nice spot beside a small lake, but the location is inconvenient if you want to do justice to Gisors.

Gisors to Rouen: 75 kilometers

Leave Gisors with **Road D10** toward **Neaufles–St. Martin** and **Vesly**. Mildly hilly cycling leads to an intersection with **D181**, where you'll swing **right** toward **Vesly**. Pedal along this busy thoroughfare through Vesly and on to **les Thilliers en-Vexin**. **Cross Road N14** in les Thilliers, and angle **right** for **Cantiers** to regain the much more pleasant **D10**. Enjoy quiet cycling through windswept fields of grain as you stay with D10 to **Guitry**. Go **left** in Guitry onto **Road D3**, then veer **right** soon after to gain **Road D9** toward **Forêt-la-Folie**.

Follow your tiny roadway to Forêt, and swing **left** through the village to regain **D10** signed for **Guiseniers**. You'll dive into a small canyon occupied by a secluded farmhouse, then climb briefly to gain more flat, open cycling. In **Guiseniers**, veer **left** opposite the **church** (it's unsigned) to stay with D10. (If you hit the junction for Villers and Harquency, you missed the turn.)

Abandon D10 about ½ km later as you go **right** for **les Andelys**. Ride to a junction with **Road D1** (this one's unsigned, too) and turn **right**, then pedal on to the brink of the hill above the Seine River. Forsake D1 as it curves right to plunge down the hillside, and take the **small road straight ahead** signed for the **Château Gaillard**. You may want to check your brake pads before you start into this one—a 15 percent downhill grade leads to an unforgettable vista of the Seine River, the city of les Andelys, and the enchanting ruin of the Château Gaillard.

Pause at the viewpoint to snap some photos and let this scene engrave itself upon your memory, then take the paved pathway leading toward the ruined castle, constructed by Richard the Lionhearted in 1196 to aid in the defense of Normandy. If you wish to visit the ruin, wheel your bicycle out onto the bluff above the Seine. To continue to les Andelys, dive **right** to stay with the paved pathway on its **precipitous descent** to the river.

Hit the **main road** below the castle and go **left** for **Evreux**, then veer **right** for **Petit Andelys**. Pause to admire the old core of the riverside city, with its 13th-century church, then join **Road D313** leading **northwest** along the Seine. To stay beside the river, keep to the **left** for **Muids** and **la Roque**, and enjoy pleasant, level cycling beneath glowing limestone cliffs. Traffic was light when we pedaled this road on a weekday morning in September, but you may encounter Paris crowds on Saturday and Sunday.

Swing **left** with D313 in **Muids** (signs for **Louviers** and **Rouen**), but veer **right** onto **Road D65** soon after to ride toward **Herqueville**. Leave the river for a time as you cut a loop in the Seine and pedal to Herqueville, then go **right** onto **Road D19** for **Connelles**. Luxurious cycling follows as you pedal past a wealth of riverside estates. Just beyond **Amfreville-sur-Seine**, angle **left** for **les Ecluses**, and continue **straight** with **Road D20** (don't take the subsequent left) to enter **Pîtres**.

Cross Road D508 in Pîtres and pedal straight ahead to an intersection with the busy **Road D321**. Go **left** here and ride a terrifying ½ km before escaping to the **right** onto **D20** for **Ymare**. A **steady climb** through trees leads to Ymare, then you'll continue **straight** (now on **Road D95**) past the **airport** at Boos. The party's over now—it's nothing but flying trucks and cars from here to Rouen. Grit your teeth, cinch up your helmet strap, and breathe a prayer; then turn **left** on N14 for the hair-raising ride into Rouen.

Fly through a long, curving downhill into this growling city of nearly half a million people, and stay with the **main road** through town, following signs for **Dieppe** and **le Havre**. The Seine River will be on your left, and the cathedral will be on your right as you pedal through the heart of the city. To find the **tourist office** opposite the cathedral, go **right** when you come abreast of the **Pont Boieldieu** and make your way along the **rue Grand Pont** to the front of Rouen's Gothic wonder, the Cathédrale de Notre Dame. You'll be able to get a good city map (a must) and a list of accommodations at the tourist office. There's a **youth hostel** on the opposite side of the Seine.

To find Rouen's municipal **campground** (it's about 5 km from the center but has frequent bus service into town), keep to the **right** when the main road branches. The left branch becomes the Dieppe-bound freeway, and your route becomes **Road N15** toward **Déville**. **Climb steadily** with heavy traffic for 2 to 3 km, and watch for **campground signs** pointing **left** near Déville's **city hall**. This exceedingly busy site is somewhat inconvenient and often noisy, but it's also the most economical way to spend time in Rouen.

Rouen is well worth any time you'll give it. In addition to the cathedral, it boasts the incredibly ornate Church of St. Maclou and the equally lovely Church of St. Ouen. The city streets are a joy for walking (although not for biking), with many half-timbered buildings and a skyline studded with soaring church spires. Several worthwhile museums and the modernistic Église Jeanne d'Arc (built on the site of her execution) add to the attractions available in Rouen.

If you're ending your cycling here with a rail hop back to Paris, there are hourly trains from Rouen to the French capital. Check in early for instructions about your bicycle.

As mentioned previously, you can make this tour a loop with the one-day ride to Dieppe. Simply leave the city with **N15 through Déville**, **le Houlme**, and **Malaunay**, then swing **right** with Road **D155** to follow smaller, paralleling roads **through Montville**, **Clères**, and **Longueville**. Best of all, why not continue with our Tour No. 2 and pedal to St. Malo from here?

TOUR NO. 2

A CHEESY COASTLINE

Rouen to St. Malo

Distance: 430 kilometers (267 miles)
Estimated time: 7 riding days
Best time to go: June through September
Terrain: A mix of hills and flatlands, pastoral solitude, and coastal traffic
Maps: Michelin Nos. 54, 55, and 59
Connecting tours: Tour Nos. 1 and 3

This ride from Rouen to the Atlantic coast of France will give you a wonderful glimpse of the farms and fields of Normandy. You'll follow the Seine River to Honfleur, then pedal past a tourist-heavy swath of beaches on the way to Bayeux. More coastal cycling leads past the D-Day battlefields, then you'll head west for an unforgettable look at le Mont St. Michel and hill-studded Brittany. One note of warning— the wind coming from the west can be tenacious on this ride. If you're unfortunate enough to encounter the Normandy gales (we were!), you may need to shorten your riding days.

CONNECTIONS. The vast city of Rouen marks the start of this tour. Hourly train connections to Paris make the city easily accessible by rail, or you can cycle in via our Tour No. 1 from Dieppe. Those who wish to see more of Brittany than this tour offers can combine the ride with Tour No. 3 from St. Malo to Angers.

INFORMATION. Two *Green Guide*s for Normandy (*Normandy Côtentin* and *Normandy Seine Valley*) and another Michelin volume entitled *Brittany* will overwhelm you with information about the regions this tour explores. For a lushly illustrated and heavy-on-history volume on Brittany, refer to the Philips Travel Guide called *Brittany*.

Because you'll be spending a good part of your time in an area marked by the indelible imprint of World War II, you might enjoy doing some background reading on the D-Day invasion or on other World War II topics, especially those pertinent to this part of France. Farther in the past, the history of Normandy and Brittany is closely tied to that of Great Britain. The date 1066 stands out in particular, as this is the year that William the Conqueror, Duke of Normandy, invaded and subdued England. As you visit this part of France, you'll see many signs of the 300-year-long link between England and France's lands along the Channel.

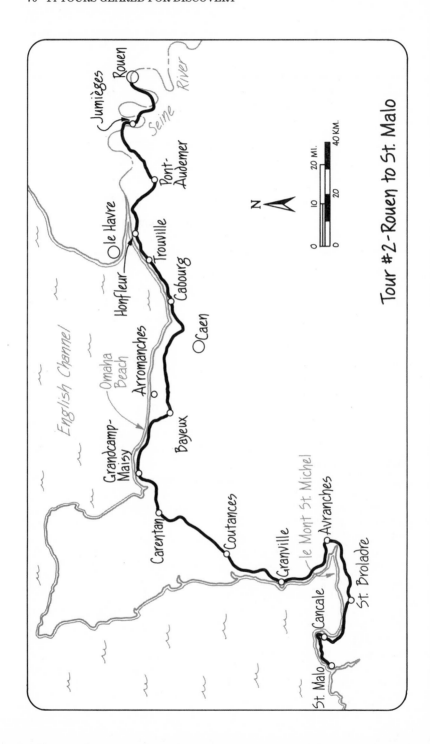

Tour #2 - Rouen to St. Malo

Campgrounds (and tourists) are everywhere in this part of France, so you should have little trouble finding a spot to plant your tent. Prices can be inflated for both rooms and campsites, however. Owing to the proximity of Paris and the heavy influx of foreign visitors, demand for tourist amenities is heavy, and prices remain high.

Seafood is (understandably) a specialty in this maritime region, and you'll be able to sample mussels, sole, cod, and a variety of other ocean delicacies, if you wish. Please refer ahead to Tour No. 3 for a discussion of Brittany's specialties, and glance back at Tour No. 1 for a taste of Normandy's delights. The Côtentin Peninsula is home to thousands of dairy cows, so you'll find a host of locally produced cheeses to select from here.

Rouen to Pont-Audemer: 70 kilometers

Please refer to the information on Rouen provided in the final paragraphs of Tour No. 1. If you arrive at the train station, you'll find Rouen's **tourist office** (opposite the cathedral) by following the rue Jeanne d'Arc to the rue du Gros Horloge and going left. Those who wish to camp should refer to the cycling directions at the end of the previous tour.

From Rouen's municipal **campground** in the suburb of **Déville**, turn **right** as you exit the campground, and cycle about 1½ km to a **T**

Normandy means cows—and cows mean milk.

intersection. Veer **left** here and pedal toward the Seine River on **Road D51**. You'll cross **Road D982** a short time later, and continue with **D51** for **Croisset**. If you're pedaling from Rouen's **center**, ride to the **right bank** of the Seine and pedal downriver. Look for the road signed for **Croisset (boulevard de Croisset)** leading away from town along the river's right bank. Stay with signs for **Croisset** as you join **D51** and continue away from the city.

This portion of the ride is very industrial and correspondingly unappealing. Traffic is quite bearable, however, and the scenery improves before long. Ride through Croisset, a riverside village with associations to the French novelist Gustave Flaubert, and push on to **Val-de-la-Haye**, the first breath of beauty after a suffocating succession of grain silos, factories, and fuel tanks. Turn away from the Seine soon after as D51 **climbs gently** to **Hautot-sur-Seine** and **Sahurs**.

Sahurs hides a neat old half-timbered church complex, and you'll swing **left** in town for **la Bouille** to abandon D51 at last. Look for the castle ruin on the opposite shore as you descend to the riverbank and a twice-hourly ferry. Hop aboard (the ride is free for bicycles) and cross to **la Bouille** and the **left bank** of the Seine.

La Bouille is a very attractive town, filled with half-timbered buildings and scarlet-dripping flowerboxes. Veer **right** onto **Road D64** for **Caumont** as you leave the ferry. Savor serene riverside cycling from here, enjoying views of the limestone cliffs and the ocean-going ships carrying goods to and from Rouen. In **la Ronce**, go **left** for **Yville-sur-Seine**, then swing **right** immediately after to gain **Road D265** toward **Yville**.

Climb steadily for about 2 km as you ascend the forested hillside, then cruise downhill toward the river once again, continuing with signs for **Yville** and the *bac* (ferry). **Dive steeply** as you finish your descent, passing the handsome château in Yville, then veering **left** on the far end of town for **Jumièges**. Follow **Road D265** and more signs for the *bac* to the river and another ferry crossing. This one is also free for bicycles, but scheduled crossings are on an hourly basis.

Depart the ferry and pedal on toward **Jumièges** with **Road D65**. Look for the **campground** you'll pass before the city if you're running late and want to call it a night. Effortless cycling leads to Jumièges, a small town overwhelmed by a massive ruined abbey. Saint Philibert founded the abbey in 654, and construction began on the present structure in 1020. The Wars of Religion and the French Revolution combined to leave the abbey what it is today—a hauntingly lovely tribute to a vast church built nearly a millennium ago. There's a rather hefty entry fee to tour the ruins. Do it if your pockets are deep enough.

From Jumièges, you'll have a couple of route options. The shortest (but steepest) ride toward Pont-Audemer begins with yet another ferry crossing. Descend to the Seine with signs for the *bac* (be sure to pause for a great view back to the abbey), cross the river, and **climb very steeply** from there. We opted for a bit less hill, mainly because Jumièges's ferry wasn't operating the day we were there. To follow our route, continue from Jumièges with **Road D143** toward **Yainville**. Climb gradually to the little town, then veer **left** for the *Marie* and *Église* to descend past Yainville's handsome Romanesque church.

Cross the train tracks and dive **left** onto a small road leading to the **ferry**. Frequent crossings and no fees for cyclists make this trip a breeze. Depart the Seine and follow **Road D65** to **la Mailleraye-sur-Seine**, then swing **right** in town on **Road N313** for **Caudebec**. Turn **left** for **Pont-Audemer** soon after, **cross Road D490**, and proceed with **Road D131** toward Pont-Audemer. Enjoy a lovely ride through the Forêt de Brotonne as you ascend a **long, steady hill** on a quiet, shaded road.

Road D131 becomes **Road D139**, and signs for **Pont-Audemer** lead through **Bourneville**, under **two freeways**, and on through a markedly busier final 8 km. Your weary legs will love the breezy descent into Pont-Audemer. If you're camping, watch for a tiny **Bar Camping** sign on the right, near the bottom of the hill. The site is primitive but the price is right.

Pont-Audemer is a charming midsize city, full of shops and hotels, tiny canals, and half-timbered buildings. Stow your bicycle and set out on foot to absorb the city's ambiance. Be sure to pause at Pont-Audemer's Church of St. Ouen. Its entertainingly ornate interior and soaring wooden roof will reward you for your attentions.

Pont-Audemer to Honfleur: 25 kilometers

This short riding day between Pont-Audemer and Honfleur should serve several purposes. It will allow you plenty of time for sightseeing in the exquisite little city of Honfleur. It will give your legs a break before the hills (and perhaps the winds) of Normandy commence. And it will encourage you to strive for an early start out of Honfleur on the following day—a must if you hope to avoid the steady stream of tourist traffic that plagues the road between Honfleur and Cabourg.

Leave Pont-Audemer with **Road D39** along the **right bank of the Risle River**. Road signs call out **Phare de St. Samson** and the **Circuit du Marais Vernier**. Enjoy a wonderfully quiet stretch of road as you cycle through Normandy at its best—half-timbered houses with thick thatched roofs, mist-shrouded apple orchards, and scores of silently chewing black-and-white cows. Pedal to an intersection with **Road D90**, and go **left** for **Honfleur**. Cross the **Risle River** and hit a **T** intersection with a much busier road.

Turn **left** here toward **Foulbec**, then veer **right** for **Conteville** to

Honfleur's harbor is a haven for anyone in search of beauty.

gain **Road D312**. Pedal through gentle hills to Conteville (there's a **campground** here), then signs for **Honfleur** lead on with D312. You'll have views of the vast port city of le Havre and the Seine estuary as you labor through rolling hills. Descend past a handsome château near **Grestain**, and push on to **Fiquefleur**. Hit **Road D180** just past Fiquefleur, but ignore the right for Honfleur and **continue straight** with the smaller road **paralleling the main road**. Pedal through **la Rivière-St. Sauveur** and follow signs for Honfleur's **center** to **join D180** into town. Despite the crowds of British tourists, Parisian weekenders, and scattered representatives from everywhere else, Honfleur is a delight.

Begin at the little city's gorgeous harbor, filled with bobbing boats and framed by three- and four-story buildings, their façades reflected in the gray-green water. If you're planning to camp, head for the **campground** to stow your bicycle and gear. It's just out of the city center, along the harbor road signed for Trouville. Those in need of a room (and in possession of a thick wallet) can seek help at Honfleur's **tourist office**, near the bus station at 33 cour des Fossés.

Once you've arranged for your lodgings and lightened your load, strike out on foot to explore Honfleur's nooks and crannies. The city is rich with delights, from its Saturday market filled with fragrant goat-cheese (*chèvre*) stands, to its unique Église Ste. Catherine, with a dark wooden ceiling constructed by the town's shipbuilders. Duck into a few of the artists' shops that swamp Honfleur, pause to paw through one of the myriad postcard racks that clog the city sidewalks, or simply sit beside the harbor and savor the view.

Honfleur to Bayeux: 86 kilometers

From Honfleur's exquisite **harbor**, take the waterside road signed for **Trouville** and head **southwest** along the coast. Enjoy pleasant cycling as you follow a narrow road between thick hedges, passing farms and luxurious vacation homes, and picking up glimpses of the ocean along the way. Gentle hills lead to **Hennequeville**. Veer **right** just beyond the town to take the **route de la Corniche** and **descend steeply** into **Trouville** with a tiny road. Pedal in along the beach and hit the heart of town.

Trouville and the adjacent Deauville are filled with tourists, hotels, and fancy restaurants, creating a scaled-down "Monte-Carlo of the north." If you pedal through in August, you may see more activity than you care to. Your beachside road will lead you to Trouville's harbor. Swing **left** along the harbor to gain the **bridge** to **Deauville**. Stay off Road D513 awhile by turning **right just across the bridge** and taking the signed *plage* (beach) route through Deauville.

Join D513 and pedal on to **Villers-sur-Mer**, with a beach that's sure to tempt all water lovers. Then **climb steeply** for about 3 km, and reach **Auberville** and a junction with **Road D163**. Veer **right** with the corniche road toward **Houlgate** (D163), and steal glimpses of a great vista in the midst of a **breakneck descent** to the sea. Ride through Houlgate, another small resort town, and rejoin the main route to struggle past **Dives-sur-Mer** and onward to **Cabourg**. Solid development and heavy traffic make the pedaling painful.

Cabourg boasts the standard seaside fare of casino, luxury hotels, and lots and lots of people. Stay with signs for **Ouistreham** from the city. Just beyond **le Home**, veer **left** off Road D514 to gain **Road D223** for **Bréville** and **Ranville**. Enjoy much saner cycling as you follow this small road toward the south. Ride through Bréville and on toward Ranville (this entire area hosted intense fighting following the D-Day invasion of 1944).

Just before **Ranville**, swing **right** for **Bénoville** and **Ouistreham**. Rejoin **D514** shortly after to cross the **Orne River** on the famed **Pegasus Bridge**, named in honor of the British 6th Airborne Division. (If you wish to visit Caen, an attraction-packed but *huge* city, you can continue straight from the junction before Ranville. You'll be about 12 km from the center at that point.) The British cemetery in Ranville holds 2,566 graves.

From the Pegasus Bridge (British Airborne Museum nearby), veer **right** onto **Road D35** for **St. Aubin–d'Arquenay**, and delight in quiet, easy cycling as you parallel the hectic coast road. (If you're particularly interested in the D-Day beaches, you may want to swing north to Ouistreham and pedal D514 along the coast. Our secondary-road route bypasses the British and Canadian beaches in this section.)

Follow D35 to **Douvres-la-Délivrande**, an attractive town with a massive church, and cycle past a somber Canadian cemetery en route to **Reviers**. Continue **straight** from Reviers, pedaling **Road D176** toward **Colombiers-sur-Seulles**. Work through a bit of steady climbing, then enjoy more gentle cycling as you pass a junction with Road D65 and the turnoff for **Arromanches** (the detour to Arromanches will add about 8 km to your ride). Continue with **Road D12** to **Sommervieu**, and swing **left** (still with D12) for **Bayeux**.

You'll hit a busy **ring road** a few kilometers later. If you're camping, go right on the ring road to find Bayeux's excellent municipal **campground** about 1 km later. To proceed to the **center** of the city, go **straight** across the ring road and dive into the heart of town. Seek out the **tourist office** on the rue des Cuisiniers, not far from the cathedral, to pick up a city map, a list of hotels, and/or directions to the city's outstanding **youth hostel**. Then settle in and enjoy Bayeux.

Although the city itself is attractive and lively, you may find yourself spending much of your time indoors while visiting Bayeux. That's because there's just so much to see. Begin with the Tapisserie de Bayeux (the Bayeux Tapestry), a 70-meter-long embroidered panel depicting the 11th-century Battle of Hastings. It's housed in its own museum/seminary. Next, move on to Bayeux's remarkable cathedral; a mix of styles makes it one of the finest churches in Normandy. Finally, visit the city's excellent Musée Mémorial de la Bataille de Normandie, if you have the time.

Bayeux to Carentan: 60 kilometers

From the **ring road** on the north side of Bayeux, continue west to the junction with **Road D6**. Turn **right** here for **Port-en-Bessin**, and pedal through easy terrain with fairly steady traffic to reach the coast. Go **left** for the **center** in Port-en-Bessin, then another **left** leads onto **Road D514** for **Grandcamp-Maisy**. Climb to a ridge above the sea, and savor the views as you continue. Ride through **Colleville-sur-Mer**, and watch for a **right turn** signed for the **American Military Cemetery**.

Pedal the short distance to the vast cemetery beside Omaha Beach.

Row after row of stark white crosses crisscross an endless emerald lawn, and the steel gray sea murmurs in the distance, its waves still weeping for the lives poured out on its beaches. Pause here awhile, and mourn with all who linger. Then ride on with signs for the **Point Fortifié WN62** to find a viewspot and monument above Omaha Beach. Read the names of those who died here, wander among the forbidding gun emplacements on the hills above the surf, and wonder how anyone survived the battle that raged on Omaha Beach on June 6, 1944.

Return to **D514** and pedal on through **St. Laurent-sur-Mer** and **Vierville-sur-Mer**. It's well worth swinging off D514 to visit **Grandcamp-Maisy**, a pretty little fishing town with a pleasant center. Return to D514 and pedal 8 km to the junction with **Road N13**. Join the hectic thoroughfare very briefly, but swing **right** to ride through the center of **Isigny-sur-Mer** and escape the trucks for a few moments.

Beyond Isigny, rejoin **N13** to cross the **Vire River**, then turn **right** just across the bridge to get on **Road D444** toward **les Veys**. Signs for **Carentan** lead on with **Road D443** to **St. Hilaire**, then you'll need to get on **N13** for the final few kilometers into Carentan. Swing **right** off the main road to pedal toward the **town center**. Carentan's well-signed **campground** is beside the marina. It's a pleasant spot with convenient access to the little city.

If you need a bed, seek out one of the hotels in the heart of town. Carentan's sole highlight is an attractive 14th-century church with a sky-piercing spire. There's a World War II museum in the city, as well, if you aren't already shell-shocked from too much battle memorabilia.

Carentan to Granville: 72 kilometers

From Carentan's **center**, hop on **N13** toward **Cherbourg**, but veer **left** for **Coutances** to get on the **ring road** leading **west**. Another **left turn** for Coutances will deposit you on the busy **Road D971**. Endure this thoroughfare for about 4 km, then dive **left** onto the much more pleasant **Road D29** toward **St. Georges-de-Bohon**. Enjoy fairly level cycling with pleasant scenes of cows and farms to remind you you're in Normandy. (At last count, there were more than 800,000 cows on the Côtentin Peninsula alone!)

Stay with D29 past St. Georges, then watch for a **right turn** about 3 km later onto **Road D57** signed for **Auxais** and **Marchésieux**. The hills pick up as you follow the quiet D57 to **Feugères**, a charming village gathered around a hefty wooden cider press. Pass countless representatives of the "three C's of Normandy" as you ride on with D57 to **le Mesnilbus**—cows, corn, and cider orchards line the way.

Signs for **Coutances** lead on through increasingly hilly terrain as you **cross Road D52** and continue **straight**, then veer **right** on **Road D53**. Pedal a very short distance and dive **left** onto **D57** once again. Endure a **long climb** to **Monthuchon**, but turn **left** on **Road D535** for **Cambernon** before you hit the main road (Road D971). Descend to a **T** intersection and go **right** on **Road D141** to follow a quiet route into **Coutances**.

You'll hit a **roundabout** on the edge of the city. Go **right** here for **Carentan**, then swing **left** on **D971** to enter the city core. Signs for the **center** and the **cathedral** will take you to the old heart of town atop the ridge. Churches, shops, and cobblestones will slow you down considerably here. You might as well plan a leisurely lunch stop and go with the flow. (The grassy crescent curving around the choir of Coutances's cathedral makes a wonderful picnic spot, if you're in the market.) Coutances's **tourist office** is located in the plaza opposite the cathedral.

To continue from Coutances, return to **D971** and **dive off the hilltop** with signs for **Granville**, but veer **right** onto **Road D20** for **Bricqueville-la-Blouette** at the edge of town. Weekday cycling in late September wasn't bad when we took this route. August may be a different story, however. Anyway, you'll enjoy easy pedaling past farms and small towns as you parallel the coast to **Brehal**, still on **D20**. In Brehal, **rejoin D971** toward **Granville**, but escape this killer road just after with a **right turn** onto **Road D597** for **St. Martin-le-Vieux**.

Reach a **T** intersection and veer **left** onto **Road D135**, and cycle this quiet route through **la Rivière** and on to **Bréville-sur-Mer**. At the intersection with the road signed for **Bréville's campground** (to the right), continue **straight** onto a tiny roadway past Bréville's ancient church. A **very steep climb** will take you back to the main road in **Donville-lès-Bains**. Go **right** to continue into **Granville**. (You can avoid the climb by taking the right turn for Bréville's campground, then entering Granville along the sea. However, many of Granville's sights are up the hill anyway.)

Granville is a fascinating seaside city, plunging down to the water from its hilltop church. A large pleasure harbor, a bathing beach, and a casino all contribute to the resort's popularity. Granville marks the northern tip of the Baie du Mont St. Michel (the bay of le Mont St. Michel), an area that sees the highest tides in Europe. Unfortunately, the thick crowds that gather here all summer help ensure remarkably high prices, too.

Seek help with lodgings at the **tourist office** across from the casino. If you're camping, there are beachside **campgrounds** at Donville-lès-Bains (you should pass them on the way in, if you take the low route) and along the road leading south of the city. (Please read the next paragraph to find a campground beyond Granville.)

Granville to le Mont St. Michel: 54 kilometers

Leave Granville with the **coast road** (Road D911) signed for **Jullouville** and **Avranches**. Watch for signs for **Camping le Vague** just before **St. Pair-sur-Mer**, and swing left to find the pleasant (but spendy) site. Stay with D911 into St. Pair, a bustling seaside resort, then pedal on with signs for **Jullouville**. You'll enjoy fairly easy cycling for a time, but soon work up a sweat with the **steep climb** to the ridgetop town of **Carolles**.

Savor enchanting views of le Mont St. Michel across the bay as you continue through hilltop fields with D911. Descend to **Dragey** and stay with signs for **Avranches** on **D911**. **Genêts** hides an old church and a fantastic view of le Mont St. Michel. You can escape D911 just outside of Genêts by swinging **right** onto the small road signed for **St. Léonard**. The route adds a little distance, a little serenity, and a lot more view.

A British cyclist pedals toward the awesome form of le Mont St. Michel.

Push on to the outskirts of **Avranches** and follow signs for the **center** to ascend a **steep hill** and gain the old core on the bluff. A ruined castle, lots of shops and bakeries, and some attractive gardens may tempt you to linger. (You'll probably want to do your supper shopping here, if you're planning to camp at le Mont St. Michel.)

Continue through town with signs for **le Mont St. Michel** and **Pontaubault**. You'll dive off the ridgetop toward Pontaubault and endure heavy traffic for a time, but escape the main road about 7 km later. In Pontaubault, **cross the river** (General Patton came across this bridge) and veer **right** onto **Road D113** for **Céaux**. Keep to the **left** when the road branches, and go **left** again in Céaux. Gain **Road D43** toward **le Mont St. Michel**, and savor spectacular views and easy pedaling as you ride beside the bay. Stay with your quiet road (becomes **Road D275**) to a junction with **Road D976**.

You'll be 2 km from the abbey of Mont St. Michel here, and a **right turn** will take you directly there. There's a wonderful **campground** at the junction. It's convenient, inexpensive, and filled with visitors from a host of countries. The adjacent motel is a good option if you're hunting for a bed, and the on-site store has some of the cheapest postcards you'll find in France. If you do stay here, be sure to venture out for a view of the floodlit abbey by night. It's a fantastic picture.

A quick bike ride (or a thirty-minute walk) will take you to le Mont St. Michel from the junction. You'll always remember this place. It's incredible from every angle. Don't let the gauntlet of tacky tourist shops in the lower streets spoil your visit to the ancient abbey church above. Ascend the streets and stairways *du mont*, paced by thousands of pilgrims in medieval times, and take the one-hour tour of the abbey complex founded by Benedictines in 966.

Le Mont St. Michel to St. Malo: 63 kilometers

Depart le Mont St. Michel with **Road D976** toward **Beauvoir**, and turn **right** for **les Polders** in Beauvoir to **cross the canal**. Once across the water, veer **left** onto a quiet road through fields. Go **left** again at the following junction, **right** at the next one, and **straight** at the next. A **left** for **St. Malo** leads to **Road D797**. (All junctions but the last are poorly signed, so rely heavily on your map.)

Swing **right** onto **D797** and endure steady traffic with views of the abbey and its bay. Carrots and cabbages fill the fields beside the road in the summer months. If traffic is too awful, you can escape D797 for a while after passing through **St. Broladre**. Otherwise, continue with the signed route for St. Malo, cycling through **le Vivier-sur-Mer**, and cruising on to **St. Benoît-des-Ondes** (now with **Road D155**).

Stranded fishing boats and signs for mussels will remind you that you're now in Brittany, a region that has always sought its fortunes from the sea. And lots of worn-out windmills, their blades long since stilled and fallen, speak of the coastal winds that sometimes whip across the water here. Climb away from St. Benoît and watch for a **right turn** signed for **Cancale** to gain **Road D76** toward the city. (There's an unsigned shortcut road before the junction. Take it if you spot it.)

Signs for the **center** lead to Cancale's old core and **tourist office**. Then stay with signs for **St. Malo** *par la Côte* (via the coast) to gain **Road D201** along the ocean. You'll have gorgeous scenes of coast and cliffs to entertain you as you pedal this winding road beside the sea. Views extend back to le Mont St. Michel and out to Landes Island. If you're cycling on a particularly hazeless day, you may even catch a glimpse of Britain's Chausey Isles.

Scores of campgrounds line the gently rolling route along the coast, and you'll enter **St. Malo** through almost nonstop city. Fight your way through the **Rothéneuf/Paramé** sprawl (you'll pass one of St. Malo's **youth hostels** along the way), and arrive at the enchanting port of St. Malo. A shimmering ocean backdrop sets the scene for this maritime city of glowing ramparts, an island fortress, and pleasure boats bouncing on their tethers. Cycle in along the seaside road, with the walled old city on your right and the harbor on your left, and seek out St. Malo's well-signed **tourist office** on the esplanade St. Vincent.

Free city maps and hotel listings will make your visit fruitful. Be forewarned—St. Malo is infinitely popular, and high-season hotel rooms are virtually impossible to find without a reservation. Besides the hostel in Paramé, there are a couple of other hostels in the city. Ask for directions at the tourist office.

If you want to camp, St. Malo offers a lofty **municipal campground**, tucked within the ramparts across the harbor (south) of the old city. It's a pleasant, scenic, and very international spot, and you'll be within walking distance of St. Malo's center. To find the campground, continue with signs for St. Servan, and climb to the little city's *Marie*, then veer right with camping signs and continue climbing.

Allow yourself at least a day or two to enjoy St. Malo, a remarkably beautiful city. You'll burn up a ton of film here, if you're a photographer. The old core within the city's massive walls is particularly enchanting, but outside scenes of bright pleasure boats, hilltop ramparts, and surf beating against a tiny island fortress are captivating, too. The nicest way to enjoy the entire panorama is to stroll along the top of the old city walls. The trip is free and unforgettably scenic.

If you're ending your Brittany journey in St. Malo, you'll be able to hop aboard a five-hour train to Paris or grab a ferry to various points in Britain (Portsmouth, Jersey, Guernsey, etc.). Otherwise, continue pedaling with our Tour No. 3, and enjoy more of Brittany en route to Angers and the Loire Valley.

You can find rain-slickened cobblestones in just about any town in Brittany.

TOUR NO. 3

CASTLES, CRÊPES, AND CIDER
St. Malo to Angers

Distance: 238 kilometers (148 miles)
Estimated time: 4 riding days
Best time to go: June through September
Terrain: Challenging hills and charming solitude
Maps: Michelin Nos. 59 and 63
Connecting tours: Tour Nos. 2 and 5

The ride from St. Malo to Angers slices through a hill-studded swath of Brittany. It's essentially a connecting tour, designed for cyclists who have just pedaled across Normandy and/or those who are bound for Angers, the Loire, or regions farther south. If you're blessed with good weather when you visit Brittany (not many are), you may want to venture west toward St. Brieuc and Quimper with what time you have. Brittany holds a host of treasures—historical, architectural, cultural, and natural. Unfortunately, most cyclists must "enjoy" the region's charms in the midst of drenching downpours and wailing winds.

We came to Brittany too late in the year to challenge its unforgiving climate, as it was almost October by the time we left St. Malo. We waited out two days of nonstop rain in Dinan, then settled for a meandering route toward the south. After just a glimpse of Brittany's many wonders, however, all we can say is, "We'll be back!"

CONNECTIONS. This tour begins in the city of St. Malo, on the northwest coast of France. It's a five-hour train ride from Paris and it's also served by ferries from Britain. If you arrive at St. Malo's train station, head for the walled old city along the avenue Louis-Martin. You'll pass St. Malo's **tourist office** near the entrance to the old city. Those arriving by bicycle via our Tour No. 2 will see signs for the tourist office as they pedal into town. Please refer to the closing paragraphs of the previous tour for more information on St. Malo.

From Angers and this tour's end, you can cycle back toward Paris with our Tour No. 5, or you might choose to pedal south, hopping onto Tour No. 6 at Chinon and riding on toward Bordeaux.

INFORMATION. An excellent *Green Guide* for Brittany and a companion volume entitled *Châteaux of the Loire* will provide you with information for your ride. For a lushly illustrated and heavy-on-

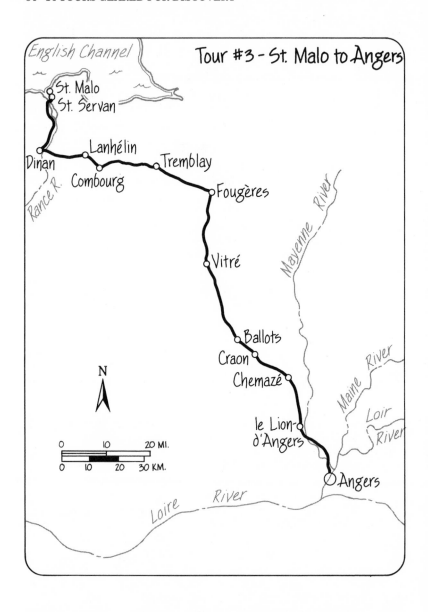

history volume on Brittany, refer to the Philips Travel Guide called *Brittany*. It's well worth it to do some extra background reading on the area, even if you're knowledgeable about general French history and culture. In many ways, Brittany is a land unto itself, from its unique Breton dialect to its costumes and its cuisine.

The area's popularity is evidenced by its host of campgrounds and hotels, so you should have no trouble finding lodgings here. Tourist-office workers are accustomed to dealing with English-speaking visitors, as Brittany is a favorite destination of travelers from Britain.

You'll work hard when you're pedaling here, but the delicious Breton food will encourage you to reward your muscles, especially after you've tackled several kilometers of the challenging Breton hills. Although most of the rest of France serves *crêpes* in one form or another, Brittany rolls up *crêpes* as only Brittany can, filled with anything from mushrooms to seafood to jam. *Crêpes* are often washed down with glasses of cool local *cidre*, while *Muscadet* from Nantes often accompanies the seafood dishes that are so prevalent on the tables here. Try out *cotriade*, a Breton fish soup, to warm your insides after a day of cycling in the Breton rain.

St. Malo to Dinan: 31 kilometers

From St. Malo's **tourist office**, continue with the signed route for **St. Servan**, and climb to the hillside town. Descend toward the **tour Solidor** and get on the **quai Solidor** leading away from town beside the water. Signs for **Dinard** and the **Barrage de la Rance** (the Rance Dam) lead onto the **boulevard de la Rance**. You'll merge with a **very busy main road** and descend to cross the **Rance Estuary** on a windswept (and rather frightening) bridge.

Climb away from the bridge with heavy traffic, then take the **left turn** signed for **la Richardais** (it's at the **first main intersection**). You'll breathe a sigh of relief as you escape the din of cars and trucks with **Road D114**. Ride a rolling route through la Richardais and **le Minihic-sur-Rance**, then pedal on toward **Plouer-sur-Rance**. Road D114 becomes **Road D12** along the way. Cross **over the main road** to enter Plouer.

You'll find two routes signed for **Dinan** just beyond Plouer. Stay with the **D12** route to the **left**. Gentle hills lead on as you **cross Road D57** and pedal on with **D12** toward Dinan. Endure a **long, forested climb** to a shaded ridgetop, then breeze through a **swift descent** to Dinan's old port area along the banks of the Rance River. (You may want to pause to enjoy this picturesque fishermen's quarter now, as you probably won't be in the mood for a return, once you've ascended to the hilltop city and settled in.)

Cycle under the **lofty main-road bridge**, then **climb steadily** to reach the old core of Dinan atop its hill. A well-signed, centrally located **tourist office** (at 6, rue de l'Horloge) can assist you if you're looking for a room. To find the small and inexpensive municipal **campground**, follow **camping signs** through the city core, then glide a short distance down the hill to **Camping Châteaubriand**. A somewhat inconvenient (but very pleasant) **youth hostel** is yet an-

Dinan's Fête des Remparts *is a medieval delight.*

other lodging option for the city.

Whatever you do, find a place to stay. Dinan is too wonderful to simply cruise through. If you're fortunate enough to visit the city on the final weekend in September, during its annual *Fête des Remparts* (festival of the walls), you'll really be in for a treat. The entire old core of Dinan is transformed into a medieval village for the two-day celebration. Banners and garlands are hung from all the buildings, and the local citizens dress in elaborate costumes, then feast and play in 14th-century fashion.

Even without its festival, Dinan is a medieval wonder, with a well-preserved old core of ancient buildings, churches, towers, and walls. Be sure to sample some regional specialties while you're here. Have a meal of freshly made *crêpes*, washed down with a glass of local cider. Or try a Brittany "sandwich"—a sizzling pork sausage wrapped in a warm *galette* (buckwheat pancake).

The narrow streets of Dinan are hung with attractive signs.

Dinan to Fougères: 74 kilometers

Leave Dinan on the lofty **bridge** across the Rance, pedaling the road signed for **Lanvallay**. Once across the river, swing **right** onto **Road D2** for **Vitré**, and ride through the roadside town of Lanvallay. Pedal a short distance (still in Lanvallay), then veer **left** onto **Road D794** toward **Combourg**. Another **left** about 2 km later will put you on the small road signed for **St. Solen**.

Cycle onward to the edge of a lovely oak forest, then angle **left** again onto the road for **St. Pierre-de-Plesguen**. **Road D68** becomes **Road D10** as you savor easy cycling through a shade-dripping forest. Ride through St. Pierre and on to **Lanhélin**, then go **right** onto **Road D73** for **Combourg**. You'll see the towers of Combourg's castle ahead as you approach the city on the busy D73. Enter Combourg (its château will be on your right) and continue **straight** for **Fougères** with **Road D796**.

Traffic is thick through Combourg's suburbs. Keep to the **right** with **D796** in **Trémeheuc**. **Climb steadily** to **Bazouges-la-Pérouse**. You'll have a wonderful view out over the valley from the ridgeline before town. Bazouges's church boasts a pretty spire. Continue on for **Tremblay** and rejoice in an exhilarating descent on a smooth-surfaced roadway. The work commences once again as you labor through a **steady ascent** into Tremblay.

Ride past Tremblay's **church** and hit an intersection with the **main road** (signed for Rennes). Go **right** here, then take the **first left** (it's unsigned) to gain **Road D113** toward **Fougères**. Look for Tremblay's **hospital** on the way out—if you pass it, you're on the right road. You'll begin picking up signs for Fougères within a few kilometers, then enjoy an hour of lovely, quiet cycling through gently rolling farm- and pastureland. Murmuring cornfields line the road, interspersed with grassy clearings where milk-laden cows mourn tardy farmers.

You'll pass several junctions en route to Fougères. Simply stay with **D113** signed for the city, and you can't go wrong. Intersect with the hectic **Road N12** just before Fougères, and go **left** here to descend past the ancient walls and towers of Fougères's castle. The route toward the **center** and the **tourist office** is heavily signed. Pause at the office to pick up a map of the city and a listing of hotels (if you need one). To find Fougères's excellent, year-round **campground**, follow the route signed for **Alençon** (N12) and watch for campground signs leading to the left. (The auto route to the campground is rather roundabout, as signed, so plan out your own, more direct route if you have a map of the city.)

Of course, the highlight of Fougères is its castle, studded with forbidding towers and defended by stout walls. A dark moat, filled by the waters of the looping Nançon River, completes the magical, medieval scene. Pay for a tour of the castle's interior, walls, and towers, then stroll the surrounding streets to gain a dozen delightful vistas of the structure.

Fougères to Craon: 69 kilometers

From Fougères's **center/castle**, follow the tiny rue de la Providence to **Road D112**. Continue **straight** across D112 and join the **chemin de la République**. This quiet thoroughfare will lead you to **Road D179**, where you'll turn **right** toward **Vitré**. Formerly the main route to Vitré, this road lost much of its traffic when the paralleling Road D798/D178 was upgraded. As such, it makes for an enjoyable and direct route to Vitré.

Cycle through fields and grazing land with gentle hills to break the monotony. You'll pass through scattered villages along the way, each with its somber war monument, still weeping for long-dead sons. The hills gain frequency and steepness after **Taillis**. Cross a main **train line** and climb abruptly. Then descend and climb again. Road D179 intersects with Vitré's **main ring road** a few kilometers from the center. Cross carefully, then turn **left** on **Road D794** soon after.

Descend with pleasing views of Vitré's castle, and follow signs for the **city center** from here. You'll pass Vitré's **tourist office** (on the left) as you loop around the old core. Dive **left** into the city's narrow, shop-lined streets to find its handsome, turreted castle. Vitré's old core is wonderfully picturesque, and you'll delight in its medieval fortress, ruling a rocky spur above the Vilaine River.

If you decide to linger here and savor Vitré's charms for an afternoon, you'll find several hotels to choose from in the city. There's a year-round **campground** on the south side of town, as well.

From Vitré's center, continue with the road past the **train station**, and follows signs for **Argentré-du-Plessis** on **Road D88**. Traffic is tolerable as you cycle through rolling hills, passing the château (open for visits) at **les Rochers–Sévigny**. Continue on to **Argentré-du-Plessis**. Go left at the **first main intersection** in Argentré, then turn **right** for **Craon** to stay with **D88**.

Ride through gentle hills and wind through villages like **Gennes-sur-Seiche**, where old men ride their bicycles homeward, balancing bending *baguettes* on rusted handlebars. Road D88 becomes **Road D127** in Gennes, and it flies like an arrow from here, shooting straight toward the steeple of each subsequent village. Pedal on to **Ballots**, where you'll swing **left** onto **Road D25** for the final 9½ km into **Craon**. The hills are gentler now, the road remains ruler straight, and the trucks roar by with a vengeance as they make a run for Craon. (If you find the going too gruesome, you can escape to the left with the small road signed for Livre, then take Road D142 into Craon.)

Enter the midsize city and follow signs for the **center**. You'll find Craon's pleasant municipal **campground** beside the swimming pool at the far side of town. Shopping and hotels complete the picture here. Craon has a large château and little else to whet your tourist appetite.

Craon to Angers: 64 kilometers

Signs for **Angers** lead away from Craon on **Road D25**, but turn **left** for **Pommerieux** about 3 km later to gain much quieter cycling. You'll have a delightfully solitary day from here until you reach the outskirts of Angers—gaze at the scenery, push through the nearly nonstop hills, and enjoy French cycling at its finest.

Leave Pommerieux with signs for **Ampoigné**, then stay with **D274** toward **Chemazé** from here. You'll hit the busy **Road D20** in Chemazé (it's a reminder of how delightful France's *small* roads are).

The magnificent château at Angers is surrounded by vibrant gardens in spring.

Go **right** here, then turn **left** immediately after to gain **Road D588** for **Molière**. Pedal past apple orchards, cows, and corn as you continue. And watch for lonely châteaux hidden in the trees along the way.

In **Molière**, take the small road (**Road V.2**) on the **right side of the church** to ride for Montguillon. You'll cross into the region of Anjou as you pedal on. Keep **left** to enter **Montguillon**, then swing **right** on the small road by the **church** with signs for **St. Martin-du-Bois**. Hit an intersection with **Road D78** in St. Martin. Go **right** here for **Aviré**, then veer **left** for le Lion-d'Angers.

A tiny road will take you to the edge of St. Martin, where an **unsigned Y** is marked by a crucifix. Keep to the **right** to cycle past more châteaux and apple orchards as you continue your journey south. Join **Road D180** toward **Montreuil-sur-Maine**, and hit the totally unpleasant **Road D101** not long after. Cross carefully to continue into **Montreuil**, then go **right** in town for **le Lion-d'Angers**.

A **left** on the dreaded **D101** will take you into le Lion, a pleasant little city famed for its horses. Pass a deluxe **campground** and hippodrome, and cross the **Oudon River** as you enter town. Go **left** immediately to swing around the city's church and old core. Then watch for a **left turn** signed for **Grez-Neuville** to lead you on from here.

Gentle hills mark the route to Grez-Neuville. Keep to the **right** at the **first intersection** in town, then turn **left** with signs for **Sceaux-d'Anjou** to descend and cross the **Mayenne River**. Take the next **right** onto **Road D191** for **Feneu** to enjoy more great cycling through trees and hill-studded farmland. You'll parallel the Mayenne to **Feneu** (and pass another neat château on the way into town), then go **left** in the city for **Champigné**. A subsequent **right** will put you on **Road D191** for **Cantenay-Epinard**.

You'll be 13 km from the vast city of Angers here, and the cycling deteriorates rapidly as you proceed. Pedal on to Cantenay and continue with signs for **Angers** to follow **Road D107** into the city. Hit a busy **roundabout** as you approach Angers, and follow signs **straight** ahead for **St. Lazaire** (don't follow the circuitous route signed for car traffic).

Continue straight with this road onto the **boulevard Dumesnil**, then cross the **Maine River** with a fantastic view of Angers's fabulous château ahead. You'll find the **tourist office** near the castle. Please refer to our Angers paragraphs in Tour No. 5 for more information on the city.

You'll have several route options from here. To pedal back toward Paris, pick up Tour No. 5 from Angers to Versailles. To continue south toward Bordeaux, reverse the ride to Chinon and hook up with Tour No. 6 from there. To head for home, hop one of the frequent trains to Paris from Angers's train station and give your hill-weary legs the rest they've been longing for.

Tour #4 - Brussels to Versailles

TOUR NO. 4

WAFFLES AND CHAMPAGNE
Brussels to Versailles

Distance: 662 kilometers (411 miles)
Estimated time: 11 riding days
Best time to go: May, June, July, or September
Terrain: Gentle hills; lots of quiet secondary roads
Maps: Michelin Nos. 2, 53, 56, 60, and 61
Connecting tours: Tour Nos. 5 and 13

This tour from Brussels, Belgium, to Versailles will provide you with a wonderful mix of riverside riding, farms and fields, cities and sightseeing. You'll see the vine-covered hills of Champagne and the cathedrals of Reims, Troyes, and Sens. Continue with our Tour No. 5 to Chartres, Angers, and back, and you'll pedal through the château-scattered Loire and Loir valleys, as well.

CONNECTIONS. The busy Brussels International Airport is the starting place for this tour. However, you can pick up the tour's beginning by air or train or pedal power. As mentioned earlier, a natural continuation of this route is the tour in the Loire and Loir valleys, so keep that in mind when you're planning, too.

INFORMATION. *Green Guide*s for Champagne, Paris, and the Île-de-France are applicable to the French section of this tour (the Champagne guide is not yet offered in English, however). You'll find an ample selection of campgrounds and hotels along the route, especially in the busier tourist spots, such as Reims, Épernay, Sens, and Troyes. Camping in Belgium is an accommodations bargain, when compared to the price of hotel rooms. Look for youth hostels, student hostels, university lodgings, or unpretentious hotels, if you're on a budget.

Write to the Belgian National Tourist Office before you leave. You'll receive bundles of literature, plus campground and tourist maps. The address is Belgian National Tourist Office, 745 Fifth Avenue, #714, New York, New York 10151. Ask for a street map of Brussels to make your arrival go more smoothly. Once in Belgium, you'll find well-stocked tourist offices in almost every midsize city, and it's usually easy to obtain guidance in English.

Potential reading material for Belgium includes *The Real Guide: Holland, Belgium, and Luxembourg* or Michelin's *Green Guide Belgium and Luxembourg*. Michelin produces an excellent map series for route finding in Belgium, and the 1:200,000 detail will probably sat-isfy all your needs. There are special cycling maps available for Bel-gium (they provide greater detail and indicate cycle routes), but you'll find them rather expensive if you're covering much ground. Maps are readily available in bookstores in the country, but it's a good idea to *arrive* with your first map already in your handlebar bag.

Belgium adheres fairly closely to the French custom of lunchtime shop closures, so you'll have to watch out for midday shutdowns if you're shopping in small stores or in rural areas. Don't expect to buy groceries on Sunday, either. Be sure to try a sweet Belgian waffle for breakfast some morning on your way to France. Buy it warm from a street vendor (not cold and sugary from the supermarket shelf). One more thing—you haven't been to Belgium if you haven't eaten *frites*. This greasy pile of fried potatoes, topped with a huge scoop of mayon-naise or a river of curry catsup, puts American French fries to shame. (It may also put your arteries into total panic.)

Once you pedal into the region of France known as Champagne, you'll have other delights awaiting you. Of course, you should be aware that this is the *only* place on earth where true Champagne is produced. The famous sparkling wine takes its name not only from the method used to make it, but also from the region where it is made. If you have any *francs* left in your food budget after sampling this ex-pensive delicacy, rely on French staples like cheese (*St. Paulin* and *Brie* are noteworthy in the north) and bread (venture beyond the stan-dard *baguette* to try *pain de campagne* and *pain complet*). These basic items are *always* affordable in France.

Brussels (Airport) to Aische-en-Refail: 51 kilometers

Belgian tourist literature laments the fact that many tourists con-sider the Belgian capital to be simply a place to set off from on their way to other European destinations. Indeed, it's a shame to skip the things that Brussels has to offer in your haste to hit the cycling trail. So, if you won't be returning to Brussels for your flight home, plan to delay your cycling a few days and take a look around while you re-cover from jet lag.

Brussels is huge, and the traffic around this city is horrendous. Add in the fact that drivers here are less than biker friendly, and you've got a good argument for leaving your bicycle in the suburbs. On our first visit to Brussels almost ten years ago, an English-speaking friend told us about his initial driving lesson in the city. "What do I do if someone gets in my way?" he asked his aggressive driving instructor. "Why, ya kill 'em!" his tutor replied. Enough said.

If you happen to arrive in Belgium at Brussels International Air-port, you can load your bicycle and gear (boxed or unboxed) aboard the quick commuter train into the city center (we took our bikes right into the passenger compartment), then look for a room near the train station. Hotel prices in Brussels are steep, but there are several **youth hostels**. Stop in at the **tourist office** in the Town Hall on the Grand-Place for help with your accommodations search. On our past visits to Brussels, we've conducted our sightseeing from two locations—from a pleasant hotel in the little community of Zaventem (near the airport) and from the quiet enclave of Camping Paul Rosmant at Wezembeek-Oppem (about 6 km from the airport). This saved us from the hassle (and danger) of cycling into the enormous capital of Belgium and allowed us to do our "touristing" from a convenient base. You can pick up a map and information on Brussels at the airport information office when you land.

From Brussels International Airport, follow road signs for **Zaventem** *Centrum* to find the small town a few kilometers from the airport (indoor lodgings here). Stay on the main road through town, passing a grassy **park** on the left, then turn **left** on **Road N2** at the next **light**. Ascend a small hill and go **right** on **Leuvense Steenweg**, then descend to pass **under** the **freeway**. Angle **left** at the following **Y**, and stay on the main route past the MP-guarded **American School**, descending a slight hill along the way. Go **left** onto **Tramlaan** at the **stop sign** at the bottom of the hill.

If you're looking for Camping Paul Rosmant (also known as Camping Wezembeek), take the first **right** onto **Warandeberg** (this may or may not be signed for the campground, depending on whether the sign has been knocked over lately). Climb a gentle hill and look for the **campground entrance** on the **right**. This pleasant spot offers nice facilities, hot showers, and a cozy clubhouse. It's open from April to September, and it provides a good base for trips into Brussels via public transport. (There's an enormous shopping center about $1\frac{1}{2}$ km away. Ask at the clubhouse for directions.)

If neither camping outside the city nor a room in the suburbs appeals to you, there are plenty of accommodations options in Brussels. You'll find lots of cars and congestion in this very international city, so please enter with caution. After you've gotten dizzy spinning and staring in the Grand-Place, overwhelmed your senses in a few of Brussels's superior museums, and had your first taste of warm Belgian waffles or a bar of the country's famous Godiva chocolate, you'll be ready to pedal.

From **Tramlaan** (the street before the campground), follow signs to the small town of **Moorsel**. Pedal through Moorsel, and veer **left** onto **Groenlaan** (a small, easy-to-miss street—look for the water tower). Keep to the right as you leave Moorsel, and **descend briefly** before taking the **first left** onto **Kruisstraat**. Stay on this road to a **junction** with **Road N3**. Cross this busy thoroughfare and enter

Leefdaal. You'll have fairly quiet riding through gently rolling terrain as signs for **Neerijse** lead you on from here.

Cycle through Neerijse's **center**, first making a **left** to ride past the **church**, then veering **right** for **St.-Agatha-Rode**. A short, **steep hill** will take you out of Neerijse, then watch for a small town sign marking a road to the **left** for **St.-Agatha-Rode**. Go left here to pedal on to this quaint village settled around its small Gothic church. From the town **center**, swing **left** for **Archennes**, then cycle to an unsigned **T** and go **left** again.

Ride through Archennes and push on to the busy **Road N25**. **Cross** carefully to enter **Grez-Doiceau**, and hit the main route through the town soon after. Go **left** here, following signs for **Jodoigne**, then dive **right** about ½ km later, turning off for **Longueville** and **Bonlez**. Keep with the main route to **Bonlez**, then go **left** for **Gistoux** on the far end of town. In **Gistoux**, swing **right** at the **stop sign**, then take the **next left** to gain the unappealing **Road N243**. Endure 11 km of unpleasant cycling as you follow the hectic, roller-coaster ride of N243 all the way to **Perwez**.

There's a rough **bike path** on the left side of the road. It makes for slow, bumpy, but safe riding—use it! At least the scenery is pleasant as you pass through rolling green farmland and small settlements. Cruise into **Perwez**, a busy Belgian market town. You'll find shopping and indoor accommodations here, if you're looking. To push on for Aische-en-Refail and the campground, leave Perwez with signs for **Aische-en-Refail**, and cycle **Road N972** toward this small town. Ride through Aische, then follow signs for the **château** and **camping** to reach your goal.

Here you'll find a pleasant, well-equipped **campground** crouched beside a moated château. The price is friendly, as is the management, and cyclists erect their tents right on the lawn of the castle, shunning the caravan "slums" across the way. Nice!

Aische-en-Refail to Dinant: 50 kilometers

You'll want to get an early start today, as a midday pause at Namur will surely be on your itinerary. From the campground at Aische, **retrace** your route through town and go **left** for **Liernu**. Hit a larger road (**Road N912**) about 4 km later, and swing **right** for **Namur**. Grab the next **left** (signed for **Dhuy**) and pedal on to this small community. Just beyond the **church** in **Dhuy**, watch for a small sign for **Warisoulx**. Veer **right** here.

Cross under the freeway, ride to **Warisoulx**, then swing **right** for **Villers-lez-Heest**. Signs for **Namur** lead on from Villers with **Road N934**. You'll begin the breezy descent to the Meuse River at **St. Marc**. Enter the sprawling city of Namur several quick kilometers later.

Cyclists can follow the lovely Meuse River between Namur and Dinant.

Signs for the *centre* will lead you to the neighborhood of Namur's major attractions—the citadel and the cathedral.

Visit Namur's provincial **tourist office** at 3, rue Notre Dame, to gather information on the city and surrounding region. The city's massive hilltop citadel is well worth a few hours of exploration, and the streets below offer a cathedral and a dozen museums to tempt you to linger even more. If things get out of hand and it's just too late to cycle any farther, Namur has a **youth hostel** and plenty of hotels for overnight visitors.

From Namur, you'll have two route options on your journey to **Dinant**. You can cycle the less-traveled but hillier road that traces the east bank of the Meuse River, enjoying lofty views and cooling forest shade, or you can take the flatter and busier west-bank route. If you do opt for the west side of the river, you'll have lots of opportunities to escape the main road. Simply dive off onto the intermittent riverside pathways that hug the shore. You'll find quiet waterside cycling with pleasant views of the river and its mansions, but you should expect a few dead ends and a bit of cobblestone along the way. We've cycled both sides of the Meuse and enjoyed both equally, so you'll have to decide for yourself.

If you plan to camp around Dinant, there's a campground just opposite the town of Bouvignes. It's on the east bank of the river, about 2 km north of Dinant. Set right on the water, the campground is a somewhat spartan, but very typical European "trailer town." It comes complete with a healthy scoop of local flavor in the form of a busy *frites* stand and an even busier *boule* (French "bowling") area, and it offers a convenient base for sightseeing in Dinant.

Dinant itself is an unqualified delight, a charming small city nestled beneath a stout fortress that towers above its onion-domed church. Take the tour of Dinant's citadel and listen to your guide tell jokes in three languages. Then descend to admire the striking stained glass in Dinant's church or join the crowds of ice-cream-eating tourists strolling the city's narrow streets. A handful of hotels provide indoor lodging options. Check at the city **tourist office** at 37, rue Grande, for more information.

Dinant to Monthermé: 73 kilometers

Leave Dinant with the main road toward **Givet** along the **west shore** of the **Meuse River**. You'll have flat and effortless cycling. We found the route pleasantly quiet on a Sunday morning in April; however, the road certainly gets its share of traffic in the summer months. If you have the time and patience, scattered snatches of **riverside pathway** allow brief escapes from the main road. Either way, you'll enjoy lovely views of Belgian towns and country mansions, water-loving kayakers and floating swans, speeding cycle racers and cruising tourers.

Cross the **Belgian–French border** just before **Givet** and continue into the handsome French city, overlooked by its hilltop fortifications. From Givet, stay with the Meuse and **Road N51** toward **Fumay**. The first portion of the ride is the pits, with lots of traffic and challenging terrain. Look for a noteworthy fortified church in **Hierges**, and enjoy mellower cycling after **Vireux-Molhain**, a personable little town with good shopping opportunities. Your legs will enjoy the break as you follow the river toward **Fumay**.

Abandon N51 as you **cross** the Meuse at **Haybes**, then follow the shoreline to **Fumay** on a much quieter road. You'll **recross** the Meuse, then endure a **stiff climb** to Fumay's attractive **central square**. This is a town worth lingering over, if you have the time. From Fumay, follow signs for **Revin** as you stay beside the Meuse and bid adieu to N51. The route is narrower from here, but cars are scarcer, too.

Signs for **Monthermé** lead on from Revin, as you hug the suddenly snaking **Meuse** and fight your way through a succession of short ups and downs. The cycling is scenic and pleasant, made more so by the loneliness of the route, and you'll arrive in **Monthermé** via the stout fortified church of St. Léger. Situated at the confluence of the Semoy and Meuse rivers, Monthermé is an attractive little town, popular with Belgian and French tourists.

The city's campground is a treat, plunked down in the grassy triangle where the Meuse and Semoy flow together. To find this pleasant and inexpensive spot, ride through town on **Road D1**, with signs for **Bogny-sur-Meuse** and **Charleville-Mézières**. Watch for campground signs just beyond a small *supermarché* on the edge of town. If you need indoor accommodations, you should be able to rustle up a bed in Monthermé. Otherwise, Charleville-Mézières is a relatively easy 21 km away.

Monthermé to Charleville-Mézières: 21 kilometers

Depart Monthermé on **Road D1** for **Bogny-sur-Meuse** and **Charleville-Mézières**. You'll get a glimpse of the four rock spires of the Rochers des 4 Fils Aymon to the left as you pedal the narrow riverside road through a handful of small towns. **Climb** away from the Meuse **after Bogny**, then make a **left** turn onto **Road D1A** (signed for **Joigny-sur-Meuse**). Escape the main road for a forested break from traffic, then **descend steeply** to cross the Meuse River and pedal on. You'll **rejoin D1** at **Nouzonville**.

More tree-lined climbing awaits after Nouzonville. Watch carefully for a **left** turn signed for **Montcy** about 3 km short of Charleville-

Mézières. Take it to gain the tiny **Road D69** toward the city. You'll descend to the river once more, then pedal into Charleville on a delightfully quiet road.

Reach the **Vieux Moulin**, a riverside museum dedicated to the city's favorite native son, the poet Arthur Rimbaud. Here, a **camping sign** leads left to the city's wonderfully situated municipal campground on the banks of the Meuse River. It's a short walk from here to Charleville's impressive place Ducale and the **tourist information** office.

Charleville has several hotels, extensive shopping opportunities, and loads of interesting pedestrian streets. You'll love the remarkably homogeneous place Ducale and the typically flashy *Hôtel de Ville*. Duck inside a few of the city's myriad churches to round out your visit.

Charleville-Mézières to Asfeld: 69 kilometers

You can look forward to a day of small roads, pastoral surroundings, and an abundance of half-timbered buildings as you set out from Charleville-Mézières. Unfortunately, you must fight your way out of one very large city before you reap the benefits of France's delightful countryside. From the campground beside the Meuse, cycle to Charleville's **place Ducale**, then go **right** to pedal on to **Road N43**. Follow **N43** out of town, enduring heavy traffic for a time, then dive **left** on a small road signed for **Warcq**.

Ride this quiet route to **Warcq**, an interesting village with a squatty fortified church (look for the lofty arrow slits) and a communal washing area. From Warcq, follow the serene and gently undulating **Road D9** through **Belval** and **Haudrecy**, marveling happily at how quickly city turns to country in France.

Leave Haudrecy with signs for **Signy-l'Abbaye** and **St. Marcel**. If you like stained-glass windows, pop inside the town church at St. Marcel. The pleasant **Road D2** leads from here through quiet, rolling farmland. Cycle past cows, tractors, and unassuming villages to arrive in **Signy-l'Abbaye**. With an excellent municipal **campground** beside the city soccer field, Signy-l'Abbaye just may tempt you to call it a day. It's a charming French village, untouched by the terrors of mass tourism.

Pedal **Road D2** toward **Lalobbe**, and settle in for more quiet roads through rolling countryside. If you're riding in the spring and you're an allergy sufferer, you may be sneezing with each stroke—the fields will be brilliant with the blossoms of pollen-heavy yellow rape. In **Lalobbe**, veer **left** onto **Road D102** signed for **Wasigny**. The tiny route climbs steeply through fields, then winds through small villages as you continue from **Wasigny** through **Herbigny**, **Hauteville**, and **Ecly** (now on **Road D11**).

Watch for the bell towers of the village churches—the design is characteristic of the area. Also characteristic are the abundant half-timbered buildings you'll see. Signs for the *route du Porcien* will indicate you're on a "tourist itinerary" of local architecture. **Road D11** runs smack into the much less friendly Road D946 in **Ecly**. **Cross** it, then continue on **Road D3** toward **Château-Porcien**. You'll join **Road D926** as you pedal into the midsize town (this may be your best chance for indoor accommodations this afternoon).

Continue with **D926**, pedaling through the green fields above the Aisne River as you cycle to **Gomont**. Then go **right** onto Road **D18B** toward **Juzancourt**. Enjoy quiet riding through Juzancourt, then look for a turn to the **left** for **Asfeld**. Take it, and glide downhill to cross the **Aisne River** and enter the outskirts of the little town.

We were exhausted by the time we got here, so we put up our tent beside the canal and watched the barges pass all evening. (Please remember that you free camp at your own risk. There is an official campground at Guignicourt, about 15 km southwest.) There's a grocery store on the right as you enter Asfeld, and the little town boasts a unique brick baroque church that's worth a look. If you're hunting for indoor accommodations, you may have to search a bit.

Asfeld to Reims: 28 kilometers

You'll have a quiet, pastoral ride ahead as you set out for the bubbly capital of France's Champagne region—Reims. Leave Asfeld with signs for **Vieux-lès-Asfeld** on **Road D926**, then veer **left** beyond Vieux onto **Road D37** for **Poilcourt**. **Cross the regional border** after Poilcourt-Sydney. Now you'll be pedaling in Champagne! You'll also notice an oddity of the French road system here—often, when French roads cross regional boundaries, their numbers change. Continue with the renumbered **Road D274** through **St. Etienne** and **Bourgogne**.

Signs for **Reims** lead onward through vast fields of grain, and you'll spot the dark towers of Reims Cathedral from about 10 km out. Begin to encounter Reims's urban sprawl not long after. Enter the suburb of **Bétheny**, and follow the **rue Bétheny** into the city. Signs for the *centre* and *cathédrale* will lead you to the **rue Jean Jaurès**. Cycle along this busy thoroughfare to a roaring roundabout, and continue **straight** toward the **cathedral**.

Reims Cathedral occupies a royal position among French cathedrals. A soaring Gothic structure with a lofty nave and exquisite stained glass, the cathedral has hosted the coronation of French rulers since 498. We carried the memory of the building with us for an entire year of cycling. Its golden stone exterior and breathtaking interior will delight you, too.

Reims's efficient **tourist office** is a stone's throw from the cathedral at 2, rue de Machault. Pick up a free map and ask for help with lodgings here. There's a **youth hostel** and university housing in Reims, and the **campground** is 3 to 4 km from the center. If you're interested in a tour of one of Reims's champagne cellars, the tourist-office staff can point you in the right direction. But don't spend too much time underground in Reims. The city has too many architectural treasures to miss.

Reims to Épernay: 34 kilometers

With a population pushing 200,000, Reims is a *big* city, and you'll have to fight your way out of the suburbs if you're looking for vine-covered hills. Either buy a detailed city map or do what we did—stop frequently to check out the transit maps at the bus stops. Follow signs for **Cormontreuil** (a suburb on the city's southern flank) as you begin. You'll gain **Road D9** south, then cycle past a vast development of **mega-stores** about 6 km out of the city center.

A succession of famous names makes pedaling through the vineyards of Champagne a bubbly pursuit.

Watch for a turn to the **right** signed for **Trois-Puits** just beyond the super mall, and swing off onto this tiny road to begin your tour of sparkling champagne villages surrounded by acre after acre of vineyards. The day's ride is rolling, challenging, but delightfully picturesque as you cycle through **Trois-Puits** and **Montore** (ride past the village church, then continue out of town) and on to **Rilly-la-Montagne**. Rilly is a charmer, with a main street lined with family mansions, their doorways labeled like a shopping list of fine champagnes. Pedal on to **Chigny-lès-Roses** and **Ludes** from here. **Climb steeply** from Ludes, and **rejoin Road D9** toward **Louvois**. You'll have more climbing (about 2 km) ahead as you ascend through trees to **Craon-de-Ludes**, then revel in a wonderful downhill glide through the Forêt de la Montagne de Reims. Watch for a regal château at the road junction near **Louvois**, and stay with **D9** for **Épernay** from here.

Avenay-Val-d'Or boasts a handsome church. As you depart **Avenay**, take the turn to the **right** signed for **Mutigny** to gain the silent **Road D201** as it tiptoes through more of the region's famously named hillside vineyards. You'll join the much less inviting **Road D1** in **Ay**, and follow signs into **Épernay** from here. Épernay offers a wonderful municipal **campground** beside its soccer stadium (well signed from the bridge across the Marne River as you enter town) or continue into the center to find the **tourist office** in the *Hôtel de Ville*.

You can ask about Épernay's indoor lodgings at the tourist office (they're few and dear from June to September) and stock up on champagne-related literature, too. Although Épernay has little in the way of historical monuments or great architecture, it does boast miles of subterranean champagne "rivers." Tour the wine cellars at Möet et Chandon or ride the underground train at Mercier. You can't admire flying buttresses forever.

Épernay to Troyes: 103 kilometers

You'll have a challenging day of hill-studded riding ahead as you leave Épernay. Vineyards, grain fields, and small villages are the rule between here and Troyes, so if you need a room, you may want to get an early start and go for a 100 km forced march (we did it once, but it wasn't fun). There are some camping possibilities along the way, so you'll have more flexibility if you're carrying a tent.

Getting out of Épernay isn't fun either. Traffic is thick and the roads are confusing. Look for **Road RD51** to the south toward **Sézanne**, and follow it to a harrowing **roundabout**, where you'll dive off onto the much quieter **Road D40** for **Avize**. Hilly cycling through endless vineyards awaits. Climb and descend, climb and descend (now on Road D10), passing through **Cuis** and struggling on to **Cramant**. Despite the rather tacky champagne bottle that marks the town,

Cramant does boast a wonderful view of the surrounding hills.

From Cramant, pedal to **Avize** and **Oger**, then join **Road D9** soon after with signs for **Vertus**. Vineyards give way to rolling wheatland now, and you can watch dozens of tractors crisscrossing the fields as you continue. **Cross** the busy **Road RD33** at **Bergères**, and stay on D9 to **Fère-Champenoise**. We shared this section of our ride with far too much truck traffic, but the pedaling is much more pleasant after Fère-Champenoise. Pause to explore the cool stillness of the church in there, then ride on with signs for **Corroy**.

A smaller, quieter **D9** leads to Corroy, a tiny town with a wonderful 12th-century pilgrimage church. Enjoy flat cycling to **Fresnay**, **Faux-Fresnay**, and **Courcemain** before abandoning D9 to ride for **Boulages**. (If your legs are beginning to fail you by this point in the day, there is a **campground** at Anglure, about 12 km from Courcemain.) In Boulages, follow signs for **Longueville**, then **Mery-sur-Seine** to gain **Road D78** along the Seine River. You'll have fairly easy cycling through **Droupt-Ste.-Marie**, **Droupt-St.-Basle**, and **Rilly-Ste.-Syre**, each with its own church, graveyard, and war memorial. But the hills increase after **Chauchigny**, and the Troyes-bound traffic picks up from **St. Benoît**. Stay with signs for Troyes to reach **Pont-Ste.-Marie**, with a remarkable church and plenty of shopping opportunities. Troyes's municipal **campground** is just beyond the bridge that spans the Seine. It's crowded and mediocre, but it provides excellent access to the city.

Continue into Troyes, following signs for the **center**, and arrive at the Cathédrale St. Pierre et St. Paul. Enter the church's cool interior and watch the lines of stone pillars unfold before you, dappled with colored sunlight and stained by windows of brilliant glass. Check in at the **tourist office** near the train station for accommodations listings and information on the city. The **youth hostel** is 5 km south of the city core in Rosières, but there are plenty of inexpensive hotels to choose from closer in.

Troyes is a wonderful city for strolling. Visit the old town to walk along the rue des Chats, lined by half-timbered houses, explore the city's wealth of churches, or simply pull up a chair in a cozy *crêperie* and fill your hungry cyclist's stomach with a taste of France. (If you're considering taking a "bite" out of Burgundy, as well, you can hook up with our Tour No. 13 from Dijon to Dijon in Troyes and pedal on from here.)

Troyes to Sens: 70 kilometers

This ride leads through the breadbasket of France, with endless acres of rolling wheatland, lots of quiet roads, and an often troublesome west wind. Leave Troyes's center on **Road N60** toward

Estissac. Cross over the **train tracks** and take the **first right**, to get on the friendlier **Road D60** out of town. Continue past the busy ring road on the edge of Troyes, following signs for **Grange l'Evêque**.

Stay on D60 through **Dierrey–St. Pierre** and continue on to **Faux-Villecerf**, then angle **right** onto **Road D23** before going **left** onto **Road D29** for **Villadin**. Turn **left** in Villadin, then go **right** to climb for **Pouy-sur-Vannes** on D29 once more. Swing down through town at **Pouy-sur-Vannes** to pedal past a lovely château, then regain the main road (now **Road D84**) for **Courgenay**. Continue past Courgenay and take a **right** soon after onto **Road D328** for **la Charmée**. Cycle through la Charmée and stay on D328, then go **right** onto **Road D28** for **la Postolle** and **Thorigny-sur-Oreuse**.

In **Thorigny**, angle **left** to ride the final 15 km to **Sens** on the up-and-down **Road D939**. Descend a moderate hill before Soucy, then continue on for Sens through **St. Clément**, arriving in the city with the mass of the cathedral rising up before you. You'll find Sens's **tourist office** near the cathedral. Sens has **youth hostels** and a municipal **campground** (south of town along the Yonne River), as well as several hotels to fit your accommodations needs.

Begun in 1140, Sens's Cathedral St. Etienne is a Gothic beauty. The building served as a model for England's Canterbury Cathedral, and it boasts fine stained-glass windows and a delightfully vast interior. Pace the pedestrian avenues around the church to discover the hidden treasures of the city.

Sens to Moret-sur-Loing: 54 kilometers

Leave Sens by **retracing** your route north to **St. Clément**, then angle **left** onto **Road D23** toward **Cuy** and **Gisy** just after crossing the **N6** auto route. Go **left** again after about 2 km to follow the small road through **Cuy**, **Evry**, **Gisy**, and **Michery**, paralleling the winding **Yonne River** along the way. Continue on **D23** through **Serbonnes** and **Courlon-sur-Yonne**, riding northwest toward Montereau-Faut-Yonne.

Road D23 becomes **Road D29** just before **Misy-sur-Yonne**, where a pretty riverside park awaits. In **Marolles-sur-Seine**, 6 km farther on, turn **left** onto the busy **Road D411** and ride toward **Montereau**. Cross the confluence of the Yonne and Seine rivers in Montereau, a city with a large church. Turn **west** onto **Road D39** immediately after crossing the river, following signs for **Champagne-sur-Seine**. This section of the ride is dull, with lots of industrial development, but the scenery improves from here.

Just before Champagne, go **left** to cross the **Seine** and enter **St. Mammes**. This busy little port town, snuggled into the confluence of the Seine and Loing rivers, must have one of the highest barge counts

Two French cyclists choose their route from Fontainebleau.

per capita in France. Pedal through St. Mammes, then veer **right** across the Loing to enter the charming city of **Moret-sur-Loing**.

Your infatuation with Moret will begin on the bridge across the Loing, where you'll gain a lovely view of the town church, its flying buttresses perched precariously above the water. Although often packed with strolling tourists, the streets of Moret are fascinating, too, and well worth an afternoon excursion. The little city's **tourist office** is at the Porte de Semois on the rue Grande, straight ahead from the bridge across the Loing. The town makes a great base for exploring Fontainebleau by bike, but you may find indoor accommodations expensive here. (If the day is young, you might consider pedaling on to Fontainebleau itself—the city beside the château has some lodgings.)

If you want to camp, go right immediately after crossing the Loing River and look for camping signs for du Lido. Stay with the **campground** signs to cross under a railroad bridge and arrive at a deluxe international site at Veneux-lès-Sablons, complete with a bar, tennis, mini-golf, and a swimming pool. Prices are steep for French camping, but the location and facilities warrant the extra *francs*.

Cyclists who have a day to spare and a yen for a bit of pleasant riding *sans baggage* should consider making Fontainebleau a day trip from Moret or Veneux. The delightful 41,000-acre Forêt de Fontainebleau boasts miles of quiet (try to avoid weekends), shaded roads, and the château itself deserves several hours of exploration. Of course, no visit to France is complete without a sun-warmed picnic, set against the backdrop of a gorgeous French castle, so be sure to pack a lunch.

Moret-sur-Loing to Versailles (via Fontainebleau): 109 kilometers

Leave Moret via the **rue Grande**, cycling past the Porte de Semois and continuing with the main road to **Veneux-lès-Sablons**. Watch for an intersection signed for the *Hôtel de Ville,* **Thomery**, and **Champagne**; go **right** here and begin following signs for **Avon**. Enter the Forêt de Fontainebleau, and pedal through two **roundabouts** with signs for Avon. Continue through **Avon** on **Road D137** (ride straight through town—don't take the truck route).

You'll veer **right** to enter the grounds of Fontainebleau Palace a short time later (no bicycles are allowed on the inner grounds of the palace, so you'll need to lock up outside the gates). A royal mansion was first constructed here in the 12th century because of the wealth of game in the area, which the French rulers loved to hunt. Today, Fontainebleau Palace is a vast edifice, richly endowed both inside and out. A tour of the interior, although far from cheap, is well worth the time and *croissant* money you'll invest.

The ride from Fontainebleau will take you along the southern edge of the Paris sprawl, zigzagging on secondary roads and getting close enough to France's overwhelming capital for a mass-transit visit from a safe base at Versailles. If you want to visit Paris (who wouldn't?), we recommend you find a friendly hotelkeeper in Versailles, or set up camp at the city's campground, stow your bike and gear, and utilize the excellent French transit system to get into the city. One word of warning about your ride today—drivers are different in the Île-de-France (the region surrounding Paris). We had more close calls and encountered more rude drivers in one day of cycling in this area than we did in a month of pedaling through parts of France more distant from Paris. Please be cautious as you ride.

Leave Fontainebleau on **Road D409** for **Étampes**, passing through fragrant forests on the way. Turn **right** on **Road D11** for **St. Martin** and forsake the busy road for quieter riding. In St. Martin, go **left** for **Courances**, crossing under the **A6** auto route. Follow the quiet country road to Courances. The city boasts a beautiful château with extensive gardens. From Courances, go **left** onto **Road D372**, then swing **right** onto **Road C3** to continue on to Moigny-sur-École.

Cross Road D948 in **Moigny** and continue with the hilly secondary route toward **Courdimanche**. Merge with **Road D105**, going right, then turn **right** again onto **Road D449** for **d'Huison**. There are many lovely châteaux to entertain you as you follow the Essone River northward. Ride to d'Huison, then turn **left** for **Longueville**. Continue on to **Boissy-le-Cutte**, and take **Road D148** to **Villeneuve**, **Étrechy**, and **Chauffour**. Angle **right** in Chauffour onto **Road D132** for Souzy. Cycle through **Souzy** and pedal on for **St. Cheron** and **Marais**.

Turn **right** onto **Road D27** just before Marais, catch a glimpse of yet another château, then swing **left** to regain **D132** to **Angervilliers**. Go right on **Road D838** for Limours in Angervilliers. From Limours, climb steeply on **Road D988**, then turn left onto **D838** again, following signs for **Versailles** toward **St. Rémy**. Follow the signs for **Milon-la-Chapelle** through St. Rémy, turning left onto **Road N306** in town, then swinging **right** for Milon-la-Chapelle.

Reach the picturesque city of Milon and climb a **tough hill** toward **St. Lambert** on **Road D46**. There are several luxurious homes scattered along the way, and you'll have plenty of time to look at them as you struggle up the hill. Go **right** onto the busy **Road D91** after St. Lambert and climb some more. Signs for **Versailles** will lead you on from here.

Head for the **tourist office** at 7, rue des Réservoirs (near the château), and seek help with lodgings there. Once you're settled in, you can pay homage to yet another fantastic French castle and end your tour from Brussels with a "royal" bang. Ask your hotel manager or the Versailles campground staff to explain the complexities of train fees and schedules before you set off for Paris. Then lock up your bike, grab your camera, and make your pilgrimage to the city.

If you're heading home from here, you can make train connections to Brussels (and its international airport) from Paris. You'll need to send your bicycle a few days in advance, then clear it through customs when you get to Brussels. If Orly Airport is your final destination, you can battle the public transit system with your bicycle and gear (a risky proposition) or cycle to the airport from either Fontainebleau (closest) or Versailles (not so close). Better yet—why not hook up with our Tour No. 5 and pedal onward from here?

TOUR NO. 5

ME AND MY CHÂTEAUX
Versailles to Angers and Back

Distance: 687 kilometers (427 miles)
Estimated time: 9 riding days
Best time to go: April, May, June, or September; avoid the July/August tourist crunch
Terrain: Wonderful river riding with few hills
Maps: Michelin Nos. 60 and 64
Connecting tours: Tour Nos. 4, 6, and 12

This delightful tour will take you from Versailles to the cathedral city of Chartres, then on to the château-studded Loire Valley. Once in the region of the Loire, you'll wind past a wealth of French castles as you savor riverside cycling, lovely scenery, and superlative French cuisine. Say farewell to the Loire at Angers, and turn toward yet another charming French river—the Loir. More châteaux await as you pedal back toward Châteaudun and the end of your cycling loop.

To maximize your enjoyment of the area, please avoid high season

A sign at the entrance to Villandry Château gives evidence of the plethora of cyclists in the Loire Valley.

at all costs. It's no secret—the Loire Valley (and its surroundings) is one of the pearls of France. Shun the hordes of tourists that "pig out" on its attractions in July and August, and sample the region's delicacies in April, May, June, or September. This will be a feast you'll never forget.

CONNECTIONS. Combine this loop ride from Versailles to Angers with our Tour No. 4 from Brussels to Versailles, and you'll be treated to a scenery-rich, attraction-packed route. Although you'll have to contend with a few stretches of intense traffic, quiet cycling on small roads is the norm for both tours. If you end your trip at the château-crowned city of Châteaudun, you'll find good rail connections to Paris.

Another possible tour hookup presents itself at Orléans (end of Tour No. 12), where cyclists arriving from Dijon can pedal on to Meung-sur-Loire and continue with this trip.

INFORMATION. There are a host of books available in English dealing with the Loire Valley. One excellent regional tourist guide is Michelin's *Green Guide* entitled *Châteaux of the Loire*. For less practical but more elaborately presented fare, turn to the Philips Travel

Guides volume for *The Loire*. If you're particularly interested in the host of castles along the route, you'll find several beautifully photographed volumes to grace your coffee table (but definitely *not* to carry in your handlebar bag). If history is your hobby, pick up a biography of this region's favorite heroine—Jeanne d'Arc (Joan of Arc).

The Loire and Loir valleys undoubtedly possess one of the highest concentrations of campgrounds and hotels of any region in France. The campgrounds here are glorious, with a great majority of them set right on a river and commanding a spectacular view of either a castle, a fortress, or a cathedral. Hotels and hostels abound in the region, as well, but you may still have to scramble for indoor lodgings in the busy months of July and August.

Cycling is delightfully easy along these twin river valleys, and you probably won't lose any weight while you're riding here—the food and wine are just too good. Nearly every town offers its own wine, and several renowned regional wines accompany a wide variety of French dishes.

Take a break from your sightseeing to sample fresh fish from the Loire River, or to taste a famous cheese such as *Port Salut*. If you want a different flavor, explore one of the many types of goat cheese (*chèvre*) produced in the Loire Valley. Mushrooms (*champignons*) and asparagus (*asperges*) seem to permeate every menu, and it's easy to see why this region is sometimes called the garden of France.

Versailles to Chartres: 73 kilometers

Look at the final paragraphs of Tour No. 4 for additional details on Versailles. Of course, you'll need to delay your journey toward the Loire at least a day or two, as you'll undoubtedly want to wander the lush grounds and amazing interior of the château at Versailles for many hours. This building makes even a simple outdoor picnic a regal affair. You won't be able to take your *baguette* inside the palace, but you will be able to feast your eyes on architecture, furniture, and paintings that bring French history to life.

Versailles makes a great base for seeing Paris, too, either from the safe haven of a hotel or the economical tent spots at the city's campground. The commute into Paris takes less than an hour. After a few exhausting days of sightseeing in the "heart of France," you'll be ready to head for back roads and farmland, so load up your bicycle, strap on your helmet, and head out.

Leave Versailles with the somewhat frantic **Road D91** toward **Dampierre** and **Rambouillet**. You'll face scattered hills along the way, with a real steepie just before Dampierre. Handsome châteaux in pretty settings await you in Dampierre and Senlisse. Road D91 leads into the busy **Road N306**. If you want to see **Rambouillet**, turn

right to pedal the unpleasant 10 km to your goal. (If you've had enough of châteaux and big-city traffic for a while, consider hopping on Road D72 at Cernay instead. Many quiet and hilly kilometers lead southwest to Sonchamp, across Road N10, and on with Road D101 to Esclimont. Regain our route in Gallardon.)

Cycle into Rambouillet's **center** to arrive at the luxurious grounds of the château. This part of France has an abundance of scenic picnic spots, and Rambouillet is one of them. All you need is a loaf of bread, a hunk of cheese, and a château. When you're finished "sharing" the summer residence of the French president, depart Rambouillet along the **main road south** (Road N10), but turn **right** onto **Road D150** for **Orphin** soon after.

Ride through Orphin and go **right**, then veer **left** to regain **D150** (becomes **Road D32**) for **Ecrosnes** and **Gallardon**. Pause to explore the large church in Gallardon before pushing on along D32 for **Chartres**. You'll see the lovely silhouette of the twin-towered cathedral of Chartres as you approach the city. Road D32 dumps you onto the growling **Road N10** just before town. Follow this to the **center** and the cathedral.

The famed stained-glass windows of Chartres Cathedral glow like a thousand jewels in the velvet-vaulted heights, and the carvings around the front altar are masterpieces of detail, reciting the life of Christ in stone. With its parks and churches, its hilly old quarter, its narrow streets, and its tantalizing alleys, Chartres is a gem of a city to linger in.

Stop in at the **tourist office** across from the cathedral for information on lodgings, city attractions, and cathedral tours. Chartres offers a convenient **youth hostel** and several hotels to choose from.

Chartres to Châteaudun: 58 kilometers

Leave Chartres to the **south** with **Road D935** toward **Dammarie**. You'll have a fairly busy 10 km to Dammarie, then angle **right** on the far end of town to gain **Road D127** toward **Fresnay-le-Comte**. Swing right into Fresnay soon after, and follow signs to **Meslay-le-Vidame**, a small town with a big château. From Meslay, continue on for **Bronville**, and go **right** on **Road D154** for **Bois-de-Feugères**.

Cross the murderous **Road N10** and angle **left** on **Road D359** for **Alluyes**, riding through flat farmland with few cars for company. Leave Alluyes on **Road D153** and pedal to **Dangeau**, then go left on **Road D941** toward **Logron**. Logron straddles the busy Road D955 and offers you a straight-shot 10½-km route into Châteaudun. This road is not fun. Postpone your entry into Châteaudun (and avoid arriving in the city on the front bumper of one of D955's fleet of automobiles), and **cross D955** to continue with **Road D23** toward **Lanneray**.

In Lanneray, go **left** on **Road D31** for **St. Denis** and **Châteaudun**. Hit the busy **Road D927** in St. Denis and join it for the final kilometers to Châteaudun. (If you need to shop for groceries, you may want to do it in St. Denis, as Châteaudun's central shopping options aren't as good.) Look for Châteaudun's fortresslike château peering down from its rocky perch as you approach the city.

Signs for the château and center will lead you upward to the hilltop city and its ancient core. If you're planning to camp, don't climb the hill! Instead, head north on Road D955 to cross the Loir River, then go right with **campground** signs to find Châteaudun's no-frills municipal camping area 1 km later. The inexpensive site features a priceless view of the city's floodlit château by night.

Châteaudun's **tourist office** at 3, rue Toufaire, can help you with indoor lodgings. There is a **youth hostel** in the city, as well as a handful of hotels.

Châteaudun to Beaugency: 48 kilometers

To pedal on toward your meeting with the lovely Loire River, leave Châteaudun with **Road D955** as it swings around the base of the hilltop *Vieille Ville*. Jog **left**, then veer **right** to gain the wonderfully quiet **Road D31** toward **Meung-sur-Loire**, passing the city swimming pool on the way. You'll have flat farmland from here to the Loire Valley. It's not terribly scenic cycling—but it is quick and easy.

Keep with signs for **Meung-sur-Loire** through acre after acre of corn. Road D31 becomes D14 and then D2, but **Meung** is signed throughout the ride. You can take a shortcut to the river and **Beaugency** by swinging right onto **D25** for **Ouzouer-le-Marche** in **Prenouvellon**, then continuing with D25 to its junction with Road D925, 12 km short of Beaugency. We'll give you the slightly longer version, via Meung-sur-Loire. From Prenouvellon, continue with **Road D2** through **Charsonville** and **Baccon**. Pick up a bit of traffic at **le Bardon**, and pedal the final few kilometers to the riverside town of Meung-sur-Loire.

With a medieval château and narrow old streets, the fortified village of Meung is worth a stop. Those wishing to see the immense but stimulating city of Orléans (about 20 km northeast along the river) might choose to make Meung a base for a day trip to the city, and a pleasant riverside **campground** in Meung invites overnight visitors. Our Tour No. 12 from Dijon connects with this ride at Orléans.

Orléans's cathedral is certainly worth a look, and there are many other attractions in the city that sent forth France's greatest heroine, Jeanne d'Arc. Cycling into this vast urban area is less than relaxing, however. Hop one of the frequent trains between Meung and Orléans instead.

To cycle on toward Beaugency, leave Meung from the **north end** of the **bridge** across the Loire River. Follow the riverside **Promenade des Mauves** away from town and pedal on to **Baule**. You'll be forced to join the busy **Road N152** for the final few kilometers into **Beaugency**. Swing **left** off the main road to enter the city, and look for the **tourist office** on the place du Martroi. The staff there can direct you to Beaugency's **youth hostel** or to the **campground** just across the river.

Visit the city's 15th-century château and its 12th-century Church of Notre Dame, or wander Beaugency's medieval streets and squares in search of buttery *croissants*. Carry your bounty to the waterfront promenade, absorbing the atmosphere of the Loire while you indulge in the joys of France.

Beaugency to Blois (via Chambord): 42 kilometers

Depart Beaugency via the **Tour St.-Firmin** and continue on the **rue Porte Tavers**. Stay with this route to **Tavers**, then go **left** just beyond Tavers's **church**. Signs for **Lestiou** lead on to the small village, followed by signs for **Avaray**. From Avaray, look for signs for **Courbouzon**, then veer **left** just past Courbouzon's **church** to descend to the flatlands along the banks of the Loire. You'll work your way **through a series of junctions** as you pedal effortlessly along the river valley.

A lone tourer savors the beauty of Chambord Château.

Arrive at a **junction** with **Road D112** and swing **left** to cross the Loire into **Muides** (there's a nice riverside **campground** here). Stay with **D112** as you climb away from the river, following road signs for **Chambord** into the luxurious **Parc de Chambord**. Sunny April weather, a fragrant forest, and the waves from picnicking French families made our first visit to the forest a delight. Be sure to stock up on lunch supplies before you enter the park, as you'll surely want to spread a picnic of your own on the lovely grounds of the château.

Stay with the well-signed route to Chambord Château, set on vast green lawns and framed by carefully trimmed plane trees. This fanciful building, with a roof said to be the work of Leonardo da Vinci, attracts hordes of tourists in the summer months. Even so, the beauty of the castle and its grounds will enthrall you for hours. Take the tour of the interior, too, if you can bear to leave the view outside.

As you leave Chambord, shun the signed route for Blois (it goes to the unappealing Road D951); follow the route signed for **Huisseau** and **Vineuil** on **Road D33** instead. You'll enjoy scenic, easy cycling to Vineuil, and you may have plenty of company if you're riding on a summer day. Just beyond **Vineuil**, another sign for Blois will try to lure you toward a main road north. Continue **straight** for **St. Gervais-la-Forêt** instead, and cross **under the main road** before gaining a **smaller road** signed for **Blois**.

Go **right** here, and continue straight across the **Loire River** to reach the **center** of the city. You'll find Blois's **tourist office** in the Pavillon Anne de Bretagne at 3, avenue Jean Laigret (to the left after you cross the Loire). The staff there will be able to direct you to the somewhat inconvenient **youth hostel** or a more centrally located hotel. If you want to camp, follow Road D951 along the left bank of the Loire River (as you approach the city, turn right before the Loire bridge), and pedal about 2 km to a somewhat ratty but convenient **campground** or 4 km to a more deluxe site.

Blois is a lively Loire city, and its streets are a delight for strolling. Visit the Château de Blois, with one of the best-preserved interiors of all the Loire châteaux, or explore the 800-year-old Church of St. Nicolas.

Blois to Chenonceau Château: 46 kilometers

Leave Blois along the **left bank** of the Loire River, pedaling the busy **Road D751** for about 4 km. When the main road swings to the left away from the river, continue **straight** onto **Road D173** for **Candé-sur-Beuvron**. Wonderful quiet cycling follows as you ride to Candé, with a handsome old bridge across the Beuvron River. Rejoin **D751** to push on to **Chaumont**. You'll pass Chaumont's municipal **campground** and **tourist information** office as you enter town.

Chaumont's hilltop château is worth a look, but you'll need to lock your bike at the bottom and ascend the asphalt pathway to the summit. A spectacular view of the Loire Valley is just one of the perks of this climb—the drawbridge-equipped Chaumont Château is a delight, and tours include a visit to the sumptuous stables.

Retrieve your bicycle and climb away from Chaumont and the Loire on **Road D114** toward **Pontlevoy** and **Montrichard**. Puff up a steady 1-km hill, then swing **right** onto **Road D27** for **Vallières** and **Chissay-en-Touraine**. A gently undulating route leads through fields and forests to Vallières. (If you want to see Amboise, another lively but touristy Loire city ruled by an impressive château, swing right onto Road D30 for Amboise from Vallières.)

To continue for Chenonceau, climb again after Vallières, staying on D27 for the 10 km to **Chissay** and the Cher River. In Chissay, turn **right** onto **Road D176** for **Chenonceau**. You'll pass a **campground** in **Chisseaux** on your way to Chenonceau, and there are campsites in Civray and Bléré (farther west) as well. The village of Chenonceaux has a small **campground** and a handful of hotels.

Spanning the Cher River with its line of elegant arches, Chenonceau Château is a delight for the senses. Thanks to the kindness and popularity of one of the château's former mistresses, it escaped the widespread destruction of the French Revolution. Hand over the entry fee for grounds, gardens, and interior, and savor the palace's matchless setting in the company of the floods of tourists doing the same.

Chenonceau Château to Chinon: 100 kilometers

You may want to consider continuing along the Cher River toward Tours and its St. Gatien Cathedral from Chenonceau, but Tours is an enormous city with a traffic volume to match. We were ready for a break from cities and sights at this point in our ride, so our route from Chenonceau was an end-run south of Tours and its sprawl. Leave Chenonceau by continuing west on **Road D176**. At **Civray**, turn **left** for **Bléré** and **cross the Cher**. Go **left** at the Y for **Thoré**, cross under the **main road**, and climb past Thoré and **les Fougères** before turning **right** for **Sublaines**.

Leave Sublaines on **Road D25** toward **Chédigny**, then turn **right** in Chédigny to gain **Road D10** toward **Reignac**. Follow the pretty riverside route through **Reignac** and on to **Cormery** (D10 becomes D17 along the way). Cormery is a lovely village with some noteworthy churches, a windmill, and an old washing house. Intersect with **Road N143** in town and go **left** here. Take the **first right** off N143 (it's signed for the **campground** and **Veneuil**).

Pedal onward past the city **campground** and keep **left** at the **Y**. **Climb briefly** but steeply to the green fields above the Indre River.

Another challenging dip and climb follows, then enjoy easy terrain to **Veigne**, continuing **straight** with the signed route for the city. Come in beside **Veigne's church**, and go **left** on **Road D50**. Grab a **right** onto the **rue Jules Ferry** just afterward (there's a difficult-to-spot sign for **Montbazon**, too).

Pedal a delightfully quiet route beside the Indre River to arrive in **Montbazon** in the shadow of the city's hilltop ruin and lofty statue of the Virgin. Go **right** on the **main road** through the lively town, then take a **left** onto **Road D17** for **Monts**. Heavier traffic will accompany you as you push on through Monts and **Artannes**, but the cycling is pleasant.

From Artannes, you can stay beside the Indre and pedal west toward the château of Azay-le-Rideau, but this route means a bit less solitude. Unless you're set on visiting Azay, swing **right** in Artannes onto **Road D121** for **Druye** and **Villandry**. Enjoy silent, flat cycling through fields of summer corn and sunflowers as you head for your reunion with the Loire River. Stay with **D121** through Druye and on toward **Villandry**.

A short, **steep descent** leads past Villandry's Romanesque village church, then go **right** on **Road D7** to gain the entrance to the **château**. Famous throughout Europe for its fabulous gardens, Villandry's château is at its most magnificent in spring and summer. Join the crowds of flower-loving tourists to wander the impressive grounds of the château, then **backtrack** to your **intersection** with D7 and wheel your bike across to find a shaded **picnic area** awaiting your *baguette* crumbs.

Continue **straight** toward the **Loire River** on this tiny, tree-lined road, then parallel the **Cher River** as it flows into the larger waterway. Keep to the **right** at an **unsigned Y** and endure a short stretch of **cobblestone**, then gain a **paved levee route** along the Loire's left bank. As you pedal on toward **Langeais**, you'll have wonderful views of the river and its many native birds—keep watch for the ungainly herons that are so abundant here.

Enjoy delightful cycling for the next several kilometers, passing under a new bridge that spans the river, then look for Langeais and its majestic château across the water as you approach the bridge into the city. (If you'd like to visit Langeais Château, famous for its richly endowed interior, pedal across to the city on the opposite bank, then backtrack to the Loire's left bank when you're finished.) To continue on toward Chinon, **cross** the bridge road with signs for **Bréhémont**, **Ussé**, and **Chinon**.

This second leg along the Loire is a bit busier than the first, but it's still quite wonderful, and you'll revel in French cycling as you glide past Bréhémont, then shun turnoffs for Rivarennes and Rigny-Ussé. Yet another opportunity to view a Loire château will present itself at the **second turnoff for Rigny-Ussé**. Go **left** here and look for the huddled white towers of **Ussé Château** on the tree-clad hillside straight ahead. **Cross** the **Indre River** (there's a great view of the château from the bridge) and continue to the castle, if you plan to visit. Some say the best thing about Ussé Château is the exterior view of the fairy-tale structure, so decide for yourself if you want to have a look inside.

From Ussé, you can either put up with a busy 3½ km on Road D7 or **retrace** your route to the **Loire shoreline** and continue with your quiet riverside road. The river route feeds back into **D7** after a handful of serene kilometers. Continue **straight** across the main road and **climb steeply** to **Huismes**. Then pedal onward with **Road D16** toward **Chinon**.

As you near Chinon, you'll hit a **roundabout** on **Road D751**. Continue **straight** for **Chinon's center** from here, and climb a final ridge before joining another main road into town. Revel in a **wild descent** past the walls of Chinon's fortified château, and fly downhill to the banks of the Vienne River. If you're hoping to camp, there's a great municipal **campground** on the opposite shore of the Vienne. Position your tent doorway correctly, and you'll have a superb view of the floodlit château by night.

Chinon's **tourist office** is up the hillside in the old core of the city at 12, rue Voltaire. Ask for help with hotels or get directions to the city's **youth hostel** (back at river level on the rue Descartes). Although the modern suburbs of Chinon are far from enchanting, the old town is a delight, clinging to the hill beneath its ruined fortress. Climb the slope to explore the scarred château, and savor the view of the medieval city, the river, and the surrounding vineyards. Then prowl the steep hillside to stare at the homes burrowed into the rock or stop at a local cave for a taste of Chinon's famous wine.

If you're in the mood for even more French wine country, consider abandoning your ride toward Angers and joining our Tour No. 6 toward Bordeaux from Chinon.

Chinon to Angers: 85 kilometers

Leave Chinon on **Road D749 south**, crossing the Vienne and turning **right** onto **Road D751** when the road branches. Go **left** after 3 km onto **Road D759**, then turn **right** for **le Coudray–Montpensier**. Angle right again for **la Devinière**. As you pedal along **Road D117**, you'll spot the châteaux of la Devinière and Chavigny on the right and the bulk of le Coudray–Montpensier commanding a hill to the left.

Just after **Chavigny**, turn **right** for **Couziers** and **Fontevraud-l'Abbaye**, cycling through a military area of forest, rolling hills, and rough pavement. Fontevraud boasts the remains of an abbey founded in 1099. Though much altered by time and plunder, those remains comprise the largest collection of monastic buildings in France. Pause for a look at the abbey church, then cruise on through the city and gain **Road D145** through the Forêt de Fontevraud.

Continue **straight** through **Champigny**, then pedal into **Saumur** along a ridge above the Loire River. Arrive at the lofty **château** of Saumur, a beautiful towered fortress with a spectacular site above the river. Plan to enjoy a picnic on the grassy grounds while you savor the château and the view. Then proceed through Saumur, following signs for **Gennes** onto **Road D751** along the left bank of the Loire.

Riding is pleasant for the 15 km to Gennes, once you escape the industrial suburbs of Saumur. You can stop at the famed mushroom caves of the Musée du Champignon along the way. In **Gennes**, angle **right** to stay along the Loire's flat **southern shore**. Ride on **Road D132** and pass through the quiet towns of **le Thoureil**, **St. Rémy**, and St. Jean. In **St. Jean**, go **right** onto **Road D751**, then ride to **Juigné** and continue **straight** to regain **D132**. Pedal the last few kilometers to a junction with **Road N160** and turn **right** on N160 to gain the **bridge** across the Loire toward **Angers**.

If you want to camp before Angers, stop at the **campground** at les Ponts-de-Cé, about 6 km before the city center. Or continue into Angers by pedaling along the busy **Road N160** and following signs for the **center**. The somber black towers of the château will draw you on. But don't let the forbidding exterior keep you from a visit—the château's flower-filled moat is a visual delight and its collection of the Tapestries of the Apocalypse is one of France's great medieval treasures.

The **tourist office** near the château can provide you with an excellent city map, as well as information on the city's hotels, **hostel**, and other **campgrounds**. If you're ending your cycling here with a train toward Paris or beyond, Angers boasts extensive rail connections and a train-station staff accustomed to handling bicycles. Please remember to prepare your bike carefully for long-distance train rides (see page 44).

Angers to le Lude: 85 kilometers

You'll have about 15 km of fairly busy cycling as you fight your way out of the Angers sprawl today, then you can look forward to delightfully quiet riding as you trace the winding course of the Loir River. From Angers's **tourist office** near the **château**, follow the **boulevard du Roi-René** southeast to its intersection with the **boulevard du Maréchal-Foch**. Go **left** here and stay with this thoroughfare to the impressive **Centre de Congrès**. Keep **left**, then swing **right** onto the **rue Boreau** as you pass the Centre de Congrès. The rue Boreau eventually becomes the **route de Briollay** farther on.

Stay with road signs for **Briollay** as you continue, and cross the **train tracks** and **Road D52**. Swing **left** to join **D52**, and endure this somewhat hectic road for a handful of hair-raising kilometers. If it's late in the day and you're looking for a **campground**, there's a pleasant riverside site at the village of Briollay, 3 km beyond the Villevêque junction. Otherwise, abandon the main road as you swing **right** for **Villevêque** onto the much more pleasant **Road D192**. Turn **left** to cross the **Loir River** in Villevêque, and ride into the adjacent town of **Soucelles**, then swing **right** onto **Road D109** for **Seiches-sur-le-Loir**. You'll hit **Road D74** just before Seiches. Go **right** here to cross the **Loir** and enter the city core. In Seiches, take the small road to the **left** signed for **Marcé**, and continue with this route **across Road N23** and over the **A11 freeway**.

Marcé is a tiny French village completely overlooked by the tourists who rush past it on the auto route. Savor its unspoiled streets as you pedal through, then hop onto the silent road signed for **Montigné-lès-Rairies**. You'll leave the level Loir Valley to cross over a forested loop in the river's route, but the solitude will repay you for your sweat. Roll through the shadows cast by oaks and poplars as you climb.

Cross Road D135 and continue with **Road C2**, then go **left** toward **Durtal** on **Road D59**. More delightful cycling follows, then you'll emerge from the Forêt de Chambiers and hit the much busier **Road D18**. Swing **left** here to pedal into **Durtal**. Even if you don't care to visit the small town, at least cycle down to the **Loir bridge** for a peek at its saucy château, flavored by a healthy portion of pepperpot roofs. From Durtal, **backtrack** along D18 toward Montigné-lès-Rairies, pass the intersection where D59 feeds in, then go **left** at the next intersection onto **Road D138** for **les Rairies**.

You'll be in for a treat from here, especially if you're riding in the off-season, as you trace a lonely riverside route past farms and small towns. Leave les Rairies with a **left** for **Cré**, and enjoy a level cruise beside the river as you stay with **Road D70** toward **Bazouges**. Bazouges boasts a picture-perfect view of its 15th- and 16th-century château, reflected in the placid face of the Loir. The comfy little town offers a wonderful riverside **campground**, too, for those who want to linger.

From Bazouges, **return to D70** and the **south shore** of the Loir, then angle **left** for **Cré** as you continue. Pedal through Cré, keeping to the **left** with **Road C3** toward **la Flèche**. More effortless kilometers follow as you savor silent cycling to the edge of la Flèche. You'll hit a hectic main road on the perimeter of town. Stay with signs for the **center** to **cross the Loir** and enter the heart of town.

If you're ready to call it a day, la Flèche has a sprawling riverside **campground** and several hotels to choose from (the first 5 km of cycling away from town are awful, so park it if you're feeling weary). The midsize city is famous for its military college, and it will delight would-be picnickers with its riverside Carmes Gardens.

To continue toward le Lude and the finish to your cycling day, leave la Flèche on the thoroughly unpleasant **Road N23** toward **le Mans**. Endure about 5 km of horrible traffic to **Clermont-Créans**, then dive **right** onto **Road D13** for **Mareil-sur-Loir**. You'll breathe a sigh of relief as you pedal the peaceful D13 to the flower-filled village of Mareil, then continue to **Pringé**. Watch for the Château du Gallerande on the left as you approach Pringé, then cycle on to **Luché-Pringé** on the banks of the Loir.

Abandon D13 beyond Luché-Pringé as you swing **right** onto **Road D214** for **Coulongé**. Watch for another right about **5 km later** and stay with signs for **le Lude** from here. Enjoy cornfields, cows, and quietness as you pedal back toward the Loir, lying in its cultivated valley. You'll make a quick descent to **Road D307** and go **right** to enter **le Lude**.

There's an excellent **campground** on the right as you approach the city center, or go **right** on **Road D305** to cross the Loir, and hunt for a hotel in the old core. Le Lude is famous for its summertime *son et lumière* performances, set on the grounds of its riverside château. Even if you can't catch a show (or don't care to spring for the hefty ticket price), the city and its handsome château are well worth exploring. There's a wonderful view of the château from across the Loir just off D305, if you decide to settle for an outside look.

Le Lude to Montoire-sur-le-Loir: 71 kilometers

Leave le Lude on **D305** toward **Vaas** and **Château-du-Loir**, but angle **right** soon after for **la Chapelle-aux-Choux**. Pedal the quiet **Road C11** along a lazy loop in the Loir, adding a few kilometers to your ride as you avoid the more direct but much busier D305. Arrive at a **T** intersection and veer **left** onto **Road D188** as you abandon the la Chapelle route and keep with the Loir's **right bank**.

You'll be forced to **rejoin D305** for the final 6½ km into **Vaas**, then you can either stay with the right-bank route and endure D305 another 8 km to Château-du-Loir or opt for a quieter and somewhat lengthier route. For a more pleasant ride, swing **right** onto **Road D30** in Vaas. **Cross the Loir** and pedal to a junction with **Road D11**. Go **left** here and follow D11 through **la Bruère** and on to **le Gué-de-Mézières**. Join **Road D10** to swing north for the final 5 km into the center of Château-du-Loir.

Pause in the attractive midsize city to prowl the many shops or view the remains of the old château (in the gardens near the town hall), then **backtrack** through the center with D10 toward **Nogent**. Hit an intersection with **Road D64** just **before the train tracks**, and veer **left** toward **Coëmont** and **Vouvray-sur-Loir**. Look for the many caves burrowed into the cliffs above the river as you trace a level route to **le Port–Gautier**. Road options abound in this part of the valley, so you can zig and zag to catch the sights or design your own direct route.

Swing **right** in le Port–Gautier to gain **Road D61** toward **Marçon**. You'll **cross the river** and go **left** a few kilometers later with signs for **la Chartre-sur-le-Loir**. Cycle into la Chartre and stay with signs for the **center** to remain on the south side of the river. La Chartre boasts an attractive old core that may tempt you to pause, then look for signs for **Tréhet** to find your way out of the city on **Road D154**. More caves line the way as you pedal through the shade of sturdy oaks on a delightfully quiet road.

Arrive in Trèhet and swing **left** to take **Road D80** toward **Ruillé** and the **Loir**. Recross the river and find a much friendlier **D305** leading **right** toward **Poncé-sur-le-Loir** and **Montoire**. Poncé is home to a Renaissance château with a noteworthy staircase, if you're in the mood for sightseeing. Cruise through the small town, then leave D305 as you veer **right** onto **Road D57** for **Couture-sur-Loir**. Once **across** the **Loir**, be sure to glance behind you for an enchanting view of the Château de la Flotte.

Pause to admire Couture's interesting church, then take **Road D10** toward **Artins**. Silent cycling leads to Artins, and you can continue with D10 from there if you're looking for the most direct route to Montoire. We weren't in any hurry on this lazy afternoon, so we turned **left** in Artins for **Souge**, then angled **right** after **crossing the Loir** (tiny tents-only **campground** here) to pedal on through the cornfields on the river's north shore.

You'll hit **Road D917** after a time, and go **right** to ride toward **Troo** and **Montoire**. A turnoff for Troo's old core will tempt you off D917 soon after, but take it from us—the climb into town is only worth it if you're *really* fascinated by troglodyte dwellings. Troo's hilltop Collegiate Church of St. Martin, founded in 1050, provides a good excuse to rest a while longer, if you do decide to make the climb.

Continue with D917 along the right bank of the Loir, and pedal into **Montoire**. This busy midsize city has plenty of shops, a handful of hotels, and a pleasant riverside **campground** to make your stay enjoyable. In medieval times, Montoire was a stop along the pilgrims' highway to Tours and Santiago de Compostela, Spain. The ancient Chapel of St. Gilles boasts 12th-century mural paintings, and the Renaissance houses in the city core are a treat, as well.

To find your way to Montoire's **campground** (about 2 km from the center), stay with signs to the **right** for **Lavardin**, the **campground**, and **St. Gilles Chapel** as you arrive in town. **Cross the Loir** and gain the **small road** along the **left bank** of the river. Pedal this shaded thoroughfare toward Lavardin to find the city's deluxe camping facility, complete with mini-golf and swimming pool.

Montoire-sur-le-Loir to Châteaudun: 79 kilometers

You'll close your Loire/Loir loop today with a finish at Châteaudun. From there, you can either backtrack toward Versailles where this tour started or hop aboard a train for Paris or other points in France. Whatever route you take from Châteaudun, you'll have pedaled past some of the loveliest castles in France on your riverside roll.

From Montoire's **campground**, continue with the shaded byway along the Loir's left bank to arrive in **Lavardin**. Swing up the little hill into the heart of town to peek at the 800-year-old mural paintings and handsome wooden ceiling of the village church. Guided tours of the extensive ruins of Lavardin's château must be arranged in advance (hardhat recommended). After you've explored the tiny village and its sights, leave Lavardin with **Road D168** for **Villavard** and **St. Rimay**.

Enjoy quiet cycling through fields of corn and sunflowers as you push on. You'll hit **Road D917** after St. Rimay. This fairly busy road provides the most direct way into **Vendôme** (13 km), but there's also a lonelier route for those with lots of time. Go **left** on D917 and **cross the Loir** to enter the cave-sprinkled village of **les Roches–l'Evêque**; a **right** on **Road D24** leads on toward **le Gué-du-Loir**.

Mild hills and light traffic will accompany you to le Gué-du-Loir, with another sprinkling of cave houses, then join **Road D5** toward **Vendôme** from there. Abandon D5 briefly to cycle a **paralleling road** through **Villiers** (another noteworthy church), then rejoin the main route until a signed **right turn** for **Naveil**. Swing right to **cross the Loir**, then go **left** on **Road C8** toward **Vendôme**. You'll meet **D917** for the final kilometers into the city and arrive near the 14th-century **Porte St. Georges**.

Recross the Loir and enter the city core through the fortified gateway. Continue straight to find the city **tourist office**. Vendôme's magnificent abbey church will be to your right. With an enchanting façade of lacy Gothic stonework and a unique freestanding belfry, the church and its surrounding buildings are worth a leisurely visit. In fact, if you have some time to spare, you may want to devote the remainder of your day to Vendôme and search out a hotel or the city **campground** rather than pedaling on.

To continue toward Châteaudun, leave Vendôme with **D917** toward the east, but angle **left** for **Areines** soon after. The cream of the day's cycling follows as you parallel the left bank of the Loir on silent roads through pleasant farmland. From Areines (12th-century church with frescoes), cycle on to **Meslay**. Go **left** very briefly for Vendôme, then swing **right** for **la Grapperie**. Pedal gentle hills to la Grapperie and stay to the **left** through the tiny town (avoid the signed route for Renay).

Continue straight with this little road, **crossing Road D111** along the way, and pedal on to **Chicheray**. Beyond Chicheray, you'll descend toward the river, then angle right onto **Road D12** for **Lignieres. Abandon D12** as you continue **straight** to stay on a tiny route beside the river to **Courcelles**. In Courcelles, swing **left** across the **Loir** to enter **Freteval**, a busy little market town popular with fishermen.

Just across the river, veer **right** with signs for the *Église* and *Étang*. Another quiet waterside road will take you out of town and past the **campground. Recross the Loir** just before **Morée**, and go **left** on **Road N157** to pedal through the village. Follow signs for **St. Hilaire** on the busy **Road D19** as you leave Morée, and escape joyfully about 2 km later as you swing **right** onto a small road signed for **St. Jean–Froidmentel**.

Savor delightful riverside riding with views of the placid Loir and the vacation homes perched on stilts above the water. You'll see fishermen exploring the eddies from their flat-bottomed boats as you pedal on to **St. Jean** (cross the river to take a peek at the village), then continue with your **left-bank** ride through **St. Claude** and on for **Cloyes**. Signs for the **center** lead into the heart of Cloyes, then swing **right** with the road (**D23**) for **Montigny**.

Cross the Loir and pause for an entertaining view of Montigny's rambunctious hilltop château, then push on with D23 to **St. Hilaire-sur-Yerre**. You'll leave D23 after St. Hilaire as you go **right** onto the small road signed for **Châteaudun** and pedal back to the banks of the Loir. Signs for Châteaudun lead on as you cross the river and cycle gentle hills with views of the city ahead. You'll hit the riotous main road (**D927**) a few kilometers short of Châteaudun. Go **right**, then veer **left** immediately to continue with your peaceful route toward the center.

A swift descent enlivened by a fantastic view of the city's towering château will take you to the base of the palace's fortified hill. If you're headed for the **center**, go **right** on Road **D955.** If you're hunting for the **campground**, go left to cross the Loir once more. (Please refer to this tour's preceding material on Châteaudun for information on accommodations and sights in the city.)

Carved horseshoes on the pilgrim hospital at Pons are signatures in stone, etched 700 years ago.

TOUR NO. 6

PEDALING PILGRIM PATHS

Chinon to Bordeaux

Distance: 436 kilometers (271 miles)
Estimated time: 7 riding days
Best time to go: April through October
Terrain: Gentle hills; lots of quiet secondary roads
Maps: Michelin Nos. 64, 68, 71, and 72
Connecting tours: Tour Nos. 5 and 7

This tour from Chinon to Bordeaux will lead you along the historic pilgrim route that once took thousands of medieval travelers from central France to Santiago de Compostela in northwest Spain. Along the way, you'll see gemlike Romanesque churches, enchanting cities rich in religious architecture, and kilometer after kilometer of lovely French countryside. Much of the route traces quiet secondary roads, so you'll have lots of time to savor the famous vineyards and silent farmland you'll be pedaling past.

CONNECTIONS. You can reach Chinon and the start of this tour by rail from Paris or simply pedal in via our Tour No. 5 along the Loire Valley. Once in Bordeaux, consider hooking up with our continuing tour along the enchanting Dordogne River (Tour No. 7). Excellent train connections link Bordeaux with other parts of France, so you should find smooth sailing if you're returning to Paris for a flight home or traveling to another section of the country for some additional cycling.

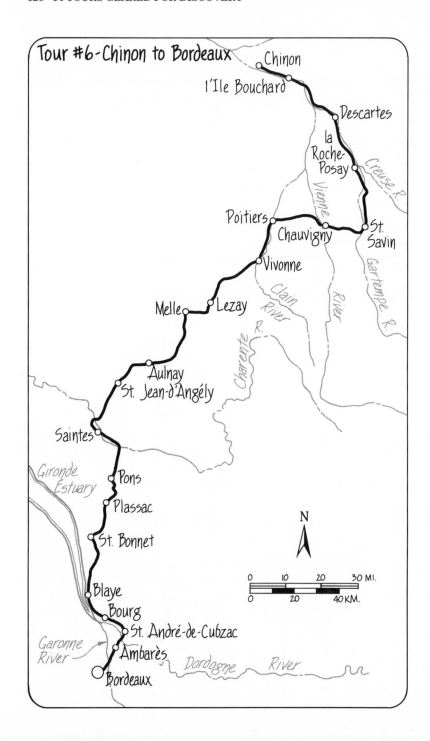

Tour #6-Chinon to Bordeaux

INFORMATION. Chinon and its environs are included in the English-language *Green Guide: Châteaux of the Loire*. However, the *Green Guide* for Poitou is not currently offered in an English version. To make your trip along the pilgrim route more interesting, try doing some background reading on the *Chemin Saint Jacques* (the way of Saint James). Look up "Santiago de Compostela" and/or "medieval pilgrimage" in the card catalogue at your local library, and go from there.

Accommodations should be no problem in this part of France, as it's visited enough to be prepared for tourists, yet not so much that it's completely overwhelmed. Nearly every midsize or larger city has a convenient campground, and there are several youth hostels in the area, as well.

On this tour, you'll begin in a respected wine town (Chinon is renowned for its red wine) and finish in one of France's most famous wine cities—Bordeaux. Along the way, you'll pedal through a part of France that's known for its Romanesque churches and its tumultuous history. Poitou has been a battleground for centuries, from 732 when Charles Martel halted the northern expansion of the Moors, to the 16th-century Wars of Religion that drenched the region's fertile, sun-baked soil with more blood.

Chinon to la Roche–Posay: 69 kilometers

A comfortable river city set on the banks of the Vienne, Chinon is dominated by the ridgetop ruins of its fortified château. Although the modern suburbs have little appeal, Chinon's old core trickles down the hillside beneath the château, its narrow streets running with enough charm to satisfy any tourist's thirst for the picturesque. Besides its modern-day reputation as a notable wine town, Chinon boasts a history-rich past enlivened by French heroes and heroines such as Charles VII and Joan of Arc. Explore Chinon's lofty scarred château, and savor the view of the medieval city, the river, and the surrounding vineyards. Then prowl the old core on the hillside to stare at homes burrowed into the rock or stop at a local cave for a taste of Chinon's famous wine.

Chinon's **tourist office** is in the old core of the city at 12, rue Voltaire. Ask for help with hotels or get directions to the city's **youth hostel** (at river level on the rue Descartes). If you're hoping to camp while in Chinon, there's a great municipal **campground** on the opposite shore of the Vienne. Position your tent doorway correctly, and you'll have a superb view of the floodlit château by night.

To begin your ride toward Bordeaux, leave Chinon on **Road D8** signed for **Briançon** and **l'Ile Bouchard**. Enjoy quiet, level cycling along the banks of the Vienne River as you draw away from town. Vineyards line the road as you pass Briançon and cruise on to **l'Ile**

Bouchard. This little city, sliced in half by the waters of the Vienne, offers shopping, a handful of churches, and a pleasant riverside **campground** (on the north bank of the Vienne) for those who might want to linger.

You'll hit **Road D757** and go **right** as you enter l'Ile Bouchard. Signs for **Richelieu** lead across the **Vienne**, then dive **left** onto **Road D18** toward **Parcay** and **Pouzay**. Delightful riding is the rule on D18, as you pe lal past farms, fields, and vineyards on a mostly level road. In **Marc ly**, swing **left** onto **Road D108** for **Nouâtre**. You'll want to pause to savor the view of Nouâtre as you cross the river. Remnants of ancient walls give the tiny town its personality.

Once across the Vienne, veer **right** onto a small road signed for **Noyers** and **les Maisons-Rouges**. Cycle this tiny thoroughfare past turnoffs for the two small villages, and continue with signs for **Port-de-Piles**. Your route will curve away from the Vienne as you follow the **Creuse River** to Port-de-Piles and a **junction** with the totally unappealing **Road N10**. Go **right** onto N10 to **cross the Creuse**, then veer **left** just afterward for **Buxeuil** and **Descartes**.

Pedal the **left bank** of the Creuse as you follow the quiet **Road D5** toward Descartes. Pass a signed turnoff for Descartes (birthplace of René Descartes), a midsize town with a riverside **campground**, then continue along the **left bank** with signs for **la Roche–Posay**. Road D5 leads on past **St. Rémy-sur-Creuse**, a neat village studded with troglodyte dwellings. Look for a lovely little château beyond St. Rémy, then enter hillier terrain as D5 climbs and descends beside the river.

In **la Petite Guerche**, make a short detour to the **left** on **Road D5A** to gain a great view from the **Creuse bridge**. Admire the riverside château that overlooks la Guerche with its stout round towers, then resume your ride along D5 toward **Lésigny**. Junctions in Lésigny are signed for **la Roche–Posay**. Keep with this route to continue your rolling ride beside the Creuse.

Pass a deluxe **campground** and hippodrome as you approach la Roche–Posay. You'll hit a **no-entry sign** as you pierce the city's central core. Auto traffic is routed to the right here. Swing left just afterward to find the heart of town. La Roche–Posay is a popular little spa city, set near the confluence of the Gartempe and Creuse rivers, but even if you're not a fan of mineral springs, it makes a pleasant stop. Medieval ramparts, a 12th-century tower, and a bristling gateway are all worth a look. There's a small **tourist office** (limited hours) on the central plaza if you need some help with indoor lodgings.

La Roche–Posay to St. Savin: 28 kilometers

You can look forward to a pleasant ride on quiet roads as you wind toward St. Savin with the Gartempe River today. Depart the center of la Roche–Posay through the **fortified gateway** on the main street, and join **Road D5** for **Vicq-sur-Gartempe** and **Angles-sur-l'Anglin**. (If you haven't already checked out the view from the bridge above the Gartempe, be sure to do it before you leave town.) Road D5 leads south from la Roche–Posay, paralleling the Gartempe River and passing the city casino en route.

Cross the Gartempe at Vicq-sur-Gartempe, and continue with **D5** toward **Angles-sur-l'Anglin**. Angles will take you by surprise—you'll descend through a somewhat ordinary looking upper town, following signs for **St. Pierre-de-Maillé**, then suddenly emerge on a slope above the Anglin River with an enchanting scene before you. An ancient castle ruin, a lovely river cut by an old wooden waterwheel, and a picture-perfect view from the bridge combine to make this village a true French masterpiece.

Press on with **Road D2** for **St. Pierre**, enduring a **stiff, short climb** away from the river. At the junction a few kilometers later, swing **left** for **St. Savin** (with **D5** once again). Enjoy effortless cycling through agricultural land as you cruise on for the 13½ km to St. Savin. You'll spot the needlelike spire of the little city's remarkable church from about 8 km out.

Enter the neighboring town of **St. Germain** and veer **right** to **cross the Gartempe** and gain St. Savin's center. If you're hoping to camp, there's a delightful little **campground** just downstream, on the left bank of the river. St. Savin's abbey church is the real treasure, though. Built in the 11th century for an abbey founded by Charlemagne, it boasts an unforgettable display of medieval mural paintings illustrating Bible scenes. (Be sure to look for a cozy Noah's ark, jampacked with seasick animals.)

If you need help with indoor lodgings or want to arrange for a guided visit to the church, check in at the city **tourist office** in the central core. A handful of hotels and grocery stores should meet your needs while you're visiting the little city. (Note: If it's early in your cycling day and you've already seen St. Savin's church, you might consider cruising on to Chauvigny for the night instead. This midsize city offers much to see, as well.)

St. Savin to Poitiers: 49 kilometers

Although this day is fairly brief in terms of distance, it offers some challenging hills and a worthwhile stop at Chauvigny, so try to get an early start if possible.

Leave St. Savin with **Road D11 south** toward **Antigny**. Begin with a short but **steep climb**, then enjoy easy cycling to Antigny, a small village ruled by a handsome old church. Veer **right** at Antigny's **church**, and pedal along a tree-lined parkway as you **abandon D11** and head west. Reach a **Y** on the edge of town, and go **right** onto the tiny **Road D33D**. Negotiate a **short, steep hill**, then pedal through open, windswept fields on a narrow, roughly paved road. You'll have nothing but silence and scenery as you stay with D33D and signs for **Fleix**. In Fleix (not much more than a dot on the map), ignore the right turn signed for Chauvigny and continue **straight** with a sign for *l'Église* instead. Stay with your lonely route past the church, then keep **left** at the **Y**. Continue with this tiny through road for several more kilometers.

Finally, when fields and solitude threaten to bore you off your bicycle seat, you'll hit a **junction** signed for **la Galisière/le Pin**. Veer **right** here, and **descend steeply**. Then climb to an intersection marked by a lone **stone cross**. Swing **right** at this junction to cycle straight toward Chauvigny. Views of the medieval city and its five ruined castles will draw you onward as you intersect with a busy **ring road** and continue **straight**.

A steep descent leads to the **main road** (**Road N151**) slicing through the lower town. Swing **left** onto N151. If you're in the mood for detours or an overnight stop, signs for the *Cité Médiévale* and the **campground** will steer you in the right direction. Chauvigny's old streets are certainly worth exploring, and the town possesses a pair of noteworthy Romanesque churches.

To continue for Poitiers, **cross the Vienne River** with N151, and veer **right** immediately afterward onto a small road signed for **Rocamat**. You'll climb away from the river, then descend once more, and savor a quiet ride along the banks of the Vienne. Push on to **Bonnes** (another interesting church), and swing **left** just **before the church**, following a hard-to-spot sign for **Poitiers**. Pedal the peaceful **Road D6** as you climb away from Bonnes and cycle on through gently rolling terrain.

Stay with this signed route for Poitiers, enjoying moderate traffic and views of fields and farmhouses. **Bignoux** marks the start of a steady hill, then you begin to pick up unappealing vistas of Poitiers's suburban high-rises as you approach the city. With a population well over 100,000, Poitiers boasts more than enough congestion for the average cyclist. However, the city's wealth of churches will repay you amply for the exhaust fumes you must endure.

Cross under a **main ring road** on the edge of town, then come face-to-face with **another main road** (signs for the center will tempt you to go left here). Go **straight across** instead, then swing **left** with another sign for the **center**. Descend steeply, and stay with a winding route to the banks of the **River Clain**. Cross the river on the **Pont Joubert** and go **left**. Next, veer **right** to climb away from the river and reach **Ste. Radegonde** church and the **cathedral**.

We'll always remember the chilly Sunday afternoon we arrived in

Poitiers. We were eating a shivering lunch beneath a portal of Ste. Radegonde when a woman who lived across the street carried over cups, sugar, a steaming pot of French-brewed coffee, and a plate of cookies for our daughter. Once you've sampled the joys of Ste. Radegonde and the 12th-century cathedral, follow the **rue de la Cathédrale** toward the center of the city.

Poitiers's **tourist office** is well signed off this street. Unfortunately, neither the **youth hostel** nor the city's two **campgrounds** are conveniently situated for sightseeing, but you should be able to find an inexpensive room with some assistance from the tourist-office staff. If you're a fan of church architecture, you may want to plan an extra day in Poitiers. The city was a major stopping point on the pilgrim route to Santiago de Compostela, and, as such, is the site of several remarkable churches. Don't skip a visit to the enchanting St. Hilaire-le-Grand, whatever you do.

Poitiers to Melle: 66 kilometers

Leaving Poitiers is less than fun, but conditions improve rapidly as you draw away from the city. To fight your way out of town, ride to the **Parc de Blossac** on the southwest edge of the city core. Join the horrendous **Road N10** toward the south, and watch for signs for the **Hermitage of St. Benoît**. Swing **left** to escape N10 and get on the somewhat quieter **Road D4** toward **Ligugé** and the **Hermitage of St. Benoît**. Then stay with D4 toward Ligugé from here.

Challenging roller-coaster hills lead to Ligugé, where you'll keep to the **right** with D4 for **Iteuil** (watch out for a confusing junction where the road branches left toward Smarves). Ligugé boasts an abbey founded by St. Martin in 361 (there's also a **campground**, if you're in the market). Continue toward **Iteuil** along the scenic and rolling valley of the **Clain River**. Gentle hills continue after Iteuil, as you push on for **Vivonne**.

Vivonne is a pleasant midsize town with a delightful riverside **campground**. Cycle past the city's old church with its attractive tower, then swing **right** for **Lusignan** with **Road D742**. Shudder as you cross the roaring **N10**, and pedal on to a **left turn** onto **Road D96** for **St. Sauvant**. Quiet cycling through open, windswept farmland follows. Keep with the signed route for St. Sauvant, pedaling D96, then **Road D29** to the city. You'll get a nice break from the somewhat monotonous fields as you pass through the tiny **Forêt de St. Sauvant** a few kilometers before town.

In St. Sauvant, go **left** for **Lezay** onto **Road D26**, then keep **right** with signs for Lezay on the edge of town. Take **Road D96** to **Courgé**, then push on with the signed route for **Lezay** on the gently rolling **Road D17**. You'll know you're in *chèvre* (goat cheese) country as you pedal past a series of fragrant goat farms on the quiet D17. Hit **Road D14** about 2 km short of Lezay, and go **right** here to cycle on to town.

In Lezay, follow signs for the **center**, then for **Melle**. You'll have two options here. You can simply stay with D14 (then Road D950) for the more direct but busier route to Melle, or you can take the slightly longer and much quieter route to the south. For the most peaceful pedaling, swing **left** onto **Road D105** in Lezay, following signs for **St. Vincent-la-Châtre** and **Chef-Boutonne**. Silent cycling leads to St. Vincent, then go **right** with **Road D305** for the final 8 km to **Melle**.

You'll crash into the busy **D950** on the edge of Melle. **Cross carefully** and continue **straight**, then go **right** onto the main road (**Road D948**) through the city. Look for Melle's **tourist office** on your left, next to the post office. The city's attractive year-round **campground** is signed to the right. Like Poitiers, Melle has enough medieval churches to provide an afternoon of wandering. Begin with the pilgrimage church of St. Hilaire, where a wonderful equestrian statue (said to be of Charlemagne) graces the main portal.

Melle to Saintes: 80 kilometers

Cycle through the heart of Melle on **D948**, and swing **left** onto **Road D120** for **Paizay-le-Tort**. Keep to the **right** for Paizay as you approach the main road (D950), **cross D950**, and continue with D120 from here. Cycle a rolling route through quiet farmland, watching for a neat old château with a circular keep, and arrive in Paizay-le-Tort. In Paizay, keep to the **right** past the **church**, and continue with D120 to **Lusseray**.

Work your way through Lusseray, swinging **left** for **Tillou**, then **right** for **Chérigné** and **Paizay-le-Chapt**. Road D120 leads to Paizay-le-Chapt, where you'll **join Road D109**, then angle **left** through town. A **left turn** will put you back on **D120** toward **St. Mandé**. Road D120 becomes **Road D129** as you pedal through the pleasant Forêt d'Aulnay. Traffic is light and terrain is gentle to St. Mandé, then continue to **Salles-lès-Aulnay**, with a noteworthy church. You won't want to linger here for long, however, as one of the finest Romanesque churches in France awaits a few kilometers farther on.

Enter Aulnay and follow signs for the **center** into the city core. Watch carefully for another sign leading **right** for the *Église Romane*, and then swing **left** for **St. Georges-de-Longuepierre**. You'll arrive at Aulnay's matchless medieval church soon after. A masterpiece of the stonecarver's art, Aulnay's little church boasts a south portal that is among the most magnificent in France. Savor the view of the building through the leaning gravestones in the adjacent churchyard, study the intricate carved portals, and pause in the quiet

The Romanesque carvings on the little church at Aulnay are among the finest in France.

of the darkened interior before reclaiming your bicycle to pedal on.

Continue past the church to an **intersection** with **Road D950** and go **left**. Descend to **cross a small creek**, then swing **right** onto **Road D107** for **Nuaillé-sur-Boutonne**. Peaceful pedaling leads to Nuaillé (another Romanesque church with a weatherworn portal), where you'll continue with D107 across the **Boutonne River**. The route is signed for **Loulay**. Just across the river, veer **left** onto **Road D220** toward **St. Pardoult**.

Pedal onward with this tiny, winding road past St. Pardoult and on to a **T** intersection, where you'll go **left** onto **Road D127** (it's unsigned). Stay with D127 to **St. Jean–d'Angély**, finishing with a rolling ride through scenic farmland. Once in St. Jean, follow signs for the **center**, and pause to view the city's unfinished church, its grand proportions marked by lonely freestanding buttresses. If you're hunting for a **campground**, St. Jean has an excellent one, within walking distance of the city center.

Leave St. Jean to the southwest, taking the route signed for the suburb of **Fbg Taillebourg** (Faubourg Taillebourg). You'll hit the busy **Road D739** as you exit the city core. Go **right** here, then swing **left** onto **Road D127** for **Mazeray**. An up-and-down ride through quiet farmland will take you past Mazeray and on to a **right turn** signed for **Fenioux**. Go right here to climb to a wonderful Romanesque church set in a tiny hillside village. Be sure to take a look at Fenioux's interesting *Lanterne des Morts* (lantern of the dead), as well.

From the church in Fenioux, continue with the road for **Grandjean**. Descend briefly and go **left** onto a second road, then swing **right** to cycle through the minute village of Grandjean. Push on to an intersection with **Road D124** and go **left**, then veer **right** soon after onto **D127** once again. Signs for **Annepont** and **Taillebourg** will lead you on through lovely hillside vineyards.

Ride past Annepont and **cross above the A10 motorway,** then sneak a look at Taillebourg's fortified castle as you pedal past. This area hosted a battle between invading Moorish forces and the armies of Charlemagne in 808. **Cross Road D114**, then the **Charente River**, as you press on for **St. James**. You'll intersect with **Road D128** in St. James. Go **left** here to pedal on to **Saintes**.

The final 9 km of the day are studded with hills that offer little comfort to weary legs. Fortunately, Saintes will console you with its many charms. Road D128 will take you to the banks of the **Charente River** as you enter Saintes. If you're camping, the city's **campground** is to the left along the river, beside a large swimming complex. Go **right** on the riverside road to gain Saintes' **center**.

The **tourist office** will be to your right (west side of the Charente) when you hit the busy city's main drag, the cours National. Pick up some information on hotels and sights while you're here. Saintes' pleasant **youth hostel** is located just across the river, near the remarkable Abbaye-aux-Dames. The hostel offers campspots for cardholders, too.

In addition to its lovely abbey church, Saintes offers a Roman arena and the wonderful pilgrimage church of St. Eutrope to make your visit memorable. If you're here in early July, you'll be joined by hordes of music lovers, as the city hosts both an ancient music festival and an international folk music festival every year.

Saintes to Blaye: 92 kilometers

From the heart of Saintes and the cours National, cross to the **east bank of the Charente River** and swing **right** past the **Arc de Germanicus**. You'll swing away from the river with the **rue Gautier**, and continue out from the city core (past turnoffs for the youth hostel and abbey). Signs for **Cognac** and **Angoulême** (via the Charente Valley) lead on as you cycle **Road D24** out of town.

Enjoy pretty views of the Charente but endure fairly constant traffic on D24 as you negotiate the 7 km to **Chaniers**. In Chaniers, veer **right** for **Courcoury**, abandoning the hectic D24 for smaller roads and quieter cycling. (If you're in the mood for a visit to one of the handful of world-famous distilleries in Cognac, continue with D24 instead.) **Cross** the train tracks, then swing **left** at a sign for **le Moulin de la Baine** (a 17th-century watermill).

Cycle past an old church and cemetery as you follow a quiet riverside road. When your route approaches D24 once again, keep to the **right** for **Rouffiac**, **Pons**, and **St. Sever** instead. Join **Road D134** to cross the Charente, and stay with signs for **Pons** as you push on. Silent cycling through cognac vineyards and cornfields will make your morning memorable. Road D134 takes you to an intersection with **Road D732**. Go **right** here, through **Bougneau**, and on to **Pons**.

Stay with signs for the **center** to gain Pons's old core. You can climb the slope to view the remnants of the city's hilltop fortress or simply pedal through the busy town below. Pons is an attractive city, sliced by many small canals and made lively by the scores of small businesses that give a French city its identity. Its prominence on the pilgrim route toward Spain is marked by remains of a medieval pilgrims' hospital, an evocative spot that was the end of many a weary traveler's earthly journey.

Leave Pons's center with signs for **Royan** and **Bordeaux**. You'll hit the busy **Road D732** on the edge of town. Look for a noteworthy priory church on the left, at the intersection. If you'd like to take a look at the pilgrim hospital, go straight across D732 and cycle less than a kilometer to reach the unimposing building astride the road. Look for the carved scallop shells that characterize the architecture of the pilgrim route, etched into the shadow-draped stones of the structure. Then return to D732 and go **right** (left if you're coming from Pons's center).

Cross over the **train tracks** and go **right** onto the tiny route signed for **Fléac**(-sur-Seugne). Signs for **Fléac-sur-Seugne** lead on as you cycle a delightfully deserted roadway. Enter the small village of Fléac, and swing **right** at a sign for **Road N137**. Pedal past the town **church** and **cross the train tracks** and a small **waterway** (look for a handsome stone bridge spanning the water), then continue to a junction with **Road D134**. Go to the **left** for the town of **Mosnac**.

Mosnac offers an out-of-the-way municipal **campground** beside its church. Swing **right** at the **church** to pedal on to **Road D146**, then go **right** here for **St. Genis**. In St. Genis, turn **left** onto **Road N137** toward **Mirambeau**. You'll catch a glimpse of the château of Plassac as you cycle past. Just beyond **Plassac**, swing **right** for **Consac** to gain yet another wonderfully tiny French road. Delightful cycling through well-kept vineyards, rolling hills, and thin forests follows.

If you're riding in the fall, as we were, you'll be entertained by scenes of men and women working the vines, plucking plump grapes that hang like raindrops between the scarlet-hued leaves. Friendly smiles, waves, and calls to join the harvest will reach you from the fields, as the pickers look up from their work to watch you pass.

In Consac, your route will first zig **left**, then swing **right** (it's unsigned), then you'll hit **Road D730** not far past town. Cross it and continue **straight** with **Road D148** toward **St. Georges**. **Parallel** the **A10 motorway** for a time, then **cross over it** as you turn toward the west. The terrain is challenging but lovely as you pedal on through vine-draped hills, enjoying vistas that reach to the Gironde estuary.

Ride through **Semoussac**, a small town with a church that's a humorous blend of divergent architectural styles, and continue to a junction with **Road D146**. Turn **left** to cycle through **St. Georges**, and pedal on for **St. Bonnet**. (There's a **campground** in St. Bonnet, if you're running out of daylight or desire.) Signs for **St. Ciers** and **Blaye** lead on from St. Bonnet, as D146 suddenly becomes a much busier (and much less pleasant) thoroughfare.

Road D146 becomes **Road D18** as you cross a regional border, and the number of prestigious wine châteaux increases as you continue south. Enjoy scenic cycling to **St. Ciers**, gazing across endless vineyards to the shimmering Gironde. In St. Ciers, keep to the **right** for **Blaye** and join **Road D255** from here. The hills flatten out and the scenery becomes somewhat monotonous as you pedal the final kilometers to Blaye. The vineyards are unceasing, however.

Blaye's **tourist office** is near the harbor (D255 will lead you to the harbor road), and you'll pass the city's major attraction on the way. The **citadel**, constructed in 1685, is the handiwork of perhaps the most famous of French military architects—Vauban. It replaced an earlier castle, said to be the burial place of the heroic warrior Roland, who fell in battle with the Moors in 778.

You'll have a treat in store if you're camping at Blaye, as the city's **campground** is planted smack in the middle of the citadel, and it comes equipped with a wonderful view of the Gironde estuary. Even if you're not putting up a tent, be sure to scramble up to the fortifications and enjoy the setting.

Bordeaux is a vast but captivating city.

Blaye to Bordeaux: 52 kilometers

Be sure to get an early start today, especially if you're planning to hunt for a room in the center of Bordeaux. Traffic intensifies as you near your goal, and you'll want to avoid the late-afternoon rush at all costs. From Blaye's **harbor road**, continue past the tourist office and ferry landing, and follow **Road D669** for **Plassac** and **Bourg** away from town. Savor pleasant cycling beside the Gironde. There's no doubt you're in wine country now—vineyards are everywhere.

Pedal to **Plassac** and continue with D669. A few kilometers later, watch for a **right turn** signed for **Roque-de-Thau** and **Marmisson**. You'll be in for a treat as you take this tiny waterside route and pedal a scenic corniche road for several kilometers. Marmisson is a delight of flower-filled yards and homes burrowed into the cliffs. Push on to **la Reuille**, then **climb steeply** to leave the water near the confluence of the Dordogne and Garonne.

Ascend toward **Bayon**, but veer **right before rejoining D669**. A sign for the **corniche road** should alert you to your turn. Cycle past Bayon's church, ruled by an intricate steeple and accentuated by a lofty virgin and child, then keep **left** when the road branches (a right will take you back to river level again). Savor a quiet ride through pampered vineyards as you continue. The turns are unsigned through here, so keep a close eye on your map.

Hit a **T** intersection and go **left**, then swing **right** to **parallel D669** for a while longer. You'll **rejoin D669** just before **Bourg**, then press on for **St. André-de-Cubzac**. Traffic remains endurable, and the mellow hills are carpeted in vines and punctuated with handsome wine châteaux. Keep an eye out for signs inviting *dégustation*, if you're feeling thirsty.

St. André is an inviting town. You can ride through the center to view the old core, or swing **right** with the sign for *Toutes Directions* to postpone your meeting with the terrifying **Road N10** as long as possible. It won't be long enough, however. Join N10 toward **Bordeaux** and breathe a prayer. Then hug the shoulder and pedal, pedal, pedal.

Ugh. This road is narrow and busy. Unfortunately, it's also the only way for you to cross the Dordogne River. The **bridge** is nothing short of suicidal—consider walking your bicycle along the pedestrian sidewalk if you hope to live to see your grandchildren. Escape the bridge and pedal through **St. Vincent-de-Paul**, cross the **train tracks**, then swing **right** onto **Road D911** for **Ambarès et-Lagrave**. Shun the subsequent signs that will tempt you toward Ambarès's center, and simply proceed with D911 from here. You'll pass the pleasant **Camping Clos Chauvet** at the junction signed for Ste. Eulalie. This is a good option if you're carrying a tent, especially if you're continuing with our Dordogne route from here. You can take public transit into Bordeaux for your sightseeing, and save yourself the headache of cycling into this enormous city.

To ride on for Bordeaux, continue with D911 through **Carbon-Blanc**. You'll hit a **junction** signed for **Bordeaux *Lac*** and the **airport** to the right (Bordeaux and St. Jean to the left). Go **right** here and reach a **roundabout** soon after. Signs for **Bordeaux *Bastide*** will lead you on. Descend to a **T** and go **left** for Bordeaux *Bastide*, then stay with this road (**Road D113**) through an unappealing industrial suburb beside the Garonne.

You'll arrive at the **Pont de Pierre** at last. Go **right** to **cross the river** and arrive in the heart of the city. The main **tourist office** will be to your right from here. Follow the riverside road north to the rue Esprit des Lois and go left. You'll be able to get help with your lodging hunt at the office. Be sure to pick up a map of this vast port city while you're in the office, too.

Bordeaux boasts a **youth hostel**, a "student house" (*Maison des Étudiantes*), and lots of cheap hotels. **Campgrounds** are less convenient for sightseeing, but you'll find sites in Gradignan and Villenave d'Ornon, to the south of the city center, if you're set on camping.

Bordeaux's major claim to fame is its wine, so you may want to begin your sightseeing at the Maison du Vin (house of wine), across from the tourist office. You can get a list of area wine châteaux here. Be sure to call ahead before you visit. Please don't spend all your time château hopping, though—Bordeaux is a fascinating city to explore on foot. A handful of first-class museums and some impressive churches can entertain you for at least a day or two, and the lively city streets and lovely Jardin Public will make your outdoor wandering a treat.

If you're putting your bike aboard a train for the trip back to Paris, please refer to our section on bikes and trains in the introductory portion of this book. Be sure to check in at the train station a few days before you hope to leave to get the scoop on bicycles from Bordeaux's baggage folks. There's a tourist office at the train station, too. Or save yourself the hassle and ride on with our Tour No. 7 to Cahors from here.

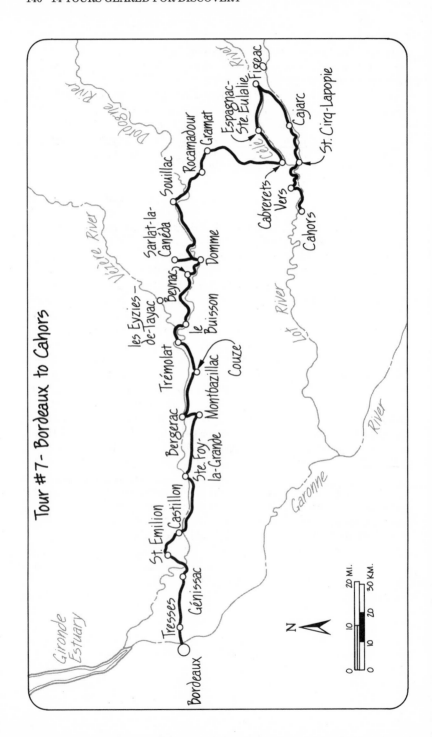

Tour #7 - Bordeaux to Cahors

TOUR NO. 7

RAVISHING RIVER ROLLS
Bordeaux to Cahors

Distance: 455 kilometers (283 miles)
Estimated time: 8 riding days
Best time to go: April through June; September or October
Terrain: Hill-studded days mixed in with riverside glides
Maps: Michelin Nos. 75 and 79
Connecting tours: Tour Nos. 6 and 8

This delightful ride along the valleys of the Dordogne, Célé, and Lot rivers will tantalize you with breathtaking scenery and tax you with breath-stealing hills. Vineyards abound for the first part of the ride, and you'll see so many incredible old villages, you'll probably find it impossible to choose a favorite.

Perhaps the one key to really enjoying this ride is timing it well. The Dordogne Valley has been "discovered" by Dutch and English tourists in recent years, and the French have savored its charms for decades. As a result, the months of July and August bring incredible crowds to the area. Avoid high season at all costs, carry lots of film, and enjoy!

CONNECTIONS. You can reach Bordeaux and the start of this tour by rail from Paris, or link together our Tour Nos. 5 and 6 to cycle south and west through châteaux and vineyards, en route to the sprawling port city of Bordeaux. Once in Cahors, you'll find frequent train connections back to Paris, or you can pedal on to Albi (as we did) and catch the start of our Tour No. 8.

INFORMATION. Michelin's English-language *Green Guide* for the *Dordogne* is an invaluable reference source for this tour. The moderate cost and negligible weight of this information-packed volume are both well worth the sacrifice you'll make to carry it. *The Visitor's Guide to France: Dordogne* by Barbara Mandell (Moorland Publishing Co., Ltd.) is another informative volume, and the Philips Travel Guide entitled *The Dordogne* is a lavishly illustrated and beautifully written book to read ahead of time (and leave at home). Scour your central library's card catalog or visit a good travel bookstore to search out other reading possibilities for this much visited (and much written of) area.

As mentioned earlier, the Dordogne Valley is woefully overvisited.

We hate to say it, but you really shouldn't consider coming here if you have to come in August. The Dordogne is too wonderful to hate, even if you have been trampled by fourteen tour groups in a single day—so don't let it happen to you! Come in May or late September and fall in love instead. Obviously, any region so popular in any country like France must have scads of campgrounds—the Dordogne does. And they're delightful ones, tucked along riverbanks and set in castles' shadows. Hotels are more difficult to come by here, as most villages are small and terribly overwhelmed with guests.

One can hardly think of the Dordogne without thinking of geese— grazing geese, fat geese, cooked geese, canned geese—and you'll probably see more *foie gras* vendors on this ride than you will in all the rest of France. Taste it once, just to say you did. *Confits* are yet another of the Dordogne's vegetarian nightmares. The production of *confits* involves preserving the innards of a goose, duck, turkey, or pig in large earthenware pots, with lots of fat for company.

On a more peaceful note, the cuisine in this region also relies heavily on mushrooms (a special type called *cèpes*) and truffles (traditionally hunted with trained pigs, although we searched high and low for such an animal, only to decide that all Dordogne pigs now reside in large earthenware pots). Walnuts are plentiful here, as well, and are to be found in delicious walnut cakes and a host of other goodies.

No discussion of the Dordogne could be complete without some mention of the region's many famous wines. Besides the renowned white wine of Monbazillac, there is the stout red wine of Cahors, the varied reds and whites of Bergerac, and, finally, the *pièce de résistance*—the infinitely wonderful wine of St. Emilion.

Bordeaux to St. Emilion: 52 kilometers

Please refer to the final paragraphs of our Tour No. 6 for information on Bordeaux. This day's ride from Bordeaux to St. Emilion, though manageable in terms of length, does present some extremely challenging terrain. Try to get an early start out of the city center. As you approach Bordeaux's **Pont de Pierre** and the Garonne River, get into the **bike lane** that ascends to the span from the south side.

Cycle away from the city core as you cross the Garonne toward the east, then swing **right** as you leave the bridge. Veer **left** just after to gain the **rue de la Benauge**. Follow this street to the **freeway**, and go **left** to find a **pedestrian underpass** after about 100 meters. Cross under the freeway and continue to the next **intersection**, then veer **left** with signs for the **Quartier Jean Jaurès**.

Stay with this route as you cross another **freeway**, then follow signs for **Haut Cenon** (upper Cenon) from here. You'll climb steadily for a time and stay with signs for **Tresses** as you get onto **Road D241**

A cycle tour along the Dordogne River offers a host of castle-ruled villages.

toward the east. Traffic is fairly thick for the early kilometers of this ride, so try to choose a departure day and time that will ensure as little congestion as possible (a weekend morning, perhaps). Press on with D241, cycling a scenic but challenging route studded with sudden dips and climbs. The vine-draped hills are lovely in every season, but you'll be in for a special treat if you pass through during the autumn grape harvest.

Ride through Tresses and continue for **Pompignac**. The traffic thins from here. One extremely steep pitch lurks among the many gentle swells leading to **Salleboeuf**. Just before Salleboeuf's center, swing **left** onto **Road D13**, then go **right** to regain **D241** signed for **St. Germain-du-Puch**. Famous Bordeaux vineyards swath the mounded hills, and you'll pedal a pleasantly quiet road past a gray, turreted château (le Grand-Puch).

Just past the **château**, swing **left** onto **Road D20** for St. Germain, but veer **right** soon after to **rejoin D241** toward **Nérigean**. Descend, then **climb steeply** to reach Nérigean, ruled by a stout 12th- and 16th-century fortified church. The building's arrow-slit windows seem to invite warriors rather than worshippers, and they provide graphic testimony of the tumultuous past of this region.

In Nérigean, turn **left** onto **Road D120**, then go **right** for **Génissac**. You'll intersect with **Road D121** soon after, and go **left** to descend into Génissac. Continue toward the banks of the Dordogne River as you pedal to the far side of Génissac and hit **Road D18**. Swing **right** onto D18 to press on for **Moulon** and **Branne**. Road D18 is a much busier thoroughfare (unfortunately) with a hefty dose of the same old hills (also unfortunate). Both your legs and your nerves will be complaining as you push on through Moulon and continue with D18 for **Branne**.

Reach a **T** intersection about 3 km later, and go **left** onto the extremely unpleasant **Road D936**. Descend to Branne on the banks of the Dordogne, and **cross the river** with signs for **St. Emilion**. Just after crossing, abandon D936 as you swing **left** onto the delightful **Road D122** to pedal onward through acre after acre of famous-name vineyards. You'll be amazed at the way every available inch of soil seems to be planted with vines in this area. The reason is the incredible reputation (and value) of St. Emilion wine—each vine is an investment in this hallowed region.

Stay with the signed route for St. Emilion as you angle **right** with D122, feasting your eyes on vineyards and treating your legs to the first level cycling of the day. Hit **Road D670** and continue **straight** across, then ascend to the hilltop city that lends this region's wine its name. St. Emilion is a stone-built beauty set among endless vineyards, and it contains a wealth of ruins, churches, cobblestones, and wine merchants. Even if you visit in the off-season, you'll find that St. Emilion also contains a wealth of tourists. Don't let the crowds spoil your enjoyment, however. This town is a gem, if a much visited one.

St. Emilion's **tourist office** is well signed as you enter the compact city. Pick up a list of the town's attractions and consider investing in a guided tour of the major monuments. You can seek help with lodgings at the tourist office, too, but expect to pay plenty if you need a bed. St. Emilion does offer a well-equipped **campground** down the hill near the Barbanne River (continue with D122 to find it). The 3 km you'll have to travel from the city center is well worth the *francs* you'll save by pitching your tent.

St. Emilion to Bergerac: 63 kilometers

If your legs feel weary as you set out on your ride today, take heart—you'll have an easy cycling day to Bergerac. From St. Emilion's **center**, continue with D122 to the north side of town, then go **right** onto **Road D243** for **St. Christophe-des-Bardes**. Continue **straight** when the road branches, and cycle onward for St. Christophe. It may seem like every inch of soil holds a vine as you draw away from St. Emilion. In a region where twenty-nine wineries hold the highest rating a French wine can receive, it's easy to see why vines take precedence over every other growing thing.

Follow signs for **Castillon** as you leave St. Christophe. You'll swing **right** off D243 a few kilometers later, joining **Road D130** toward **Castillon**. Run into **Road D17** on the edge of Castillon, and go **right** to cross the **train tracks** and ride toward the **center**. Castillon is a busy little market town—a good spot for breakfast if you haven't eaten your obligatory *croissant* as yet. **Cross Road D936** in town, then angle **right** for **Sauveterre** and **Pujols** to cross the **Dordogne River** with D17.

Once across the river, take the **first left** (it's unsigned) to gain a wonderfully quiet road beside the water. Vineyards share the land with tobacco fields as you pedal on with delightful vistas of the Dordogne. Begin picking up signs for **Ste. Foy-la-Grande** as you stay with your tiny route beside the water. You'll **join Road D130** at **Flaujagues**. Begin a **long, steady climb** through vine-mantled hills soon after.

The views will recompense you for your labor as you ascend with ever-widening vistas. Reach the crest of your climb, then descend to **Pessac-sur-Dordogne**. Signs for **Eynesse** and **Ste. Foy** lead on with D130 along the river. Silent cycling will carry you to Eynesse and on with D130 toward Ste. Foy. Swing **left** for Ste. Foy onto **Road D130E7** to stay with your flat riverside route when D130 climbs away.

You'll run smack into the much busier **Road D672** a few kilometers short of Ste. Foy. Go **left** here, **cross Road D936**, and continue straight for the **center** of Ste. Foy. A pleasant waterfront promenade, a plethora of shops, and lots of activity all combine to make Ste. Foy a pleasure. We sampled some of the most delicious bread we ever hope to eat in this busy city, purchased so fresh from the oven that we nearly needed potholders to slice it. (This region's *pain de campagne* is magnificent—be sure to try it!)

Cycle straight through Ste. Foy's busy center, paralleling the left bank of the Dordogne. Pass the **church** and continue to a **junction** on the edge of town. Go **right** here for **Pellegrue**, then swing **left** at the next intersection onto **Road D18** for **Eymet** and **Monbazillac**. Stay with D18 to **St. Philippe**, then go **left** onto **Road D18E6** toward Monbazillac. This secondary road becomes the equally quiet **Road D14** when you cross a regional boundary.

Savor easy, silent cycling past verdant vineyards as you follow signs for **Issigeac** and **Monbazillac**. You'll pick up views to the northeast of Bergerac and vistas of the hilltop château of Monbazillac as you approach the finish of your riding day. **Cross Road D933** and continue to a **junction** with **Road D13**. To the right, a brief climb will lead you to Monbazillac Château, crowning a vine-clad ridge. The detour is well worth it, if you have the time, as the 16th-century château has been skillfully restored by the Monbazillac Wine Cooperative.

To ride for **Bergerac**, pedal **north** on **D13** and descend gently toward the Dordogne. Stay with D13 as you cross a **main ring road**, then press on to the **bridge** spanning the river. Bergerac's attractive old core awaits on the right bank of the Dordogne. You'll find the city's pleasant municipal **campground** on the left bank (follow signs a short distance downriver from the bridge). To continue into the city **center**, simply cross to the north side of the river.

The compact old town is a treat for walkers, and several museums and churches will tempt you to venture indoors. Bergerac's excellent Musée du Tabac gives evidence of the city's prominence in the tobacco industry. If you need a bed, Bergerac has a handful of hotels to select from. Ask for help at the well-signed **tourist office**.

Bergerac to le Buisson: 48 kilometers

From the **south end** of the **bridge** spanning the Dordogne River in Bergerac, get on the busy **Road N21** toward **Agen**. Make your escape very soon after, angling **left** onto **Road D19** for **St. Nexans**. A subsequent **left** will put you on **Road D37** toward **Couze**. Continue 1 ³/₄ **km** to an unmarked road veering **left**, and take this quiet thoroughfare along the banks of the Dordogne. Continue **straight** through the following junction, and enjoy flat, effortless cycling past dozens of sweet-smelling tobacco sheds.

You'll **rejoin D37** (it's unsigned) a few kilometers later, and continue beside the river with light traffic and pastoral scenery. **Cross Road D21** and continue **straight** for **Couze**. When your route branches with both ways signed for Couze, keep to the **left** on **Road D37E1**. A brief climb leads to **Varennes**, then a quick descent finishes with the scenic, riverside ride to Couze. Couze is an interesting Dordogne village, characterized by shadowy dwellings burrowed into the cliffs.

Swing **right** in Couze to get on **Road D660** for **Beaumont**, then veer **left** just past the **school** (there's a hard-to-see sign for **St. Front**) to join a tiny road ascending steeply along the hillside. Wonderful views of the river and the forest-shrouded hills will reward you for your laboring lungs. Descend abruptly to the bridge into **Lalinde**, but stay on the **south side** of the river with **Road D8E4** toward **le Buisson**.

You'll join **Road D29** as you keep **left** beside the river, and savor a scenic ride to **Badefols**. Traffic is a bit heavier through here, but you'll still have time to look for river birds and vistas as you pedal.

About 2 km beyond Badefols, swing **left** for **Trémolat** onto the much more serene **Road D28**. This route will lengthen your ride to le Buisson by a handful of kilometers, but the detour is worth the effort. Road D28 becomes **Road D31** as you dive into the **Trémolat Meander** (a particularly scenic twist in the Dordogne) and **cross** to the **right bank** of the river.

Just across the **Dordogne bridge**, swing **left** for **Limeuil** and enter the tiny town of Trémolat. Trémolat is a charming little village, boasting strong associations with the pilgrim route to Santiago de Compostela. Before heading out on D31, you may want to pause to view the domed interior of Trémolat's 12th-century church. It displays an architectural style characteristic of the region.

Leave Trémolat with **D31** toward **Limeuil**. A **long, wearying ascent** is interrupted by a **quick descent** to cross a creek, then you'll make another **short, steep climb** to reach a lofty viewpoint above the Dordogne. Pause for a dizzying peek straight down to the river, and admire the striking limestone cliffs that hold the writhing waterway in its course. An exhilarating descent leads to Limeuil, and you'll cruise in beneath the city's piled stone houses. (If you're interested in making a trip up the Vézère River to visit the famous prehistoric caverns around les Eyzies-de-Tayac, Limeuil will be your departure point. Those who cycle to les Eyzies will probably want to continue to Sarlat-la-Canéda via Road D47 rather than return to the Dordogne and our described route.)

To continue with the Dordogne Valley from Limeuil, join **Road D51** toward **le Buisson**, and cross the **Vézère River**, pausing to admire the striking confluence of the Vézère and Dordogne. Stay with D51 as a busier road adds its le Buisson–bound traffic. Pedal on to the banks of the **Dordogne**, and **cross** the river to enter le Buisson. A riverside **campground** and indoor accommodations options await you here. If you have a half-day to spare, you may want to stow your gear in le Buisson and pedal the 6 (mostly uphill) km to Cadouin and its famed 12th-century church. The church boasts remarkably flamboyant cloisters.

Le Buisson to Sarlat-la-Canéda: 48 kilometers

Be sure your camera is loaded and ready for your ride today—you'll be pedaling through some of the most famous of the Dordogne's villages en route to the valley's undisputed queen, Sarlat. From le Buisson, cross to the **right bank** of the Dordogne River and veer **right** with the signed route for **Bigaroque** and **le Coux**. Pedal a tiny road to Bigaroque, a picture-perfect village of flowers and glowing stone, then press on to **Coux** (maps say Coux-et-Bigaroque), where you'll join **Road D703** for **St. Cyprien**. When the road curves right to cross the Dordogne to Siorac, angle **left** for **Mouzens** instead, and stay with the suddenly quiet D703.

Revel in easy, scenic cycling as you ride to St. Cyprien with its barnlike church. Continue **straight** through St. Cyprien's center, then go **right** with D703 for **Beynac**. Traffic intensifies as Road D50 adds its collection of trucks and autos from the south side of the river, but you can entertain yourself with château spotting as you continue up the gradually narrowing valley. If you're pedaling in the fall, you'll be able to exchange greetings with the locals gathering walnuts in roadside orchards. In addition to orchards and châteaux, campgrounds abound along this section of the river—an indication of the region's almost pathetic summertime popularity.

An enchanting vista of the crenelated walls and turrets of Beynac's lofty castle will draw you toward the city along the winding banks of the Dordogne. This is a sight you won't soon forget. The lower town is lovely, too, especially when its timeless stones are glowing in the golden caress of the morning sun. If you want to view Beynac's castle from a closer perch, you can lock your bicycle in the lower city and climb the hill for a visit. The panorama of the Dordogne Valley is spectacular from the lofty fortress.

Reach a **junction** just beyond Beynac, and stay with signs for **la Roque–Gageac** to pedal on beneath towering cliffs. Lofty châteaux will delight you as you cruise on to la Roque–Gageac, a luminescent village of yellow stone, hemmed in by vertical slabs of rock. Continue with D703 for another 3 km and hit a **T**. You'll swing **right** here for **Cénac** and **Domme**, then **cross** the river with **Road D46**.

Enter Cénac and veer **left** for Domme to begin a **long, steady climb** toward the ridgetop *bastide*. You'll probably be dripping by the time you reach the touristy town of Domme, 2 km later, but the climb is worth it for the vista of the Dordogne Valley and the varied charms of the famous fortified city. Stand on the Barre Belvedere and stare at the cliffs plummeting to the distant banks of the Dordogne, then marvel at the audacity of the Protestant Captain Vivan. In 1588, he led thirty of his men up the unguarded cliff face and overwhelmed the sleeping town before it could resist his forces.

Backtrack down the hill and **across the river**, then pedal on for **Vitrac**. You'll swing **left** for **Sarlat** a few kilometers later, and begin a gentle **climb** of about 7 km on the somewhat busy **D46**. Cruise into the sprawling (and infinitely popular) city of Sarlat-la-Canéda, an effervescent beauty built of glowing sandstone. Although this city attracts far too many tourists for its own good, it's easy to see why. Sarlat is a medieval gem, with a carefully restored old core that invites hours of delightful strolling.

Look for the **tourist office** on the place de la Liberté in the Hôtel de Maleville. You can pick up a walking map of the *vieille ville* (old town) here. If you're visiting in high season and arrive without reservations, don't expect much help from the busy staff. Off-season rooms are spendy but plentiful in Sarlat. A convenient **youth hostel** and some nearby **campgrounds** round out the lodging options. Staying in Sarlat is worth the struggle, however, as you really can't do justice to the town with bike and bags in tow.

Once you've stowed your gear, set out on foot to explore the narrow streets and glowing buildings of the old town. Resist the scores of shops and concentrate on the cathedral, the museums, the architecture, and the ambiance of this delightful Dordogne city.

Sarlat-la-Canéda to Rocamadour: 59 kilometers

Begin your ride today by enjoying a fast downhill **backtrack** to **Vitrac**. You'll begin seeing new territory as you push on with **D703** for **Carsac**, enjoying gently rolling pedaling along the right bank of the Dordogne. **Montfort Château** will soon appear before you, ruling a rocky butte above the road. Ascend steadily to the **Cingle de Montfort**, an impressive viewpoint above the snaking river, and gaze down on the hundreds of geese grazing the Dordogne's shoreline, stuffing themselves in preparation for their inevitable French fate.

A delightful descent leads to Carsac, a tiny stone village huddled around a squarish Romanesque church. Swing **right** in Carsac to join the busy **Road D704** toward **Cahors**, cross the **river**, then dive **left** onto **Road D50** for **Veyrignac**. More up-and-down cycling follows, and you'll pass hordes of geese and forests of walnut trees as you pedal to **St. Julien-de-Lampon**. The hills ease a bit from here, and you'll parallel the river on a wonderfully quiet road shaded by poplars.

Pass through a series of small villages "stuffed" with *foie gras* merchants as you approach **Souillac**. A short distance beyond **Cieurac**, recross the **river** and pedal to a junction with **Road D703**. Go **right** here to gain the center of **Souillac**. (There's a large supermarket about 1 km to the left on D703—this is probably your best shopping option of the day, especially if you're camping at Rocamadour.)

Souillac's major attraction is its handsome abbey church, loaded with carvings and boasting the region's characteristic domed ceiling. If you're running low on daylight or energy at this point in your day, consider stopping at Souillac (**campgrounds** and hotels), as a killer climb awaits en route to Rocamadour. A centrally located **tourist office** can provide information on the town and its surroundings.

From Souillac's abbey church, continue to the thoroughly unpleasant **Road N20** and go **right** for **Cahors**, **Rocamadour**, and the **Grottes de Lacave**. Endure horrible cycling for a brief kilometer, then exit **left** onto **Road D43** for Rocamadour and the Grottes de Lacave. You'll savor scenic, easy riding as your road runs between the cliffs and the Dordogne, then climb to **Pinsac**. A quick descent leads to a **bridge** across the river (be very careful here—the bridge is surfaced with tire-grabbing grooves). **Cross** the Dordogne and **climb again**, bidding adieu to the famous river for the final time.

The views will recompense you for your labors as you puff uphill, then descend to cross the **Ouysse River**, enjoying an impressive vista of a clifftop château. Signs for **Rocamadour** lead on—and up. Endure a **punishing ascent** for 4 or 5 km. If you're cycling through late-afternoon heat, as we were, you'll suffer here. You'll also notice a startling change in the landscape, as you trade the lush Dordogne Valley for much drier, sparser terrain.

The climb eases for the final few kilometers of your ride, then you'll arrive at the lofty community of **l'Hospitalet**, the commercial outpost of Rocamadour. The "hospital" in l'Hospitalet's name is an indicator of the pilgrim roots of Rocamadour, a city that once drew in religious travelers by the thousands—travelers who often needed sustenance and medical care upon arriving at their goal. Today, travelers who land in l'Hospitalet are "sustained" by four-star hotels, deluxe campgrounds, restaurants, and overflowing postcard racks, yet Rocamadour still retains its almost supernatural charm.

Your small road will take you to a **junction** with the busier **Road D673**, where you'll go **left** (to the right is the clifftop château and city access for those who wish to walk). Rocamadour's many campgrounds are well signed from the following junction. There's a wonderful **campground** right at the junction, with friendly managers and excellent access to the city. If you're seeking a hotel, swing **right** to follow the winding, swiftly descending road to the valley floor.

Your first look at Rocamadour will take your breath away, especially if the sun's early rays caress the almost vertical city, its streets and stairways hanging beneath fortresslike churches and crowning ramparts. It's easy to imagine why so many medieval travelers made the difficult journey to this place. Not only is it visually enchanting, it's filled with religious treasures and impressive architecture.

Stash your bicycle and gear and pace the steep stone streets and stairways, ignoring the tourist shops to pay homage to the 11th-century basilica and surrounding chapels. If you visit Rocamadour during July or August, or around the first two weeks of September when the annual *pèlerinage* (pilgrimage) occurs, don't expect to find a room without reservations. In off-months, you should have more luck. As mentioned earlier, campgrounds are plentiful around l'Hospitalet.

Rocamadour to Cabrerets: 58 kilometers

You'll have a tough and solitary day of cycling ahead as you set out from Rocamadour and head toward the pretty Célé Valley. If you need to trim this tour a bit to make up for lost time or enthusiasm, you can skip the Célé and ride a more direct route to Figeac (see the following paragraphs). Those who can pedal the entire route should do it, though, as the Célé Valley is a lovely corner of France.

From **l'Hospitalet**, get on **Road D673** toward **Gramat** (if you're leaving from the lower town, take Road D36 toward Gramat instead). Pedal 4 km along the ridgeline, then swing **right** onto the unpleasantly busy **Road N140** for Gramat. Tough it out on N140 for the 8 km to Gramat, a midsize town without much charm. You'll have a couple of options here. You can cut off almost an entire day of cycling by heading straight for Figeac (a potential route would be to take N140 to Road D35 for Issendolus, then ride on through Lalinié, Assier, Reyrevignes, and Lissac to arrive in Figeac).

Our route as written (and recommended), however, is to head toward the lower end of the Célé Valley, rack up some additional scenic kilometers, and reach Figeac on your second day of cycling from Rocamadour. To do this, swing **right** onto **Road D677** for **Cahors** and **St. Cirque–Lapopie** in Gramat. Descend through town, cross the **train tracks**, and dive **left** onto the tiny **Road D14** for **Reilhac**. This road gives new meaning to the term "lonely"—but you'll have lots of attractive farm buildings and scores of sheep for company as you battle through an afternoon of exhausting hills and sometimes rotten road surfaces.

You'll be crossing the Gramat Causse as you ride toward the Célé Valley. This limestone plateau presents a dry landscape studded with oak and juniper, and sheep are plentiful in the rocky fields. Just after entering **Reilhac**, veer **right** onto a hard-to-spot road signed for **Lunegarde**. A brief descent with **Road D42** leads into a **stiff climb** to Lunegarde's ridgetop church. Look for a wooden "cage" for shoeing horses in this delightfully untouched village.

More rolling terrain leads on to **Fontanes-du-Causse**, then continue with D42 toward **Caniac-du-Causse** as you pedal through a dry oak forest characteristic of the area. A **punishing climb** leads on from Caniac as D42 heads toward **Sénaillac-Lauzès**. In Sénaillac, go **right** on **Road D17**, then veer **left** to regain **D42** toward **Orniac** and **Cabrerets**. A much-deserved downhill glide leads to **Road D653**. **Cross** it and push on through more rolling hills past Orniac and on for Cabrerets. You'll have 3 km of **precipitous downhill** cycling to arrive in the Célé Valley. A final **left** will put you on **Road D13** into Cabrerets.

Cabrerets is the leaping-off point for your journey up the deep valley of the Célé River. The little town boasts a 15th-century château, but its major claim to fame is its proximity to the fantastic **Grotte du Pech Merle**, a mile-long cave filled with prehistoric art. Throughout the Célé Valley, indoor accommodations are scattered and somewhat sparse. If you're camping, you'll be able to choose among a host of appealing campgrounds, however.

Cabrerets to Figeac: 45 kilometers

From Cabrerets, the riverside **Road D41** leads toward **Figeac**. If you're pedaling in off-season, you'll have delightfully quiet cycling on this mostly level route. The summer months bring campers, boaters, and sightseers to the area, and traffic picks up markedly. Small towns, tobacco fields, and a twisting river held in place by majestic overhanging cliffs will provide your scenery as you ride.

You'll probably want to stop for photographs several times as you draw away from Cabrerets with the gently climbing road. Pass the **Fontaine de la Pescalerie**, a pretty waterfall marking the emergence of a subterranean river, and pedal on beneath precipitous rock walls. **Sauliac-sur-Célé** is an ancient village tucked into the cliffs, and more enchanting towns follow close behind it. The remains of a Benedictine abbey grace **Marcilhac-sur-Célé**, while **St. Sulpice** boasts a medieval castle.

If you only pause in one Célé village en route to Figeac, consider making **Espagnac–Ste. Eulalie** the one. This handsome little town on the left bank of the Célé seems untouched by the 20th century. Silent stone streets, rustic buildings, and a priory church with a handsome bell tower will make your tour a delight. We made use of the town's wonderful *gîte d'etape*, an inexpensive hostel-type lodging situated in the old priory complex, and passed a memorable evening in the cozy village.

From Espagnac, continue with D41 along the Célé's right bank, and enjoy easy pedaling past **Corn** and **Boussac**. Shun the first turn for Béduer, and watch for a signed **right turn** onto **Road D18** (also for **Béduer**). Take this road to cross the river, climb briefly to an **intersection** with **Road D19**, then swing **left** for **Figeac**. Cycle this rolling road along a green hillside above the Célé. Road D19 become **Road D662**, and you'll stay with D662 as you **recross the river** and go **right** to gain Figeac's **center**.

Figeac offers two conveniently located **campgrounds**, and the city's **tourist office** is well signed as you enter the downtown core. The office staff will be able to help with your lodging hunt, if you're looking for indoor accommodations.

Figeac's medieval streets are a delight for wandering, made more so because they seem devoid of tourists, in comparison to the glut in cities like Sarlat and Rocamadour. Pause in the quiet plaza beside the church of St. Sauveur, and watch the local retirees gather for *boule* matches in the shade, then climb to the church of Notre-Dame-du-Puy for a view of the city and its surrounding fields.

Figeac to Cahors: 82 kilometers

Your final day of cycling between Figeac and Cahors is a lengthy one, offering scattered hills and several worthwhile pauses, not the least of which is the enchanting village of St. Cirque-Lapopie. If you're camping, you'll have several opportunities to turn this into a two-day ride. Those in need of a bed will encounter fewer options. Either way, you'll want to get an early start, as the hill out of Figeac is long and hot in the midday sun.

As you leave Figeac, **recross the Célé** and retrace your route along **D662** toward **Cahors**. About 5 km out of Figeac, take a **left** for **Faycelles** and the **Vallée du Lot**, and climb away from the Célé with D662. An unrelenting **3-km ascent** will take you to the ridgetop, then stay with D662 toward **Cajarc**, and dive into a wonderful descent beneath the lofty village of Faycelles. Cruise downhill to the **Lot Valley**, where signs for **Cajarc** will lead you on.

The river valley is wide and agricultural at your first meeting, and you'll glide along a delightfully quiet, level road along the right bank of the Lot. **St. Pierre–Toirac** is ruled by a formidable Romanesque church (you'll have a short, steep climb through town to view it), and a lovely vista of the yellow-stone castle at **Larroque-Toirac** will greet you next.

Press on with the riverside route, passing golden-leaved poplars and fields filled with tobacco and corn. Continue on to **Cajarc**, a bustling little city with the best shopping you'll see before Cahors. The bulging postcard racks in town offer the first real taste of tourism you'll experience along the Lot.

In Cajarc's center, keep to the **right** and then the **left** with D662 for **Cahors**. When the road **branches** a few kilometers past town, stay to the **right** with D662 once more. Climb briefly to gain a spectacular corniche road above the river. You'll be pedaling along sheer, orange-hued cliffs as you peek down on the cultivated Lot Valley and gaze at **Calvignac** on its lofty perch across the river.

Descend to the valley floor before **Larnago**. You can cross the Lot just before Larnago with **Road D143** for **Calvignac** if you want to see the ridgetop city or visit the Cénevières Castle. This route will put you on the quiet **Road D8** along the **left bank** of the Lot. (On the solitary off-season Saturday we pedaled the Lot, we were delighted with the scenic and silent D662, so we stayed with that road along the right bank of the river.)

Savor the treasures of the Lot as you cycle onward—breathing in the sweet aroma of the tobacco drying in sheds beside the road, feasting your eyes on wooden corn cribs overflowing with their yellow harvest, and marveling at the round stone dovecotes (pigeon houses) that are a pleasant oddity, characteristic of the region. **La Toulzanie** is a unique village, its houses shoved into the overhanging cliffs. Continue with your level route to **Tour-de-Faure**, then swing **left** to **cross the river** toward **St. Cirq–Lapopie**.

There's a **campground** near the riverbank, then you'll **climb very steeply** for about 1½ km. Your first look at St. Cirq–Lapopie will make your already pounding heart beat even faster. The city owns an incredible site, clinging to its cliff above the river like a hesitant leaper. Its buildings and walls seem to be contemplating a suicidal dive into the rushing water. Finish your agonizingly steep ascent in the heart of the tiny city. This place is a gem in April or October—the rest of the summer season it's packed with visitors.

Explore St. Cirq–Lapopie's narrow streets, and climb to the crumbling walls of the castle for a wonderful view down on the settlement's tiled roofs and leaning buildings. The view of the Lot River, flowing far below the castle between verdant green shores, is a vista worthy of long study. St. Cirq's **tourist office** is in the Château de la Gardette, near the 15th-century church. Ask for information on the town and surrounding region from the helpful staff.

Leave St. Cirq with **Road D40** for **Cahors** and **Bouziès**, and savor an incredible stretch of cycling as you "tightrope walk" along a **twist-**

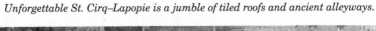

Unforgettable St. Cirq–Lapopie is a jumble of tiled roofs and ancient alleyways.

ing corniche road that hangs from the cliffs like a tangled kite string. Peer downward to the confluence of the Lot and Célé rivers, then make the speedy descent to **Bouziès** and pedal **across the Lot.** Rejoin **D662** as you veer **left** for **Cahors**. The valley widens out before **Vers**, where you'll go **left** onto the somewhat busy **Road D653.**

Veer **left** again just after, taking **Road D49** toward **Arcambal**. Cross the **Lot** and climb with this small road, enjoying solitary, scenic cycling. When you hit a **road sign** proclaiming **"Arcambal 6 km,"** swing **right** for **Mondies** onto an almost minuscule paved road. You'll feel like you're pedaling on a hiking path as you climb through trees and cliffs, trying not to think about the nearly vertical drop to the river a few feet to your right. This is an amazing stretch of cycling.

Emerge from your solitary detour at **Galessie**, and go **right** onto **Road D8** (it's unsigned). You'll hit **Road D911** soon after, and swing **right** again to pedal the final 8½ very busy kilometers into Cahors. Gentle hills and far too many cars will make the kilometers pass much too slowly. Stay on D911 beside the Lot as you enter Cahors, enjoying views of the city's tiled roofs and towers. When you reach the **Pont Louis Phillipe, cross the Lot** to gain the **boulevard Gambetta**. Cahors's large, well-stocked **tourist office** is on the left, a short distance along the boulevard.

If you want to camp, the city offers a riverside municipal **campground** on the left bank of the river, just beyond the Pont Louis Phillipe. The tourist-office staff can provide a listing of hotels and sights. The lively boulevard Gambetta is a good introduction to this bustling city, and you'll note a decidedly southern flavor to the town. Stow your bicycle and gear, and join the natives for an evening stroll. Then duck inside the pleasing St. Stephen's Cathedral, pausing to admire the 12th-century carvings on the famous north door.

If you're returning to Paris and a flight home from Cahors, there are several trains per day between the cities. Cahors also has good rail connections to other parts of France. We tagged a ride along the Tarn River (see our Tour No. 8) onto this Dordogne/Célé/Lot meander, and we endured a two-day push from Cahors to Albi that was filled with hills and lonely countryside (Road D6 toward the south will get you started, if you're interested).

TOUR NO. 8

UNTARNISHED BEAUTY
Albi to Avignon

Distance: 429 kilometers (267 miles)
Estimated time: 6 riding days
Best time to go: April through October
Terrain: Horrendous hills and spectacular scenery
Maps: Michelin No. 80
Connecting tours: Tour Nos. 7, 10, and 11

This tour is not for the weak of heart. The hills are gruesome—we admit it. But if you can get in shape, and if you can lighten your load, and if you can put up with more than a little physical pain, you're definitely in for the ride of your life. Words like spectacular and awesome can hardly begin to capture the scenery you'll see as you follow the Tarn River northeast from Albi, then join the amazing Ardèche for its incredible journey toward the Rhône. But spectacular it is, and awesome, too. Pedal it. Experience it. And come up with some superlatives of your own.

CONNECTIONS. Although Albi does have train connections to Paris, it'll take a bit of planning to get there. At the time of this writing, Albi had one direct train from Paris per day (arriving early in the morning). The majority of trains reach Albi via Toulouse. If you can't make the Paris–Albi connection, you'll probably want to take a direct train to Toulouse, then hop a one-hour commuter from there. Those cycling into Albi should consider hooking up with our Tour No. 7, Bordeaux to Cahors. A tough, two-day ride will take you from Cahors to Albi and the start of this trek. If you're interested in pedaling a two- or three-week loop, you could connect this tour with Tour No. 10 from Avignon to Carcassonne, then push north from Carcassonne to arrive at Albi and this tour's start.

INFORMATION. Unfortunately, the Michelin *Green Guide* for the *Gorges du Tarn* is not available in English at this time. However, *Languedoc* from Philips Travel Guides is a lovely introduction to the area. Your ride along the Ardèche River and the subsequent journey south toward Avignon is covered in the *Green Guide Provence*, an excellent investment for this and other tours out of Avignon.

Tour #8 - Albi to Avignon

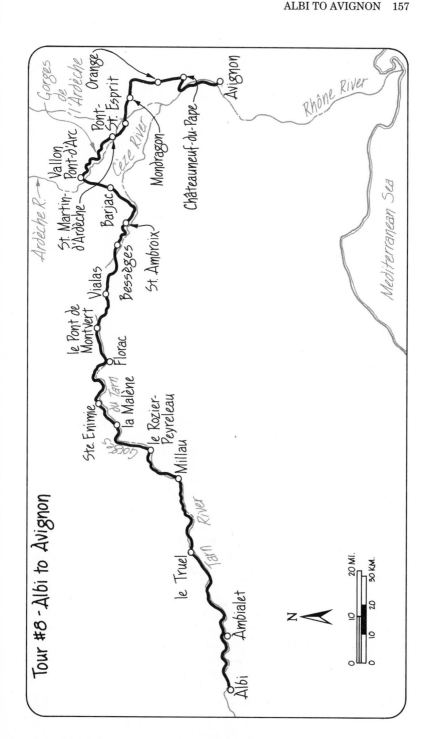

This is a somewhat lonely corner of France, and, as such, it's limited in terms of tourist amenities. With a little advance planning, you'll still find adequate facilities for your needs. You just won't be deluged with them. Campgrounds are well distributed along the rivers this tour follows. Hotels are a bit more scarce, centered in midsize cities and tourist spots. Try to carry a little extra food in your panniers each day. This will allow for a hill-fueled appetite and some long stretches without shops.

When you do find food here, we think you'll like it—and not just because you're hungry enough to eat a discarded tire tube. The fare in Languedoc is hearty and filling. Perhaps the rugged landscape has something to do with that. Everyone gets hungry, if they have to travel very far.

Try out a plateful of real *cassoulet* if you get the chance, not the supermarket variety served in a tin can. Albigensian stew is a specialty of Albi. *Tripe* is a special treat for the strong of stomach. Be sure to check out *Roquefort* cheese while you're here—you'll pedal so close to *Roquefort* caves, your nose may add some permanent wrinkles. And if you need an inexpensive wine to soothe your muscles at day's end, the wines in this region are some of the best of the *vin de table* class we've ever tasted.

Albi to le Truel: 80 kilometers

With one of the most remarkable churches in France, a lively downtown core, and a scenic river setting, Albi is a delightful French city, well worth a day or two of sightseeing. Don't be so eager to set off up the Tarn that you skip the charms of Albi.

If you arrive at Albi's small central train station, you'll have about a 2-km trek to the north to reach the cathedral and adjacent **tourist information office**. Ask for a list of hotels and/or campgrounds from the well-equipped staff (there's a **campground** 2 km east of town). Since Albi is the capital of its region (the *département du Tarn*), you'll also be able to gather information on the Tarn River at the office. Ask for a list of campsites and *gite d'etape* options in the Tarn Valley, if you're in the market for cheaper accommodations.

Albi's massive 13th-century cathedral is a complete delight—from its somber red brick exterior and fortresslike lines to its incredibly ornate interior embellished with fantastic frescoes, stone carvings, and the largest organ in France. Devote a few hours to the cathedral, then explore the surrounding streets, pausing to admire the stained-glass windows of the Église St. Salvy or to view the controversial art of the Musée Toulouse-Lautrec.

While you're in Albi, be sure to stock up on necessities for your ride along the Tarn. Several tunnels dot the route, some of them unlit. If your bicycle doesn't have a light, you'll want to purchase one at a bike shop—or at least carry a dependable flashlight, as we did. Buy your maps at one of Albi's bookstores, and gather a day's worth of groceries (if you're cooking) at one of the city's supermarkets. You won't see another large city until Avignon, at tour's end.

To begin your ride along the Tarn, leave Albi's center by **crossing the river** on the **Pont du 22 Août 1944** (the date Albi was liberated during World War II). Pause for a great view from the bridge of the Tarn, the Palais de la Berbie, and the cathedral. Once across the river, go **right** for **Cagnac–les Mines** and work your way out through the newer part of town. Abandon the Cagnac route as you swing **right** again with signs for **Lescure** and the *Église Romane*. Stay with signs for the *Église Romane* if you want to take a look at Lescure's Romanesque church.

In **Lescure**, hop onto **Road D70** for **Arthes**, and pedal on to this little town beside the Tarn River. Leave Arthes with **Road D100** for **St. Grégoire**, but keep to the **right** with **D70** toward **Sérénac** when the road branches a short distance out of town. Cycle the serene and scenic D70 along the rock-studded river, enjoying easy riding until the valley narrows and the road crashes headlong into a **steep hill**. Climb steadily, then swing **right** onto **Road C5** for **Lougouyrou** to escape the remainder of the ascent (don't worry—you'll have more than enough hills later).

Coast downhill to river level once again, and pedal a narrow, undulating road beside the water. Road C5 becomes **Road D700** as you continue in the shade of plentiful chestnut (edible variety!) and oak trees. Tall poplars add bursts of golden color to the riverbanks in autumn. Intersect with **Road D74** just before **Ambialet**, and veer **right** to enter this attractive little town overlooked by an 11th-century church. (There are a **campground** and a *gite d'etape* in Ambialet, if you're in need of lodgings.)

Cross the Tarn with D74 and swing **left** on **Road D77** for **Villeneuve-sur-Tarn**. When the road **branches**, swing **left** again, joining **Road D700** for **Courris**. **Recross the river** and pedal through a **short tunnel** (it's lit), then glide onward as your road follows the route of an old train line, climbing gently as the river falls. Ride to **Trebas** and cruise on with **Road D172** toward **Lincou**. More delightful cycling follows, as you ride in the shadow of ancient vineyards clinging to the terraced hillsides.

Keep to the **right bank** of the Tarn as you glide through Lincou. A few kilometers beyond town, **cross to the left bank**, and push on to **Brousse-le-Château**. This pretty little village boasts a ruined castle and a hotel/château beside the water. Pause on the bridge across the Tarn for the best view of the town.

You'll have two options from Brousse. We continued on the **left bank** of the Tarn with **Road D902**, then went **right** on **Road D200** for **St. Izaire**. Road D200 crosses the Tarn and runs smack into an unlit and very unnerving **440-meter tunnel**. Don't try it without a good light! (You can avoid the tunnel by climbing with Road D54 for Broquiès from Brousse-le-Château.)

Beyond the unlit tunnel, we decided not to brave a subsequent tunnel and swung **left** for **Broquiès** instead. A steady 3-km ascent leads to the hilltop town, then go **right** on **Road D25** for **St. Izaire**, only to dive right back down the hill again. Careen downhill past steeply sloped vineyards and grazing sheep, then keep to the **left** onto **Road D200** for **la Jourdanie** and **le Truel** to stay on the Tarn's **right bank**.

Endure a short, **steep** (and probably exhausting, at this point in your day) **ascent** past the dam at **la Jourdanie**, then pedal on along the backed-up Tarn to reach the small resort town of **le Truel** and its pleasant municipal **campground**. (Le Truel's campground is on the left bank of the Tarn, just beyond the city.)

Le Truel to le Rozier–Peyreleau: 64 kilometers

Prepare yourself for a challenging day of cycling as you cruise through le Truel and swing **right** to **cross the Tarn** just beyond the city. Once across the bridge, veer **left** for **Ayssènes** with **Road D200**, and head into a **long, steep climb** past another Tarn dam. Continue with **Road D510** on the **left bank** of the Tarn when the route for Ayssènes crosses the river. A second **long and tiring climb** follows. Revel in a quick descent toward **Pinet**, a picturesque town perched above the river.

Cross the river/reservoir on the dam at Pinet, and climb to a **junction** signed for **le Viala du Tarn**. Take this road (**D200**) along the river and ready your legs and lungs for the longest, most **punishing climb** of the day. An extremely steep pitch will take you right up the canyon wall, ascending on a silent road lined by oak and chestnut trees. The colors are exquisite in October—crimson, orange, and golden hues stain the nearly vertical hillsides. And streamers of gray fog cling to rocks and tree branches, as if seeking desperately to avoid a tumble into the murky Tarn, its sluggish waters languishing in the belly of the canyon.

Crest the hill at last, then continue along a winding road that hugs the hillside, easing into a gradual descent back to river level. You'll join **Road D73** toward **St. Rome-de-Tarn**, and continue on beside the river. If you want to visit St. Rome, a hilltop town with shopping, indoor accommodations, and a **campground**, you'll have to cross the Tarn and climb once more. Otherwise, stay on the **right bank**, con-

A riverside road claws its way through solid rock along the Gorges du Tarn.

tinuing with **Road D96** for **Candas**.

Savor easy riverside cycling past small farms and terraced vine-yards. Swing **right** onto **Road D41** about 1 km before **Candas**, and climb steadily to the little Tarn village. Then pedal on with the de-lightfully undemanding D41 to reach the busy city of **Millau**. Set at the confluence of the Tarn and Dourbie rivers, Millau is the liveliest town you've seen since Albi, so take advantage of your visit to gather groceries and supplies.

Angle **left** at the **first main road** you hit as you enter Millau, then follow signs for *centre ville* to find the main thoroughfare through the city core. You'll pass the **tourist office**, as well as several shops, a handful of hotels, and a couple of churches as you cycle Millau's main drag. If you stop to shop here, be sure to purchase a hunk of the *bleu* cheese this area is famous for. At the far end of the downtown core, reach a **roundabout** and a rather ugly **fountain**. Take the route for **Montpellier-le-Vieux** from here.

Cruise down to the **Tarn River** once again, and cross with **Road D991**. Veer **left** just across the river to take the route signed for **Paulhe**. Pedal past scores of **campgrounds** and cherry orchards on the tiny **Road D187**. At Paulhe, go **left** once more, joining **Road D506** toward **Aguessac**. **Cross the river** and go **right** on the busy **main road** (**Road N9**), then swing **right** again soon after onto **Road D907** toward the **Gorges du Tarn**.

Revel in effortless riding and savor spectacular vistas of the river and the rocky heights that rule it as you pedal on. You'll pass dozens of campgrounds trumpeting the popularity of this scenic portion of the Tarn, but, with any luck, you'll be pedaling in the off-season and won't have the accompanying crush of tourist traffic to remind you this is *not* an undiscovered corner of France. Pass **Rivière-sur-Tarn** ruled by the impressive **Mont Peyrelade**, a rocky bluff reminiscent of an ancient castle ruin, then cruise on past **Boyne** with your riverside road.

Beyond Boyne, look for a Romanesque gem beside the water, a tiny church with medieval origins, then cycle onward to the picturesque city of **le Rozier–Peyreleau**. This "twin town" perched above the Tarn serves as the gateway to the most famous section of the river gorge. Le Rozier is a crossroads for rock climbers and long-distance walkers, too, and, as such, it's a busy little village.

Stroll the postcard-packed main street and climb to le Rozier–Peyreleau's hilltop church, if you have the energy. Those who stay in town can choose between a riverside **campground**, a couple of hotels, and a lofty *gite d'etape* (in the hilltop ruin) for lodging possibilities. Spend the evening savoring the town, and be sure to load your camera and loosen up your trigger finger—tomorrow's ride is a scenic odyssey you'll long remember.

Le Rozier–Peyreleau to le Pont-de-Montvert: 80 kilometers

From le Rozier, continue with **D907** toward **Florac** as you stay along the **right bank** of the Tarn. Climb gently, cycling through a handful of short tunnels cut into the crowding cliffs. There's a **campground** at **les Vignes**, where D907 becomes **Road D907Bis**. The scenery picks up intensity with every passing kilometer as you pedal a narrow, winding road overhung by massive bulges of solid rock. The native trees are majestic in their autumn finery. Oaks, poplars, and vine maples don flowing boughs of crimson, gold, and orange in September and October.

Gaze upward to the ridgeline on the opposite side of the valley, and marvel at the rock formations clinging to the heights in grotesque poses. The rushing Tarn, not yet tamed by the dams in the lower reaches of the valley, is a crystal-clear slash of icy water. Cycle onward through **la Malène**, reveling in more spectacular natural scenery. **Ste. Enimie** is the largest town along this lonely section of the river, and it offers a modern **tourist office**, several surrounding **campgrounds**, a few small stores, and many reasons to linger.

A handsome 17th-century bridge gives testimony to the wild nature of the Tarn. One of its spans was swept away in a flood in 1900. Look for the flood's high-water mark on a plaque in Ste. Enimie's church, or simply gather a picnic lunch in town and eat it on the riverbank,

A beaten sign warns of rough cycling ahead as you follow the writhing course of the Tarn River.

drinking deeply of the beauty of this picturesque village.

Bid farewell to the most striking section of the Tarn as you **climb steadily** with D907Bis from Ste. Enimie, gaining a lofty route above the river valley. **Castelbouc** boasts an old château with a marvelous position on a pinnacle of river rock. Stay with signs for **Ispagnac** and **Florac** as you pedal on. The valley is much wider and less fantastic now, but scattered sights will still delight you. Watch for the ancient bridge spanning the Tarn at the turn for Quézac.

Continue with D907Bis as you pass through **Ispagnac** (shopping, hotels, and a **campground** here), then cycle on for **Florac**. You'll join **Road N106** and pick up too much company about 5 km short of Florac. Florac is a midsize city offering good shopping and indoor accommodations. Unless you need groceries or a bed, escape N106 a few kilometers short of the city by veering **left** onto **Road D998** for **le Pont-de-Montvert**. There's a very nice **campground** on D998, near the junction. If it's late or you're weary, stop here, for now the day's real work begins.

Start into a **long, steady climb**, first on the left bank of the Tarn, then on the right. Road D998 is never overly steep, but the ascent is unrelenting. If anything, the climb picks up intensity as you approach le Pont-de-Montvert. After almost **20 km of uphill pedaling**, you'll be hurting by the time you roll into **le Pont-de-Montvert**.

On the plus side, though, you'll be riding through some truly lovely country. Tree-clad hillsides will invigorate you with their stunning colors in the fall, and vistas of the shimmering Tarn will fill you with elation. When we pedaled this road on a weekday in October, we were passed by very few cars, and the quiet riding allowed us lots of time to savor the scenery. Despite the natural beauty, we were more than ready to be finished with cycling when we finally coasted into le Pont-de-Montvert, a cozy riverside village with a handful of small shops and an unassuming municipal **campground**. If you need a room, you should be able to rustle up something in town.

Le Pont-de-Montvert to Barjac: 80 kilometers

As you begin your ride today, you'll be heading into the rugged **Parc National des Cévennes**, a mountainous area popular with hikers and outdoor types. The good news is that you did most of your climbing en route to le Pont-de-Montvert. There is a little uphill left, however, and you'll find it right away as you **climb steadily** for about 4 km with D998. The ascent eases as you approach the summit at **Col de la Croix de Berthel** (1,088 meters), crest the hill, then descend toward **Vialas**.

The road is steep and twisting as you writhe downhill past a hikers' wonderland of trails and trees and mountain scenery. At the junction just **before Vialas**, swing **left** onto **Road D37** to take the best route down the hill (D998 goes down, then up again). Cycle through Vialas with D37, and **rejoin D998** after a short time. Views of the Luech River in its forested canyon will entertain you as you coast downhill.

You'll hit another **junction** about 2½ km short of **Génolhac**. Unless you want to see this city for some reason, swing **right** for **Bessèges** onto **Road D17**. When you hit **Road D906** soon after, go **right** and continue your descent with a marked increase in traffic. As you approach **Chamborigaud**, turn **left** on the **unsigned small road** just before the main road crosses the river into town.

Cycle this quiet route along the river, marveling at how delightful a tiny French road can be. Just how tiny is this road? Well, you'll cycle right under someone's front porch along the way!

Join **Road D29** toward **Peyremale** after a time, and continue gently downhill past several small villages and a host of **campgrounds**. Your rocky river canyon will lead you to the little town of **Peyremale**. Swing **right** onto **D17** toward **Bessèges** here. Enter Bessèges, a midsize city with shopping opportunities, and **cross the river** with signs for **St. Ambroix**. **Road D51** leads on through easy terrain toward St. Ambroix, but you'll have more than enough traffic to contend with as you continue.

Watch for the ruined castle above **Meyrannes**, and stay with D51 to a junction just before St. Ambroix. **Join Road D904** here to enter St. Ambroix, a pretty town with lots of shopping, several hotels, and some nearby **campgrounds**. Sliced by the Cèze River and ruled by a ruined castle, this little city makes a good stopping place if you're in need of a break.

In St. Ambroix, veer **left** on **D51** once more, following signs for **St. Jean-de-Maruéjols** and **Barjac**. Continue with your easy route along the Cèze River, passing a host of campgrounds along the way. You'll lose a hefty portion of your traffic when Road D37 exits to the right for Uzès. Stay with D51 through **St. Jean**, pedaling past vineyards and fields of lavender. Road D51 becomes **Road D979** as you cruise into Barjac, a pleasant midsize town with shopping and hotels.

Barjac to St. Martin-d'Ardèche: 50 kilometers

You'll want to get an early start today. Although you'll be cycling only 50 km, a combination of incredible scenery and excruciating hills awaits. Allow yourself as much time as possible to appreciate—and struggle through—your ride along the spectacular Gorges de l'Ardèche.

Leave Barjac with the road signed for **Vallon Pont–d'Arc** and the **Gorges de l'Ardèche**. You'll climb steadily as you draw away from town, then enjoy easier riding as you press on, first with **D979**, then with **Road D579**. Cycle through **Salavas** with its ruined castle, cross the **Ardèche River**, and hit a junction with **Road D290** just beyond. Stay with **D579** to enter **Vallon Pont–d'Arc**, a self-proclaimed tourist town with lots of shopping, several hotels, and a **tourist office**. If you're interested in a one-day float trip on the Ardèche, inquire at the tourist office or one of the many outfitters in town. Seeing this wild section of the river from water level is a once-in-a-lifetime opportunity.

To continue with your cycle tour along the Ardèche, **return to the junction** with **D290** and follow signs for the **Gorges de l'Ardèche**. You'll pass one **campground** after another as you head southeast on D290, and the traffic level will depend largely on the time of year you're visiting the area. The summer months bring hordes of kayak and canoe enthusiasts to the Ardèche, as well as hundreds of car travelers simply passing through to enjoy the scenery. However, if you're cycling in early spring or late fall, you should have relatively peaceful pedaling on D290.

A few short **tunnels** will greet you first, then you'll get your first view of the massive **Pont d'Arc**, a natural stone bridge that spans the river with incredible bulk and beauty. Kayaks and canoes are more plentiful than *baguettes* in a *boulangerie* on this section of the river, and the viewspots along the shoulder of the road may be packed with autos. Despite the crowds, the Pont d'Arc retains its majestic aura—this is an amazing creation, carved by time and water.

Continue with the road as it curves around and up to a wonderful **viewspot** for the Pont d'Arc, then cycle on past **Chames** and the gorge's final **campground**. Now the river valley will begin to exact its toll, as you head into a truly **gruesome hill**. The ascent goes on and on, and the grade is challenging. Reach a **long tunnel** (it's lit) and don't hope for the end yet. Continue upward, dripping sweat and cursing all road builders and guidebook authors. At last, you'll reach the summit and begin your clifftop, panoramic ride.

As the views unfold dramatically with each twist of the writhing road, your legs will recover, your mood will improve, and you may even forget the hill behind you. The vistas are unbelievable—vertical cliffs scream downward forever, their cries silenced by a splash into the twisting river, and the Ardèche is gray and distant, far below, its icy waters slipping through channels of solid stone.

Once you've conquered the day's first big hill, you'll have several subsequent ups and downs. There's nothing quite as punishing as the first climb, though, and you'll get lots of opportunities to rest as you pause at one vista after another. Don't miss the viewpoint of the **Maladrerie des Templiers**, where those who dare to peek into the abyss are treated to a breathtaking vista down to a lovely loop in the Ardèche, with the river singing between soaring limestone cliffs.

The final 5 km to **St. Martin–d'Ardèche** are mostly downhill, although a few brief ascents will remind your legs just how hard they've worked since leaving Barjac. St. Martin offers a handful of **campgrounds** and a view of the hilltop ruins at Aiguèze. Undoubtedly, you'll share your site with lots of weary boaters. If you need a bed, check in the small downtown core, or struggle on to **Pont–St. Esprit**, a much larger city about 10 km farther on.

St. Martin–d'Ardèche to Avignon: 75 kilometers

Swing down to the **riverside road** as you cycle through St. Martin, then go **under the Ardèche bridge** and take a **left** for the **Aven d'Orgnac**. Curve up and around onto the bridge, and **cross to the right bank** of the Ardèche. Continue straight to a **junction** with **Road D901**, and go **left** here for **Pont–St. Esprit**. Pass the signed turn for **St. Julien-de-Peyrolas**, and take the **next right** (it's unsigned) to gain **Road D343** toward **St. Paulet-de-Caisson**.

You'll descend briefly to cross a small **creek**, then grumble at a **short, steep climb** (especially if you're still recovering from

yesterday's ride) before gaining easier cycling through well-kept vineyards. Pedal quiet farmland to **St. Paulet**, where you'll swing **right**
at the first junction, then continue **straight** with **D343** toward Pont–
St. Esprit. Enjoy easy cycling to the edge of this busy Rhône city, famous for its remarkable 13th-century bridge spanning the river.

Hit a **roundabout** as you approach Pont–St. Esprit, and take
Road D23 for **Bollène**. Descend into the **city core** and run smack
into a second **roundabout**, where you'll get on **Road D994** to **cross
the Rhône** on the ancient (also long and busy) bridge. Once across
the river, take the **first right** (it's poorly signed) onto **Road D44** for
Mondragon. You'll revel in a wonderful escape from traffic as you
pedal this level road to the large **Canal de Donzère–Mondragon**.

Cross the canal, then cycle **over the freeway**. You'll encounter
the only-for-the-suicidal **Road N7** next. Cross it and continue
straight into **Mondragon**. Mondragon is a charming village, overlooked by a ruined castle and squeezed between the river valley and
the vine-clad hills. Swing to the **right** through town with **Road D26**,
then veer **left** on **Road D152** for **Rochegude**. A **long, steady climb**
ensues, but you'll be treated to pleasing views of acre after acre of
rocky Côtes-du-Rhône vineyards as you struggle up the hill.

The road levels after about 6 km, then continues to a junction with
Road D12 for **Orange**. Go **right** here, descend to **Road D11**, and go
right again. Stay with signs for Orange as you coast downhill through
the wonderful vineyards around **Uchaux**. You'll reach the valley floor
and go **right** on **Road D976**, then pedal on to **Road N7**. Now this
only-for-the-suicidal road is (unfortunately) also for you.

Grit your teeth for the short distance into Orange, and arrive at the
Roman city's amazing **Triumphal Arch**. Oh, for a better setting—the
traffic on N7 roars past this gorgeous Roman structure, spewing exhaust and noise on either side. Even so, the stoic stones continue
standing, paying timeless tribute to a civilization long since fallen.

If you're considering an overnight stop in Orange, in hopes of doing
justice to its pair of remarkable Roman monuments, there's a **campground** just off N7, near the Triumphal Arch. Continue with the
main road into the city, and hit a **T** intersection on the edge of the old
core. Go **right** here to find the main **tourist office**, or follow signs for
theater parking and cycle to the **Roman Theater**. (If you don't mind
walking, simply push your bicycle straight ahead through Orange's
pedestrian shopping core, then angle left to find the theater.)

To continue toward Avignon, swing to the **left** around the **Roman
Theater**, and cycle past the adjacent parking area, following signs for
Avignon and **Carpentras**. Pedal a short distance to a **right** turn
signed for **Châteauneuf-du-Pape**, and veer right to gain the delight-
fully scenic **Road D68** through mile after mile of famous vineyards.
This ride is lovely in all seasons—in the erupting green of spring, in

the fruity purple lushness of late summer, in the dying gold and crimson of fall, or even in the barren brown of winter.

You'll have mostly uphill pedaling to Châteauneuf, but views of the hilltop papal fortress will draw you on. However, your progress may be slowed by the countless wine châteaux tempting you off your bicycle with roadside *dégustation* (tasting) signs (especially if you're familiar with the world-famous wine produced in the fields around Châteauneuf-du-Pape). As you approach the city, watch for a **right** turn signed for the **château**. If you want a close-up look at the onetime fortress of the Avignon popes, take a right to climb steadily to the ridgetop ruin. The view from the top is magnificent on a clear day.

Otherwise, simply continue with **D68**, and keep to the **right** with signs for *centre ville*, then descend with the main road through the tidy little town of Châteauneuf. There's a **campground** nearby. Get on **Road D17** signed for **Roquemaure**, and make a short zig to the northwest, pedaling through more picture-perfect vineyards. You'll intersect with **Road D976** 6 km later. Go **left** here, **cross the Rhône**, and endure far too much traffic on the way to Roquemaure.

Swing **left** onto **Road D980** for **Avignon** just before **Roquemaure**, and cycle through this pleasant village before continuing with the cliff-shadowed D980 toward the south. Pedal your level, somewhat busy route past **Sauveterre** and on to **Villeneuve-lès-Avignon**. This lively town has charms of its own well worth pausing for; however, you may decide to push on to Avignon and backtrack later for sightseeing. Villeneuve's 14th-century fortifications are impressive and beautiful, and you'll get a nice view of the walls and towers as you cycle through on **D980** with signs for **Avignon**.

Watch carefully for a **left turn** signed for **Avignon** that will lead you up onto the **Rhône bridge** and out onto the **Ile de la Barthelasse**. You'll get a great view of Avignon from the bridge as you pedal across. If you're planning to camp or stay at the hostel-like *auberge* within the wonderfully situated **Camping Bagatelle**, swing down to the right off the bridge with signs for the Ile de la Barthelasse. Camping Bagatelle is huge and often packed, but it provides access to one of the most spectacular views of Avignon by night you'll ever hope to see.

To continue into the heart of Avignon, pedal to the **left bank** of the Rhône on the bridge. You can dive into the old core of the city right away by piercing Avignon's old walls via the **Porte de l'Oulle**. However, an excess of traffic, narrow thoroughfares, and one-way streets in the city center will probably necessitate a cautious dismount once inside.

To pedal directly to Avignon's **train station** or **tourist office**, you're better off staying outside the walls and making a **counterclockwise** loop on the peripheral road. Look for the train station opposite the **Porte de la République**, and enter the old core of the city at this gate to find Avignon's deluxe tourist office about three blocks away on the cours Jean Jaurès. You can ask for a listing of hotels from the office staff. If you visit during July, when Avignon holds its renowned theater festival, you'll have to scramble for a room. Otherwise, you should find plenty of accommodations options in this exceedingly popular city.

Once you're settled in, savor Avignon's lively old core, surrounded by 14th-century walls. Walk the café-lined streets to le Palais des Papes (the Palace of the Popes), and pay for a tour of the impressive complex that was home to a series of popes between 1309 and 1403. Savor the wonderful collection of art in the Petit Palais Museum, or climb to the park and gardens gracing le Rocher des Doms, a bluff overlooking the Rhône and the evocative 12th-century bridge known as the Pont St. Bénezét.

If you're ending your cycling tour in Avignon, rail connections to Paris are frequent and direct. Those with more time in their schedules and more kilometers in their legs should consider hooking up with either our Tour No. 10 from Avignon to Carcassonne or our Avignon-to-Avignon loop (Tour No. 11), which takes in many of the charms of Provence and the Camargue.

RIVIERA ROCK
AND CLASSICAL PROVENCE

Nice to Avignon

Distance: 337 kilometers (209 miles)
Estimated time: 6 riding days
Best time to go: April, May, June, September, or October
Terrain: Fairly easy throughout
Maps: Michelin Nos. 83 and 84
Connecting tours: Tour Nos. 10 and 11

This tour from Nice to Avignon provides a tantalizing look at both the French Riviera and the wonderful region of Provence. You'll endure brief sections of heavy traffic as you make your way west, as this area is heavily populated and often overwhelmed with tourists. However, we've attempted to route you onto quiet roads whenever possible. After all, silent roads and pastoral scenery are what cycling in France is all about!

CONNECTIONS. You can reach Nice and the start of this tour by plane or train, or you can combine this ride with some cycling in Italy (as we did) and pedal in along the Italian and French rivieras. If you wish to extend this tour, continue with our ride from Avignon to Carcassonne (Tour No. 10), or add in some of the attractions of Tour No. 11, an Avignon-to-Avignon loop.

INFORMATION. Michelin's English-language *Green Guide* books, one for the *French Riviera* and one for *Provence*, are both invaluable references for this ride. Another option is the less practical but more attractive Philips Travel Guide for *Provence*. Be sure to read *A Year in Provence* (and, if you like it, *Toujours Provence*) by Peter Mayle, and consume a literary feast about the region.

Of course, the Riviera is crowded and extremely popular, so high-priced tourist lodgings are plentiful here. Things thin out a bit when you hit Provence, but you'll still have no trouble locating campgrounds or hotels. Many Provençal towns host annual festivals—from music to saints' days to bullfights. Check a guidebook listing to find out what's going on and when (Michelin's *Provence* has a list), then make reservations or avoid arriving without them.

It's unusual not to feel compelled to mention wine when discussing just about any region in France, but perhaps we can safely skip it for

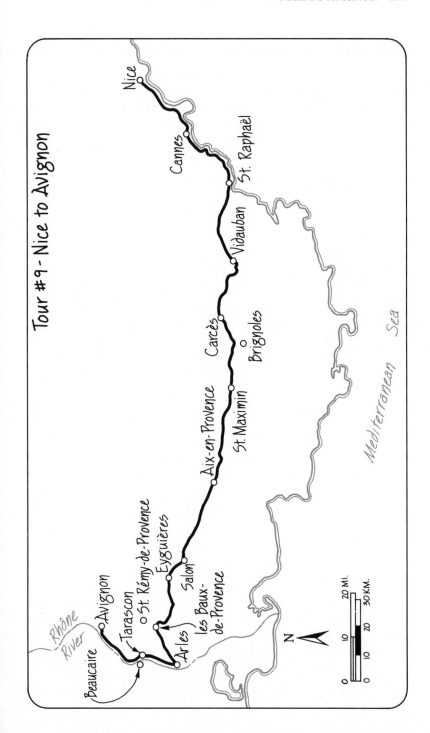

the Riviera and simply ignore it for Provence (don't worry—you won't go thirsty). You will eat well here. Provençal fare is unique to France. It's heavy on garlic and olive oil, flavored with a breath of Spain and a whiff of North Africa.

Couscous is everywhere along the Mediterranean coast, holding equal footing with *ratatouia* (a vegetable stew), but perhaps giving way to *bouillabaisse* (the ever-present Provençal fish stew). If you're feeling really brave, try *catigau* (Rhône eel in sauce). If you're not quite that adventurous, sample *saucissons* (sausages) from Arles instead. The almond-flavored *calissons* from Aix-en-Provence are a wonderful sweet treat.

Nice to St. Raphaël: 77 kilometers

Nice is a thriving Mediterranean metropolis, packed with department stores, theaters, night life, and traffic. If you arrive at the train station in the heart of the modern city, you'll find a busy **tourist office** there to assist you in your quest for accommodations. Pick up a hotel listing, campground information (if you're camping), a city map, and any material on the area you can find in English. There are several cheap hotels near the train station, but the area lacks charm. Since neither one of Nice's two **youth hostels** is centrally located, we recommend you head for the old city (*vieille ville*) to search for budget accommodations. (Please note that if you're visiting Nice during high season, you'll find hotel rooms scarce and dear. Utilize the tourist-office staff for assistance.)

Nice's old city is a fascinating enclave within the modern city, full of tangled streets, smoky cafés, and hidden churches. Get a room, stow your gear, and strike out on foot to explore. After you've exhausted the alleyways of the *vieille ville*, head for the Promenade des Anglais along the sea and join the waves of walkers there. Modern Nice has attractions of its own, with scores of shops and restaurants. If you're a museum lover, you'll probably need an extra day in Nice to sample the city's outstanding selection.

Leave Nice by cycling west along the **Promenade des Anglais**, following signs for **Cannes**. Pass the Nice airport and continue on the busy **Road N98** for about **2 km** before veering **left** for **Villeneuve-Loubet-Plage**. Follow the road along the sea to **Antibes**, a midsize Riviera city with a pleasant old core. You can add some scenic riding to your day by cycling the small road around the Cap d'Antibes and rejoining Road N98 beyond.

Otherwise, follow signs for **Cannes** onto **Road N7** as you pass through Antibes, and **abandon N7** about **8 km** later, angling **left** for **Palm Beach**. Cycle around a small promontory and enter Cannes along a lovely waterfront road. Pass a tree-filled city park where men bowl in the afternoon sun, and continue on through the city, following the seaside **Road N98** to **la Napoule-Plage**.

Climb a long hill just beyond **Théoule-sur-Mer**, then descend to ride along the **Corniche de l'Esterel**, a strikingly scenic route that winds beside the sea from Cannes to **St. Raphaël**. You'll have views of the inland peaks of the Massif de l'Esterel, as well as looks at the Mediterranean, the red cliffs, and the scattered mansions tucked among them as you ride.

There are several **campgrounds** between **Agay** and **St. Raphaël**, including some deluxe, Riviera-priced sites near the city. St. Raphaël is a pretty resort town with a harbor full of expensive boats and a tidy downtown core. Take a final look at the opulence of Riviera life in St. Raphaël. Pastoral, peaceful Provence is ahead.

St. Raphaël to St. Maximin: 90 kilometers

Ride through St. Raphaël on **Road N98**, and follow signs for **Aix**. Turn inland with N98, then cycle through **Fréjus**, an ancient Roman town with the remains of the oldest amphitheater in France. Veer **left** for **Aix** and **Road N7** just before the **train tracks**, then turn **right** at the **T** to pass under the **tracks** and N7. Go left onto **N7** for **Aix**.

Cycle along the comfortably wide shoulder of the uncomfortably busy N7 for the 24 km to **Vidauban**. Take a brief break from the traffic on the way by pedaling through **le Muy** when the main road makes a loop around the handsome town. Pass through **Vidauban** and turn right for **le Thoronet**, leaving the traffic on N7 behind. Ride a winding route on **Road D84** beside the **Argens River**, passing fields of vines and deep forests on the quiet road.

Leave the river to climb to **le Thoronet**, and cycle **through town**, continuing uphill to a **turn** toward **Carcès**. Go **right** to **regain D84**, then descend to cross the **Argens River** and join **Road D562** toward **Carcès**. Cycle the rolling 7 km into Carcès and follow signs for **Brignoles**, continuing on **D562**. Pedal **gradually uphill** for the 12 km to **le Val**. You'll fall in love with rural France as you cycle quiet roads past olive groves and vines, exchanging *bonjours* with smiling fieldworkers along the way.

Just past the center of **le Val**, turn **right** on **Road D28** for **Bras**, and climb gently beside the Ribeirotte River. **Ascend steeply** through a scraggly forest of aspen and oak. Reach the ridgetop, keep **right**, and descend into the small town of **Bras**. Follow signs for **St. Maximin** in Bras, and stay on **D28** for the final 10 km to that city. The road is level most of the way.

St. Maximin is a midsize town with a good selection of shops and a handful of inexpensive rooms. Visit the Gothic church or explore the narrow streets of the city core, and nibble on a crispy *baguette*.

A boulangerie *in southern France offers delicious fuel for a hungry tourer.*

St. Maximin to Aix-en-Provence: 38 kilometers

Follow signs for **Aix** out of St. Maximin and pedal **steeply uphill** on **N7** for about 4 km. From the crest, you'll have mostly downhill and level riding the rest of the way to Aix-en-Provence. Traffic is heavy on N7, but you'll make good time through the easy terrain. Views of the rocky white mountains to the north increase the pleasantness of the ride. (If you don't mind cycling a little extra distance in exchange for quieter roads, swing right off N7 to ride through Pourcieux, then continue to Pourrières and Puyloubier. You can pick up Road D17 into Aix from here.)

If you stay on N7, you'll follow the course of the **Arc River** into a scenic canyon, then continue into **Aix**. Look for signs for the **center** (*centre*) as you climb a gradual hill on **cours Gambetta** to enter the city. Continue straight, walking your bicycle through a bustling pedestrian area on **rue d'Italie**. Proceed to **place Forbin**, where **cours Mirabeau** angles left toward the beautiful Fontaine de la Rotonde.

Cours Mirabeau is Aix-en-Provence's lovely main boulevard. Lined with cafés and dotted with fountains, it leads to the main **tourist office** on place Général de Gaulle (on the left across from the fountain). Get a city map, literature on the city, and accommodations information at the tourist office. There's a **youth hostel** in Aix, and there are lots of hotels in the streets around cours Mirabeau. If you want to camp, you'll find an assortment of **campgrounds** 3 to 5 km from the center.

Spend your afternoon strolling beneath the plane trees, browsing in the city's many bookstores, or sitting at a streetside café and watching people watching people.

Aix-en-Provence to les Baux-de-Provence: 67 kilometers

From the Aix tourist office, take **avenue Bonaparte** to **boulevard de la République**, and continue on past a large **supermarket**, then veer **left** at the next intersection onto **Road D10**. Cycle under the **train tracks** and over the **freeway**, then go straight on **Road D17** for **Eguilles**. Climb steadily to Eguilles on the quiet secondary road. Veer **left** onto **Road N543** at Eguilles, then continue straight onto **D17** for **Salon-de-Provence** and **Pélissanne**.

Descend gently to Pélissanne, an attractive small town, and swing **left** onto **N572** toward Salon. At the far edge of Pélissanne, go right to **regain D17**. Pedal the 5 km to Salon's **center**, entering on a long boulevard lined with plane trees. Come to a **T** by the fountain and town hall. Go left to get a look at the city castle, built between the 10th and the 15th centuries.

Return past the fountain (walk—it's the wrong way on a one-way) and turn **right** by the **large church**. Continue on this street to a junction with **Road N538**. Veer **right** toward **Avignon**, then go left a **short distance** later to gain **D17** for **Eyguières**. You'll have short ups and downs for the 9 km to Eyguières, another pretty Provençal town approached by a long, tree-lined boulevard. In Eyguières, swing **left** onto **Road N569**, then go **right** onto **D17**. Intersections aren't well marked.

Pedal away from the city on D17 toward **les Baux-de-Provence**, climbing gently, then continuing on level terrain. The lush fields of vines give way to dry, rocky olive groves as you continue west toward **Arles**. Descend a short hill to the **D5 junction**, and go **right** toward **Mouriés** and **les Baux-de-Provence**. There's a **campground** at

Maussane, and it makes a good base for cycling to les Baux and St. Rémy (uphill) without your bags.

If you need a room, you can pedal the 9½ km from Maussane to **St. Rémy** on **D5**, then backtrack to visit les Baux-de-Provence on the following day. St. Rémy has several Roman remains, including a triumphal arch and a mausoleum, but you'll have a stiff climb to reach the town.

Whatever you do, don't skip a visit to les Baux. It's an amazingly situated village, perched on a stern outcropping of stone and guarded by the walls of a medieval castle. To reach ancient les Baux, turn onto **D5** for St. Rémy at **Maussane**. Ride gradually uphill for 2½ km, then turn **left** for **les Baux**. Pedal **steadily uphill** through shimmering olive groves with the stone city on the ridge luring you on. Pass through the modern tourist village to arrive at the long-dead city on the ridgetop (entry fee), then pace backward through the centuries to gain a spectacular view from the summit of the hill.

Les Baux-de-Provence to Arles: 20 kilometers

Continue **around the hill** from les Baux, following signs for **D17** and **Arles** as you descend past olive groves. Go **right** on **D17** to pedal the final 13 km into Arles. Ride through **Fontvieille** and continue on to **Montmajour Abbey** with the 12th-century Church of Notre Dame. The abbey's massive walls command a hill beside the road.

Turn **left** onto **Road N570** and follow signs for Arles's *centre* into

The Alyscamps of Arles, an evocative spot, was captured on canvas by van Gogh.

town. There are several inexpensive hotels in the charming city, and you'll have a host of sights to induce you to an afternoon of wandering. Begin at the **tourist office** on the **boulevard des Lices**. To reach the office, head for the Roman arena as you pedal into town, and continue south past the Roman theater to the pretty Jardin d'Eté. The tourist office is just beyond the garden.

If you're planning to do some heavy-duty sightseeing in Arles, invest in a *billet global*, an overall ticket for the arena, the theater, and several other attractions. It will save you a fistful of *francs* and introduce you to one of the most personable cities in Provence. Don't miss Arles Cathedral with its elaborately carved portal depicting the Last Judgement, then take a melancholy walk along the Alyscamps, a quiet lane whispering with golden-leaved trees and lined with empty Christian tombs. Vincent Van Gogh painted this spot when he lived in Arles.

Arles to Avignon: 45 kilometers

Although the ride from Arles to Avignon isn't a long one, you can expect a battle if the wind is blowing down the Rhône. Unfortunately, it usually is. From Arles's **tourist information** office, continue away from the city core with the **boulevard des Lices**, then swing **left** onto the **boulevard Emile Combes** (with the main road). Pedal on to a busy **roundabout** at the **place Lamartine** and stay with signs for **Fontvieille** and **les Baux**. Cross **under** the **train tracks**, then veer **left** at the traffic **light** approximately 100 yards farther on. You'll go **right** immediately afterward onto the **avenue de Hongrie**.

Keep to the **left** at the subsequent **Y** (it's unsigned) to gain **Road D35** toward **Tarascon**. Signs for Tarascon lead north with D35, and you'll lose most of the traffic as you draw away from Arles. Enjoy effortless cycling to **Lansac**, and continue with **D35** toward **Tarascon**. Look for the riverside château in the distance as you approach the city. You'll hit a **junction** marked by a hard-to-spot sign for **Cellulose du Rhône** (a factory) and go **left** to cross the **train tracks**. Keep **right** at the subsequent **roundabout** to cycle into Tarascon, entering the city through unappealing industrial suburbs.

Look for signs for *centre ville* as you enter town. Tarascon offers a **youth hostel** and a **campground**, if you're considering an overnight stop. In the heart of town, you'll hit the main road crossing the Rhône toward Beaucaire (you can go left here to view that city and its château, leaping the Rhône with the bike lane on the bridge). To stay on the left bank of the Rhône and continue toward Avignon, **cross** the **main road**, and go **left** along it very briefly. Then dive **right** just **before the Rhône bridge** with signs for **Vallabrègues**. Pedal past Tarascon's hulking fortified **château**, and continue out of town on a quiet road beside the river.

Keep to the **left** for **Vallabrègues** to gain **Road D183**, then stay with signs for **Avignon** to join **Road D183A** as you depart Vallabrègues. With a **campground** and a tiny bull ring, the little village might tempt you to linger, but cruise onward along the flat, orchard-dotted valley, making your way north toward Avignon. You'll run smack into **Road D402** as it leaps the Rhône toward **Aramon**. Go **left** here, **cross the river**, then dive **right** onto **Road D2** for **Avignon**.

Several kilometers of flat, busy cycling follow, then stay with signs for **Villeneuve-lès-Avignon** to cycle past the first and gain the **second** of Avignon's two auto bridges across the Rhône. (The turn onto the bridge is signed for **Avignon**.) Pedal onto the bridge, and watch for a turn for the **Ile de la Barthelasse**. If you're hoping to camp or to claim an inexpensive bed in Avignon, **Camping Bagatelle** is your best bet. Swing **right** off the bridge to loop around to the campground (there's an *auberge* inside with hostel-type lodgings).

To continue into Avignon's **center**, pedal onward with the Rhône bridge to reach the left bank and the city walls. Avignon's **tourist office** at 41, cours Jean Jaurès, is on the opposite side of town, not far from the train station. Probably the simplest way to reach the office is to stay **outside the walls** and cycle the circling road until you come abreast of the station. Then dive **left** through the city gate to get on **cours Jean Jaurès**. The efficient and helpful staff at the tourist office can supply you with a city map, a list of accommodations, and information on the sights.

Visit Avignon's Papal Palace (Palais des Papes), where the roaming and Rome-less popes settled in for 100 years. The palace is a handsome structure, and it totally overwhelms the little church beside it. Then climb to le Rocher des Doms, a wonderful park with a superb view of the Rhône and the 12th-century Pont St. Bénézet. Avignon's old core has many fine buildings, lots of tempting shop windows, and the self-satisfied look of a popular tourist town.

If you're ending your tour here, you should be able to make train connections to Paris without difficulty. Otherwise, pedal on with our Tour No. 10 or No. 11 to see more of Provence and/or the Camargue.

TOUR NO. 10

SOLITARY HÉRAULT HILLS

Avignon to Carcassonne

Distance: 335 kilometers (208 miles)
Estimated time: 6 riding days
Best time to go: April through October
Terrain: Lots of lonely hills
Maps: Michelin Nos. 80 and 83
Connecting tours: Tour Nos. 8, 9, and 11

This ride from Avignon to Carcassonne combines some wonderfully lonely cycling with impressive sights like the Pont du Gard, little-known delights like Pézénas, and much-loved gems like St. Guilhem-le-Désert and Carcassonne. Along the way, you'll be challenged by the hills, charmed by the scenery, invigorated by the villages, and soothed by the solitude.

CONNECTIONS. You'll probably be cycling this tour as a continuation of either Tour No. 8 from Albi or Tour No. 9 from Nice. As such, you'll be arriving in Avignon in the best way possible—on the seat of your bicycle! If you are just beginning your French pedaling here, however, you'll probably land in Avignon's train station, on the south side of the old city. The **tourist office** is nearby, and you should be able to get a city map (and your bearings) there.

If you have the time to do some additional cycling after completing the Avignon-to-Carcassonne ride, consider creating a loop trip by making the leap from Carcassonne to Albi and the start of Tour No. 8. Or preface your ride to Carcassonne with our Avignon-to-Avignon loop (Tour No. 11), and experience the captivating Camargue en route to Arles and les Baux, two of the gems of Provence.

INFORMATION. Please refer to our Information paragraphs in Tour Nos. 8 and 9 for recommended books and tasty tidbits pertinent to this ride.

Avignon to Uzès: 45 kilometers

Please review the Avignon paragraphs of either Tour No. 8 or Tour No. 9 for background information on the city. To begin your ride toward Carcassonne, leave Avignon's old core by cycling **west** across the **Rhône bridge** (Pont Edouard Daladier) and crossing over the **Ile de la Barthelasse**. Once across the river, go **right** for **Villeneuve-lès-**

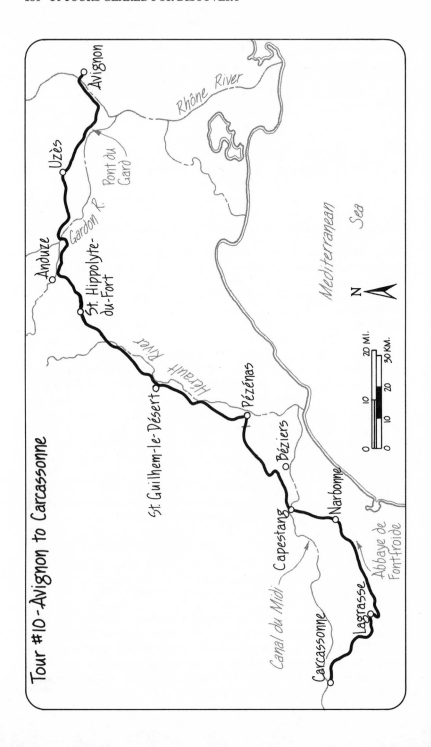

Tour #10 - Avignon to Carcassonne

Avignon and **right again** just afterward for **Aramon**. You'll swing around and **under the Rhône bridge** to find your way to the busy **Road D2** along the river's **right bank**. Pedal the flat thoroughfare away from town and south along the Rhône valley. Escape D2 happily as you swing **right** onto **Road D126** to enter **Aramon**.

Keep to the **right** as you pedal through this attractive fortified village, and hop on the road signed for **Théziers**. Lovely, pastoral cycling follows as you enter the Provence of poetry and legend. Look for shimmering olive trees, slender green cypresses, rocky vineyards, and barren ridges set against a sky of dancing blue. You'll pass the gemlike Romanesque church of **St. Amand** just before **Théziers**.

In Théziers, swing **right** for **Remoulins**, and pedal **Road D19**, then **Road D19B** as you continue with the signed *route des Vins*. You'll see as many cherry orchards as you do vineyards as you cruise on toward Remoulins. Cross under the **A9 freeway** and intersect with the disagreeable **Road N100** just before Remoulins. Go **left** here to cycle toward the city, and continue **straight** at the **roundabout** with signs for the **Pont du Gard/Rive Droite**.

Pedal Remoulins's main street past several *pâtisseries* (be sure to gather your picnic for the Pont du Gard on the way through town), then keep **left** at the far end of the city with more signs for the **Pont du Gard/Rive Droite**. You'll cross the **Gardon River** and go **right** on **Road D981** toward France's most famous aqueduct. Pass a **campground**, a **tourist office**, a parking lot, and loads of postcard racks as you near your goal. Somehow, the Pont du Gard soars above it all, triumphing through the beauty of its design, the ingenuity of its construction, and the longevity of its rule.

The massive Roman aqueduct makes a spectacular picnic spot, and you can wheel your bicycle out onto the ancient stones of the span to claim your seat. You'll find a great photo angle if you descend to the Gardon River with the path that leaves from the far end of the aqueduct. And be sure to explore the top tier of the span (if you're not afraid of heights!) to see the channel that allowed the Romans to carry water from the Eure River all the way to Nîmes.

Road D981 crosses the Gardon in the shadow of the Pont du Gard. Continue with D981 to join the **main road** from Remoulins (becomes D981) and go **left**. Traffic is fairly steady on this thoroughfare, although it's wide and straight. (You can escape the cars and lengthen your ride to Uzès by several kilometers if you take the small roads to the south of D981.) Otherwise, pedal a flat, busy 13 km to **Uzès**. As you approach the hilltop city, you'll pass the turnoff for Road D979 and Nîmes, then the ring road signed for Anduze.

Climb into the city **center**, swinging **right** to reach the **cathedral**. Uzès's cathedral boasts a unique freestanding tower. The lovely Tour Fenestrelle is just one of the architectural treats in this compact city.

Mottled plane trees line a quiet road near Uzès in southern France.

Head for the **tourist office** on the avenue de la Libération (west end of town), and ask for information on hotels or the nearby municipal **campground**.

Stash your bicycle and gear and head out on foot to explore the old core of Uzès, pausing to admire the attractive place aux Herbes and the imposing Duche d'Uzès (ducal palace). Uzès has a picturesque skyline, studded by medieval towers. If you visit the city in early August, you may get in on the annual *fête votive* (patron saint's day)—just don't get trampled by the bulls that thunder through the city streets!

Uzès to Anduze: 46 kilometers

Leave Uzès with **Road D982** signed for **Anduze**. You'll descend briefly, then cycle a plane treelined roadway toward the west. Cycle past **Arpaillargues** and push on to a **right turn** signed for **Collorgues**. Take this to gain the wonderfully quiet **Road D120**. You'll negotiate a series of **gentle hills** as you pedal past vineyards, olive groves, and fruit orchards. Collorgues is just one of the many enchanting old villages on the route.

In **Collorgues**, swing **right** on **Road D114** for **Baron**, then go **left** for **St. Dézéry** to **regain D120**. St. Dézéry is another gemlike city, tucked into the cultivated hills. Turn **left** onto **Road D720** toward **St. Chaptes**, then dive **right** onto the **unsigned road** just below the little city's **church** and **fountain**. Descend briefly and continue **straight** out of town. You'll know that you're still on course when after a short distance you pick up signs for **Road D226**.

Follow D226 to **Moussac**, and go **right** at the first road (unsigned), then **right again** (this time for **Alès**). Immediately afterward, take an **unsigned left** onto the **route de Font de Barre**. You'll be pedaling **Road D18** toward **Brignon** as you continue. As you near Brignon, swing **left** onto **Road D7** toward the city, cross the **Droude River**, then dive **right** for **Cruviers-Lascour** to gain D18 once more.

Vineyards line the quiet roadway as you stay with D18, then **Road D18A2**, and pedal through **Ners**, an enchanting little town that literally overhangs the street. Cross under a **train bridge** and angle **left**, then run smack into the wild **Road N106**. Grit your teeth and turn **left** onto N106, cross the **Gardon River**, and escape to the **right** on **Road D982** toward **St. Hippolyte-du-Fort**. If your day is like ours was, you'll notice a marked increase in traffic from here to Anduze. The cycling is scenic and effortless, however.

Pedal D982 beside the Gardon River, then push on through more lovely vineyards with the purple shoulders of the Cévennes hunched on the horizon. **Cross Road N110** and continue straight with D982 for **Anduze**. You'll pass lots of campgrounds as you near the river (now the Gardon d'Anduze) once again. When D982 veers left toward Tornac and St. Hippolyte, keep to the **right** with **Road D907** for **Anduze**.

Cruise up the increasingly narrow valley, and arrive in Anduze, a picturesque village set on an impressive spot in the river gorge. Although often overrun with tourists, Anduze retains its small-town charm. Narrow streets, an architecturally rich town square, and a beautiful natural setting all contribute to the little city's appeal. Look for Anduze's **tourist office** on the main street, opposite the old clock tower.

Anduze is surrounded by **campgrounds**, and it offers a simple *gite d'etape*, as well as a handful of hotels, for those in search of indoor accommodations. If you have some time to spare, you may want to make the city your base and spend a day visiting the nearby **Grotte de Trabuc**, a cave inhabited in the Neolithic period, or the **Musée du**

Desert, a monument to the Protestant resistors who suffered and died under the 17th-century Edict of Nantes.

Anduze to St. Guilhem-le-Désert: 67 kilometers

You'll have a couple of route options between Anduze and St. Hippolyte. If you crave solitude and don't mind some very challenging hills, take Road D133 for Monoblet from Anduze's center. Find your lowest gear, ignore your legs' complaints, and enjoy some very lonely cycling. We were hauling a ton of baggage and a toddler in a bike trailer on this trip, so we opted for an easier (but more trafficked) route. To avoid some of the hills, **backtrack** on **D907** about 4 km to the junction with **D982**. Swing **right** on D982 for **St. Hippolyte**, and keep to the **right** when the road branches just afterward.

Cycle through rolling hills as you leave the valley of the Gardon d'Anduze, and enter a dry landscape of scrub oaks and rocky vineyards. Auto traffic is a noticeable, but not unpleasant, companion on the ride. Pause for a look at **Durfort**, an enticing medieval village, then push on through gentle hills to **St. Hippolyte**. You'll find good shopping in this busy village overlooked by a crumbling fortress. Gather supplies for lunch, and keep to the **right** through the city center, staying with signs for **le Vigan** and **Montpellier**.

Run into the busy **Road D999** on the outskirts of the city, and veer **right** toward **Ganges** and **le Vigan**. Endure a frightening 4 km on the roaring main road, then dive **right** to swing around and **across D999**. Signs for **St. Bauzille-de-Putois** will alert you to this turn onto **Road D195**. Savor effortless cycling on a delightfully silent road as you pedal past scores of vineyards and campgrounds, paralleling the tiny Alzon River.

Road D195 becomes **Road D108** as you continue. Reach the pleasant village of **St. Bauzille**, and intersect with **Road D986**. Go **straight** across this main road to dive into the heart of town. (If you're interested in caves, the Grotte des Demoiselles is nearby.) Swing **left** onto St. Bauzille's **Grand Rue**, and pedal down the little town's main drag. You'll hit a **no-entry sign** not long after, but the accompanying *"Sauf bicyclettes"* means it's permissible for cyclists to go on. **Continue straight** to a **second no-entry sign**, then angle **right** to regain **D108** toward **Causse-de-la-Selle**.

Pedal across the **Hérault River** and stay with D108 toward the south, negotiating sporadic hills along the way. Keep to the **left** when D108 swings right for Brissac and its fortified château, and stay with signs for **Causse-de-la-Selle** and **St. Guilhem-le-Désert** on **Road D4**. You'll regain the Hérault's company at **St. Etienne–d'Issensac**, where a beautiful three-arched bridge spans the river and a Romanesque church squats on the opposite bank. Savor your last bit of

A weathered sign points the way along a quiet road to St. Guilhem-le-Désert.

level, riverside cycling on D4 before beginning a **5-km climb** to
Causse. The ascent is steady but not excruciating.

Another 2 km of **steeper climbing** comes after Causse, then
plunge into a **wild, serpentine descent** through rocky hills to meet
the river once again. If you're cycling in autumn, you'll be treated
to a blurred but lovely palette of muted colors as you fly downhill.
Pedal on beside the kayak-dotted Hérault to arrive at **St. Guilhem-
le-Désert**, and swing **right** to climb steeply into this dark village of
narrow streets, leaning buildings, shadowy archways, and whispering
fountains.

St. Guilhem is a wonder, that's for sure. The only trouble is, you'll
wonder how half the population of Europe knows about it. Visit in the
off-season, and you'll love the place. Show up on a weekend in July or

August, and you may hate it. Fortunately, we've only seen St. Guilhem at its best, shrouded in the grays and golds of autumn, with silent, shadowed streets and singing streams and scarved local women chatting in the church plaza. But even if you visit with the tourist crowds, you'll be able to admire this exquisite medieval village, ruled by hilltop ruins and the poetic lines of its Romanesque church.

Stop in at the well-signed **tourist office** for advice on accommodations. Rooms in the little city are probably scarce and expensive, but there are several **campgrounds** in the area (we stayed in one near St. André-de-Sangonis, a bit farther on).

St. Guilhem-le-Désert to Capestang: 82 kilometers

Leave St. Guilhem with **D4** toward the south, passing the somewhat touristy **Grotte de Clamouse** and arriving at the 11th-century **Pont du Diable**, an ancient stone bridge that spans the rocky Hérault with haunting symmetry and strength. Keep to the **right** with D4 for **St. Jean-de-Fos**, and climb away from the river once again. Vineyards and rolling hills will take you past St. Jean, **Lagamas**, and on to **St. André**. Go **right** on the **main road** through St. André, then veer **left** for **Brignac** less than 1 km later. You'll pass a year-round **campground** as you pedal **Road D130** to Brignac.

From Brignac, continue with D130 for **Canet** and **Aspiran**. You'll swing **left** on **Road D2** in Canet, then go **right** for **Aspiran** to regain **D130**. Quiet roads and carefully tended vineyards will make your pedaling pleasant as you **cross Road N9** and climb into Aspiran. Continue straight through this attractive village surrounded by vines, staying with signs for **Paulhan**. Then swing **right** onto **Road D130E** for **Adissan** when the road branches just outside of town.

Join **Road D30** before Adissan and pedal into town, then go **left** for **Roujan**. Stay with D30 through **Nizas**, climb away from town, and swing **left** onto **Road D30E5** toward **Pézénas**. Revel in a **long, gentle descent** to Pézénas. You'll hit a **main road** on the edge of the city. Turn **right** for the **center**, and pedal across the **Peyne River**. To see the heart of the old town and/or the city **tourist office**, dive **right** off the main drag past the post office and the place du 14 Juillet.

Pézénas's old streets are definitely worth a look. Lock your bicycle, grab your valuables, and take a walk. Unique doorways, cozy courtyards, and interesting old buildings will make your strolling satisfying. In addition, Pézénas appears to be delightfully undiscovered, and you'll be able to enjoy a "natural" French city as you explore. Be sure to dive into one of Pézénas's well-stocked *pâtisseries* before you hop aboard your bike again.

Leave Pézénas with **Road D13** toward **Bédarieux** (it's signed off the northwest end of the cours Jean Jaurès). This will be one of the busiest roads you encounter all day. Fortunately, you'll only have to put up with it for about 4 km. Escape to the **left** for **Alignan-du-Vent**, and pedal **Road D33** through Alignan and on toward **Abeilhan**. Beautiful vineyards and fine views toward the west and the mountains of Haut Languedoc will carry you past Abeilhan and on to the **right** with **D33** toward **Espondeilhan**.

In Espondeilhan, veer **left** onto **Road D15** for **Béziers**. You'll pedal a busy roadway lined with plane trees as you climb steadily toward the little Romanesque church called **Notre Dame des Pins**. Then descend past **Lieuran-lès-Béziers**, and push on to a **right turn** onto **Road D39** for **Corneilhan**. Intersect with **Road D909** and veer **right**, then swing **left** just after to regain **D39**. Corneilhan is yet another inviting little town along the route today. Go **left** for **Béziers** in the city, then turn **right** for **Lignan**.

Stay with signs for **Lignan** as you pedal **D39** through more of the vineyards that carpet this sun-blessed region. You'll run into **Road D19** in Lignan. Go **left** here for **Béziers**, and endure steady traffic for about 2 km. A **right turn** signed for **Narbonne** will put you on a much more pleasant thoroughfare. Cross the **Orb River** on a **harrowing bridge** (use the pedestrian route to avoid the grooved metal surface on the roadway), keep **straight** at the next junction, then swing **right** on **Road D14** to ride through **Maraussan**. A **left turn** signed for **Maureilhan** will deposit you on **D39** once more.

Pedal this silent road past grape-laden vines, then join **Road D162** to enter Maureilhan, a handsome town with remnants of ancient fortifications. Hit the roaring **Road N112** in the city, and continue **straight** across with signs for **Capestang**. A tiny **D39** leads on toward your goal. You'll come in beside the serene **Canal du Midi**, shadowed by leafy plane trees, as you approach Capestang. Swing **left** to **cross the canal** and enter this compact city ruled by the soaring bulk of its unfinished church.

Capestang offers grocery stores, a handful of hotels, and a **campground.** Its major attraction is its massive 13th- and 14th-century church, but its situation on the scenic Canal du Midi brings in scores of boating tourists in the summer months. There's a free "youth campground" on the banks of the canal, but don't expect much in the way of facilities.

Capestang to Narbonne: 18 kilometers

From Capestang's **church and center**, continue toward the **west** and descend to **Road D16**. Go **left** here for **Narbonne**. Traffic is fairly steady on D16, but it's not unpleasant, and you'll have flat and easy cycling past plenty of vineyards. On a clear day, the view toward the south extends to the Pyrenees. On a windy day, you'll be fighting

Corbières vineyards are everywhere on the mounded hills before Carcassonne.

gales howling out of the west. Road D16 becomes **Road D413**, then **Road D13** as you cross regional lines.

Enter **Cuxac-d'Aude**, a busy little city on the banks of the Aude River, and endure a steady increase in traffic from here. Grit your teeth and sprint toward Narbonne, with the mass of the city's ill-fated cathedral piercing the skyline ahead. About 1 km short of Narbonne, your road will swing left to join the main road (Road N113) into town. **Continue straight** instead, and pedal a small roadway toward the center, with the train tracks on your left.

You'll hit a **T** intersection at the **canal** that cuts through Narbonne. Veer **left** here, **cross N113**, and continue **straight** for the **center**. Head for the Cathedral of St. Just, or seek out Narbonne's **tourist office**. It's on the place Salengro, just north of the cathedral. You'll find an outstanding selection of English-language literature in the office, and you can get information on Narbonne's **campground** (1½ km from the center) or a listing of hotels and pensions from the office staff.

Narbonne's cathedral is an architectural freak, but it's a magnificent one. The church was begun on a grand scale in 1272, but it was never completed. As a result, the lofty Gothic choir has been left without a nave. Explore the lovely interior, exchange winks with the staring gargoyles in the cloister, then continue on to the Archbishop's Palace right next door. You'll be delighted by the sights this southern wine town has to offer, and you can use the tourist-office map to direct your wandering.

Narbonne to Carcassonne: 77 kilometers

The ride to the walled city of Carcassonne provides scenic pastoral surroundings and lots of quiet cycling. However, the wind coming out of the west can be a fierce enemy on the Narbonne–Carcassonne ride. If the gales are howling when you're ready to head out, consider delaying a day or hopping aboard a commuter train for the trip. We tried to fight the tempest one morning—and ended up being blown right back to Narbonne's campground!

Hop on the growling **Road N113** running south through the center of Narbonne, then swing west with this main road to pedal out of the city, following signs for **Carcassonne**. You'll have to endure this thoroughly unpleasant thoroughfare for about 4 km, hugging the shoulder and choking on truck exhaust, then grab a **left** turn onto **Road D613** for **Bizanet** and the **Abbaye de Fontfroide**. Aaah. . . .

Much more pleasant cycling follows as you pedal a quiet road past a ruined hilltop château, mournfully guarding its vineyards. Stay with **D613** when the road branches to the right for **Bizanet**. Cross under the Carcassonne-bound **freeway**, and pedal on to a left turn signed for the **Abbaye de Fontfroide**. If you have the time for a 4-km (roundtrip) detour, consider making a visit to this secluded 11th-century abbey.

Cruise on with D613 toward **St. Laurent**, negotiating gentle hills on a delightfully peaceful road. You'll be pedaling past the vineyards that produce Corbières wine as you glide through St. Laurent, then climb to a junction with **Road D3** toward **Lagrasse**. Go **right** here and ride through **Tournissan**, a small town set on a long avenue of spotty-trunked plane trees.

Climb steadily for a time, then enjoy a **swift descent** into the rocky **Alsou Gorge**. The road hugs the little river as it curves and bends toward **Lagrasse**. Be sure to pause in this delightful village, its medieval streets tucked into the vine-swathed hills of the river valley. A ruined abbey, an ancient bridge, and a picturesque market square make the little town a treat. There's a **campground** here, if you decide to linger.

From Lagrasse, continue with the twisting river gorge as it fights its way through rock-encrusted hills. You'll have a gentle climb before **Pradelles-en-Val**, then pass **Monze**, a tiny village snuggled into a blanket of vines. Rolling hills commence as you follow the roller-coaster route of D3 past **Fontiès d'Aude**, across the **freeway**, and on to **Road N113** toward **Carcassonne**.

Rejoin N113 for the final hectic kilometers into **Carcassonne** (you can escape to the right on Road D303 through Berriac for a time, if the traffic is unendurable). You'll see the turreted walls of the old town (la Cité) on a hill above the road as you approach your goal.

You can turn off N113 to climb the hill to la Cité, but if you're look-ing for a cheap room, continue on to the modern town on the banks of the Aude River and do your looking there instead. Seek help from Carcassonne's **tourist information** office at the place Gambetta. There are a few hotels within the walls of la Cité, but you'll pay plenty for the atmosphere. There is a superbly situated **youth hostel** on top, however.

If you want to camp, watch for a sign for Carcassonne's **camp-ground** just before N113 crosses the Aude to enter the modern city. The campground is an easy walk from both la Cité and 20th-century Carcassonne. Plan to spend several hours exploring the cobblestone streets of la Cité, and be sure to visit the beautiful Cathedral of St. Nazaire with its impressive collection of stained glass. A walk along the golden-hued walls of la Cité at dawn, with a view of the snow-capped peaks of the Pyrenees beckoning from Spain, will make your visit a memorable one.

If you're ending your cycling at Carcassonne, head for the train sta-tion and load your bicycle aboard a baggage train toward Paris and its airport (or points beyond). Please remember that you'll need to send your bicycle two or three days in advance to ensure it arrives on time. Those with the time and inclination for more riding could continue with the Canal du Midi toward Toulouse or swing north toward Albi and the start of Tour No. 8.

TOUR NO. 11

A LOVABLE LOOP
Avignon to Avignon

Distance: 254 kilometers (158 miles)
Estimated time: 6 riding days
Best time to go: April, May, June, September, or
October
Terrain: Windswept flatlands and friendly hills
Maps: Michelin Nos. 80 and 83
Connecting tours: Tour Nos. 8, 9, and 10

If you're looking for an easy six-day loop in an attraction-packed area, check out this tour from Avignon to the Mediterranean and back. You'll visit some of the top tourist spots in the Camargue and Provence, and the relatively effortless cycling on the route should leave you lots of time for sightseeing. One warning, though—if you attempt this tour when the *mistral* is roaring south down the valley of the Rhône River, you'll work very hard whenever you're not riding with the wind.

Plan to savor long pauses in Nîmes, Aigues-Mortes, Arles, and les Baux-de-Provence, and spend an afternoon exploring the twin towns of Beaucaire and Tarascon. With a city as full of charms as Avignon to mark the start and finish of your ride, you'll be glad you came—and went—and came again.

CONNECTIONS. Tag this tour onto the end of Tour No. 8, arriving on a hill-studded route from Albi; or add it to the little tour of Provence in our Nice-to-Avignon ride (Tour No. 9). If you cycle this route as a continuation of either of those two tours, you'll arrive in Avignon in grand French style—on the seat of your bicycle. If you are just beginning your French pedaling here, however, you'll probably land in Avignon's train station, on the south side of the old city. The **tourist office** is nearby, and you should be able to get a city map (and your bearings) there.

A third hookup option presents itself with Tour No. 10 Avignon to Carcassonne. You can use this ride through the flatlands of the Camargue as a warmup for the Hérault hills, then head west toward Carcassonne and the heartland of Languedoc with Tour No. 10.

INFORMATION. Please refer to our Information paragraphs in Tour Nos. 8 and 9 for recommended books and tasty tidbits pertinent to this ride.

Tour #11–Avignon to Avignon

Gardon River

oUzès

oAvignon

Pont du Gard

o Nîmes

Beaucaire o

o Tarascon

St. Rémy-de-Provence

les Baux-de-Provence

o Arles

Rhône River

St. Gilles o

0   5   10 MI.

0   10   20 KM

N

Aigues-Mortes

Stes. Maries-de-la-Mer

Mediterranean Sea

Avignon to Nîmes (via the Pont du Gard): 65 kilometers

Please read the Avignon paragraphs of either Tour No. 8 or No. 9 for background information on the city. To begin your ride toward Nîmes, leave Avignon's old core by cycling **west** across the **Rhône bridge** (Pont Edouard Daladier) and then crossing over the **Ile de la Barthelasse**. Once across the river, go **right** for **Villeneuve-lès-Avignon** and **right again** just afterward for **Aramon**. You'll swing around and **under the Rhône bridge** to find your way to the busy **Road D2** along the river's **right bank**. Pedal the flat thoroughfare away from town and south along the Rhône valley.

Escape D2 happily as you swing **right** onto **Road D126** to enter **Aramon**. Keep to the **right** as you pedal through this attractive fortified village, and hop on the road signed for **Théziers**. Lovely, pastoral cycling follows as you enter the Provence of poetry and legend. Look for shimmering olive trees, slender green cypresses, rocky vineyards, and barren ridges set against a sky of dancing blue. You'll pass the gemlike Romanesque church of **St. Amand** just before **Théziers**.

In Théziers, swing **right** for **Remoulins**, and pedal **Road D19**, then **Road D19B** as you continue with the signed *route des Vins*. You'll see as many cherry orchards as you do vineyards as you cruise on toward Remoulins. Cross under the **A9 freeway** and intersect with the disagreeable **Road N100** just before Remoulins. Go **left** here to cycle toward the city, and continue **straight** at the **roundabout** with signs for the **Pont du Gard/Rive Droite**.

Pedal Remoulins's main street past several *pâtisseries* (be sure to gather your picnic for the Pont du Gard on the way through town), then keep **left** at the far end of the city with more signs for the **Pont du Gard/Rive Droite**. You'll cross the **Gardon River** and go **right** on **Road D981** toward France's most famous aqueduct. Pass a **campground**, a **tourist office**, a parking lot, and loads of postcard racks as you near your goal. Somehow, the Pont du Gard soars above it all, triumphing through the beauty of its design, the ingenuity of its construction, and the longevity of its rule.

The massive Roman aqueduct makes a spectacular picnic spot, and you can wheel your bicycle out onto the ancient stones of the span to claim your seat. You'll find a great photo angle if you descend to the Gardon River with the path that leaves from the far end of the aqueduct. And be sure to explore the top tier of the span (if you're not afraid of heights!) to see the channel that allowed the Romans to carry water from the Eure River all the way to Nîmes.

Road D981 crosses the Gardon in the shadow of the Pont du Gard. Continue with D981 to join the **main road** from Remoulins (becomes D981) and go **left**. Traffic is fairly steady on this thoroughfare, although it's wide and straight. If you want to see the charming midsize city of **Uzès**, stick with it. Otherwise, dive **left** for **Collias** after about 3 km, and pedal the much more enjoyable **Road D112**. Go **left** again a few kilometers later for **Collias**, then follow **Road D3** to the little town (**campground** here).

In Collias, swing **right** onto D112 toward **Sanilhac**, and continue through vineyards, orchards, and fields of asparagus with your quiet route. Pedal toward **Pont St. Nicolas** from Sanilhac, and enjoy a gentle downhill glide to the Gardon. You'll hit **Road D979** coming from Uzès (those who made the detour to visit Uzès will join our route here), and go **left** to enter the tiny village of **Pont St. Nicolas**, named for its 13th-century bridge.

An amazed tourer stands within a vast arch of France's unforgettable
Pont du Gard.

Cross the **Gardon River** and pause to enjoy the scene, then prepare yourself for a **long ascent** as you climb away from the river with D979, snaking upward through a rocky canyon. Things level out after about 7 km, then pedal onward through a **military area** and past a French military base. Pick up views of Nîmes's high-rise buildings as you plunge down an olive-sprinkled hillside into town.

Reach the edge of Nîmes and continue the **main route** (becomes the avenue Vincent Faita). You'll hit a sign for the **center** leading onto the **boulevard Saintenac**—follow it. Endure hectic city cycling onto the **boulevard Gambetta**, then watch for a sign for the **Maison Carée**. Go left here onto the **rue Auguste** to find Nîmes's **tourist information office**. You can claim a city map and a list of accommodations here. Unfortunately, Nîmes's municipal **campground** has an inconvenient location far to the south of the city center. If you hope to do any sightseeing, hunt for a cheap hotel instead. Or claim a bed at the city's **youth hostel** (the management may allow camping for hostel cardholders).

The first-century Roman arena in Nîmes is an impressive monument to the city's prominence in the Roman world, and the city's busy streets, glittering shop windows, and brightly lighted movie theaters give testimony to its modern-day prominence. Be sure to visit the Roman arena and the cathedral, and take a walk up the hill to the Tour Magne for an impressive view of the sprawling metropolis. The extensive gardens around the tower make a great spot for a picnic.

Nîmes to Aigues-Mortes: 45 kilometers

Your early kilometers of pedaling will be far from idyllic today as you fight your way out of Nîmes and its urban sprawl. Ride carefully! From the city's Roman arena and **place de Arenes**, angle **right** onto the **rue de la République** and stay with this busy route to the **boulevard Jean Jaurès**. Go **left** here and cycle this hectic road to a **roundabout** on an even more hectic ring road. Go **right** onto the **ring road** and pedal to the next **roundabout**, where you'll go **left** with signs for **Générac**.

Continue away from Nîmes on the surprisingly busy **Road D13**, passing the city's municipal **campground** along the way. Intersect with **Road D135** and go **right** at the roundabout with signs for **Générac**. Grab a **left** shortly after to continue with **D13** toward **Générac**. Pedal through orchards and vineyards, and keep to the **right** through Générac to gain **Road D139** for **Beauvoisin** and **Vauvert**.

Traffic finally eases as you cycle to Beauvoisin and continue with signs for **Vergèze** and **Vauvert**. You'll be pedaling through an area of Provence known as the Camargue as you zigzag south toward Aigues-Mortes. The Camargue is a marshy plain created by the Rhône River, and it holds rice fields, vineyards, and a 33,000-acre reserve for migratory birds. If you're lucky, you might spot a flock of pink flamingos on your ride. As for the much-touted wild horses of the Camargue, they seem to have all signed on as "hired hooves" for the myriad "dude ranches" in the area.

Cross Road D135 and swing **right** onto **D56** for **Vergèze** shortly afterward. You'll abandon D56 as you continue **straight** with **Road D139** and ride toward **Perrier**. Look for the factory buildings of the famous bubbly water straight ahead as you veer **left** onto a **tiny road** crossing a **canal** (there's a small road sign for **St. Pastour**). Keep to the **right** at the subsequent **Y** (it's unsigned), and cycle this silent road past greenhouses and nurseries to reach an unsigned intersecting road (Road D104). Continue **straight** across and hit **Road D979** soon after.

Go **left** on D979 and pedal to the wild **Road N313**. Cross carefully and continue **straight** on the small road through the fields (don't go left into Aimargues). You'll encounter a short section of roadway with no-entry signs (for no apparent reason). Continue through with caution to hit **Road N572**.

You'll pick up signs for **Marsillargues** here as you continue **straight** on your small-road route, cycling past vineyards and fields of asparagus. Cross the **Vidourle River** and enter **Marsillargues**, then angle **left** through town to find the road signed for **Aigues-Mortes**. Pedal this route to **Road D979** and continue **straight** across into **St. Laurent–d'Aigouze**, then go **right** onto **Road D46** toward **Aigues-Mortes**.

Keep to the left through St. Laurent to stay on D46, then cycle onward past windswept rice fields and grazing white horses to reach the lonely **Tour Carbonnière**, northern outpost of the walled city of Aigues-Mortes. Pedal on with D46 to an intersection with **Road D58**, and stay with signs for **Aigues-Mortes** to reach this touristy little town surrounded by wonderfully preserved medieval walls.

Saint Louis sailed from this port on a crusade to the Holy Land in 1248. Climb to the top of the wall for a view of the city and the sea. You can walk the entire circuit if you have the time. Venture down into the streets of the city if you dare, and be prepared for the neon pink flamingos, fragrant lavender sachets, plastic Camargue horses, and a host of other "tourist attractions" offered by the shops that line the way.

Look for the city **tourist office** on the place St. Louis. You can line up your own personal "wild" horseback ride here or simply inquire about accommodations. The city has a handful of hotels and a deluxe **campground**.

Aigues-Mortes to Stes. Maries-de-la-Mer: 30 kilometers

From the center of Aigues-Mortes, **backtrack** to **D58** and go **right** with signs for **Stes. Maries-de-la-Mer**. Pedal past rice fields and vineyards with no hills to slow you down and steady traffic to urge you forward. Endure 13 km on D58, then dive **right** on **Road D58E** for **Stes. Maries-de-la-Mer** (**via** *bac du Sauvage*). The turn comes just before D58 crosses the Petit Rhône.

You'll lose much of the traffic as you cycle this tiny thoroughfare (now **Road D85**) to a **free ferry crossing** of the Petit Rhône. Depart the twice-hourly ferry and pedal to a **T** intersection, then swing **right** onto **Road D38** for **Stes. Maries-de-la-Mer**. You'll see the little city's white houses glowing beneath the hulking form of its fortified church as you approach this tourist-haunted Mediterranean resort. If you're camping, try out the **campground** before the city, as the one we stayed at on the other side was gigantic, expensive, and less than wonderful.

Stes. Maries' **tourist office** is on the main seaside road, and you should be able to get help with accommodations there. If you arrive at the end of May, when the gypsy pilgrimage to the crypt of the servant girl Sarah brings thousands of European gypsies to the city, or during the busy months of summer, when the Mediterranean beaches bring thousands of European sunbathers to the city, expect to scramble for lodgings. If you arrive in November, as we did, expect to find an attractive but rather forlorn little tourist village with empty streets and boarded-up businesses.

Whenever you arrive in Stes. Maries, don't skip a visit to the town's bristling 12th-century church, keeper of the relics of *"Sainte"* Sarah. The church also claims relics of two of the three Palestinian Marys, said to have landed here on their flight from the Holy Land following the death of Christ. Climb the church tower for a magnificent vista of the city, the Camargue, and the sea. Then descend to stroll the streets of Stes. Maries, to explore the surrounding beaches, or to take in a Camargue-style bullfight (the bull lives to tell the story) in the city's compact arena.

Stes. Maries-de-la-Mer to Arles: 44 kilometers

From Stes. Maries' **tourist office**, take the route signed for **Arles**, then stay with signs for **Arles** *par Cacharel* to gain **Road D85A** toward the north. You'll have extremely pleasant cycling (*if* you're not struggling against the *mistral*) as you pedal past flat fields filled with flamingos, herons, ducks, and horses. In case you begin to wonder, the million or so signs you'll see advertising *Promenades a cheval* are inviting you to partake in "wild" horseback rides in the Camargue. Exchange one saddle for another, if you dare.

Savor silent cycling for about 10 km, then swing **right** onto **Road D570** for **Arles**. Traffic is unrelenting on this busy thoroughfare. Fortunately, you'll have a wide shoulder to find solace in, so steer straight and pedal hard. Continue for 14 km to a junction with **Road D37**. It's decision time here. If you would like to see more of the Camargue, with its unique scenery and abundant bird life, swing right for Salin-de-Giraud and Méjanes, cycle along the Étang de Vaccarès, then follow Road D36 to Arles. To take the more direct route to Arles, veer **left** onto **D37** for **St. Gilles**.

The road is surprisingly quiet as you pedal north past acre after acre of farmland. Those with an interest in medieval stone carving should make the short detour to St. Gilles and its outstanding Romanesque church, continuing with D37 to Road N572 and pedaling the busy 3 km into the midsize city. If you're headed for Arles like a horse for the stable, however, leave D37 by going **right** onto **Road C113** for **Gimeaux**. Pedal this delightfully minuscule road past farms and grazing land, and steal peeks at bulky black bulls and skittish white horses.

We made Gimeaux without a single car having passed us. Angle **left** in **Gimeaux**, then swing **right** with signs for **Arles** to get on **Road C108**. Cycle on to a junction with **D570**, and continue **straight across** to get on **Road D36A** signed for Arles's **center**. Stay with signs for the center as you cross the **Rhône River**, continue on the **rue Anatole France**, then angle to the **right** onto the **rue Gambetta**.

The rue Gambetta leads onward to a busy tree-lined boulevard. Go **left** to follow the **boulevard des Lices** to Arles's well-signed, well-stocked, and well-staffed **tourist information office**. Ask about camping, and the staff here will provide you with an excellent city map. Please refer to the paragraphs on Arles in our Tour No. 9 for information on this charming city.

Arles to Tarascon: 42 kilometers

From Arles's **tourist information office**, cycle away from the city core with the **boulevard des Lices**, then swing **left** onto the **boulevard Emile Combes** (with the main road). Pedal on to a busy **roundabout** at the **place Lamartine** and stay with signs for **Fontvieille** and **les Baux** from there. Ride along the busy **Road N570** to another **roundabout**, and veer **right** onto **Road D17** toward the **Montmajour Abbey**, **Fontvieille**, and **les Baux**.

A steady flow of auto traffic will accompany you as you enjoy easy cycling with views ahead to the rocky Alpilles of Provence. Pedal beneath the hulking ruin of **Montmajour Abbey** squatting on its hilltop, and push on with D17 to **Fontvieille**, a pleasant midsize town. Those familiar with the writer Alphonse Daudet might swing to the right off D17 to view the **Moulin de Daudet**.

Continue with the route signed for **les Baux**, with ever-improving views of the rugged Alpilles. Pines, vines, and olive orchards line the road. About 3 km beyond Fontvieille, turn **left** for **les Baux** onto **Road D78F**. You'll catch a glimpse of the hilltop city of les Baux as you make your turn, then climb gently with the sun-baked road. The ascent steepens as you near les Baux. You'll hardly notice, though, as the majestic landscape will claim all of your attention.

Make a **very steep** final push to les Baux, swinging **right** off D78F less than 1 km from your goal. Les Baux-de-Provence is a medieval fortress ruling a rocky spur of the Alpilles. The long-dead village (*Ville Morte*) boasts a magnificent view of the surrounding area, while the little settlement that has sprung up below is filled with artists' studios, shops, and small houses. Lock your bicycle and pay the entry fee, then climb the steep avenues of this medieval ghost town, letting your imagination outrun your legs.

From les Baux, **backtrack** to the junction with **D78F**, and go **right** for **Maillane** and **St. Rémy-de-Provence**. **Climb very steeply** through a rocky wasteland of abandoned bauxite quarries. The roadside scenery is fantastic. Immense mounds of rock tower above your ribbon of asphalt, hewn into giant building blocks by bauxite hunters, then left to throw their shadows on the barren ground. Reach the crest of your climb and pause to savor an incredible view south to the shimmering Mediterranean Sea (you can take the small road to the right to ascend to an even loftier viewpoint).

Continue downhill with your road (now **Road D27**), and enjoy a twisting descent through barren rocks. The view to the north extends to Avignon. You'll hit an **unsigned junction** about 5 km from les Baux. If you would like to visit the Roman city of St. Rémy-de-Provence (mausoleum and commemorative arch), veer right to cycle the Vieux Chemin d'Arles toward the city. Otherwise, turn **left** on this small road to pedal a wonderfully quiet route past farms and orchards to **St. Etienne-du-Grès**.

Intersect with **Road D32A** in St. Etienne, and go **left** with signs for *centre ville* and **Fontvieille**. This route becomes **Road D32** and you'll keep to the **right** for **Arles** to arrive at the hectic **Road N570**. (The 12th-century Chapel of St. Gabriel, near the junction, has a wonderfully carved west doorway.) Go **left** for **Arles** on N570, then grab the **first right** onto the tiny road for **Lansac**.

Enjoy more silent cycling to Lansac, then turn **right** onto **Road D35** for **Tarascon**. Look for Tarascon's riverside château in the distance as you approach the city. You'll hit a **junction** marked by a hard-to-spot sign for **Cellulose du Rhône** (a factory) and go **left** to cross the **train tracks**. Keep **right** at the subsequent **roundabout** to cycle into Tarascon, entering the city through unappealing industrial suburbs.

Watch for signs for *centre ville* as you enter town. Tarascon offers a **youth hostel** and a **campground**, if you're looking for budget lodgings, and Beaucaire, just across the Rhône, also has a centrally located **campground**. In the heart of Tarascon, you'll hit the main road crossing the Rhône toward Beaucaire (you can go left here to view that city and its château, leaping the Rhône with the bike lane on the bridge).

To stay on the left bank of the Rhône and find Tarascon's medieval castle, **cross** the **main road**, and go **left** along it very briefly. Then dive **right** just **before the Rhône bridge** with signs for **Vallabrègues**. You'll reach Tarascon's hulking fortified **château** soon after. The nearby Church of Ste. Marthe is said to contain the body of Saint Martha, sister of Mary Magdalene. (According to the legend, Martha came to Provence via the same craft that brought the three Marys to Stes. Maries-de-la-Mer.)

Spend an afternoon exploring Tarascon and Beaucaire, twin Rhône cities with a 700-year rivalry. Tour their two castles, stroll their busy town centers, and enjoy the river atmosphere that gives these French cities their unique character.

Tarascon to Avignon: 28 kilometers

Because the ride from Tarascon to Avignon follows the same route as the latter portion of our Tour No. 9 from Nice to Avignon, please refer to the final riding day of that tour for your directions from here. Once in Avignon, you'll be able to make train connections back to Paris and a plane for home, or hook up with Tour No. 10 and pedal on to Carcassonne.

TOUR NO. 12

A WINE-DING RIVER ROUTE
Dijon to Orléans

Distance: 511 kilometers (318 miles)
Estimated time: 9 riding days
Best time to go: June through September
Terrain: Brisk hills; a mix of crowds and solitude
Maps: Michelin Nos. 64, 65, and 69
Connecting tours: Tour Nos. 5, 6, and 13

This tour from Dijon to Orléans offers a delightful blend of famous vineyards, challenging hills, and pleasant riverside riding. You'll get a close-up look at Burgundy, famous for both its wine and its cuisine, then you'll work your way south toward the Loire River. Pedaling the Loire above Orléans, you'll have an opportunity to see some of the river's less touristed attractions, and the charming cities and impressive churches along the route will make you glad you came.

CONNECTIONS. The large city of Dijon is the starting point for this tour. If you arrive by train from Paris, there's an **information desk** at the main station on the west side of town. Several trains per day connect Dijon with Paris, and the ride takes about 2½ hours. Be sure to obtain a city map before heading out into the busy city streets.

You can pedal into Dijon with our Tour No. 13, an attraction-packed loop tucked between Dijon and Paris. Hop onto the loop in Troyes or Sens, then cycle onward to Dijon. Yet another sprawling city marks the route's finish. Orléans offers fast and convenient train connections to Paris, or you may choose to pedal on with the Loire and Tour No. 5, sampling even more of the delights of this château-sprinkled river valley.

INFORMATION. The Michelin *Green Guide* for *Burgundy* and the one for *Châteaux of the Loire* are invaluable reference volumes for this tour. Prentice-Hall's *Insight Guide Burgundy* is a beautifully illustrated guide to the region, less oriented to specific sites than to a general understanding of the area's culture, cuisine, and history. Check out the Philips Travel Guide entitled *The Loire*, as well.

Campgrounds abound in the Loire Valley and, in our opinion, the campsites in this region command some of the most scenic locations in France. We'll always remember the view of Nevers by night, enjoyed from the doorway of our tent. Although the campgrounds in Burgundy aren't quite as wonderful, they are adequate and affordable, and ho-

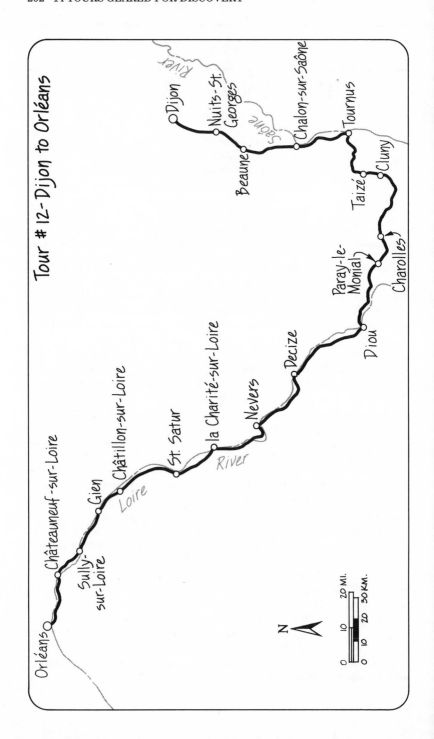

tels are plentiful in both regions. Avoid the summer months of July and August whenever possible, as both Burgundy and the Loire Valley are well known and much visited by Europeans.

You'll be in for a treat as you explore the food and drink of Burgundy. Don't burn out your taste buds on Dijon's famous *moutarde* your first day out—save your senses for the many flavors this region is famous for. If you're adventurous, try Burgundian snails. For a "slower" introduction to the sometimes exotic tastes of a new culture, sample *boeuf bourguignon* (Burgundian beef) instead. This dish, like many others here, depends on a wine-enhanced sauce for its unique flavor. One day of pedaling the hills around Dijon will show you why wine is such a major element of the Burgundian table. Vineyards are everywhere, and Burgundian wine has earned the praises of scholars and connoisseurs since Roman times. Sip the flavors of Burgundy if you choose, or simply savor the loveliness of the vineyards that characterize the land. Either way, you'll rejoice in the richness and beauty of this corner of France.

Dijon to Beaune: 40 kilometers

Famed as the capital of Burgundy, Dijon is a big and busy city with much more traffic than you'll care to see. Stow your bicycle and explore Dijon on foot or with the aid of public transport. You'll have a safer and more enjoyable visit if you do. Those beginning at Dijon's train station can obtain accommodations listings at the **information desk** there. Or seek out Dijon's **tourist office** on the place Darcy, not far from the station (walk along the avenue Maréchal Foch).

Dijon offers a huge **hostel** and a score of hotels for those in search of indoor accommodations. The city's busy **campground** on Lac Kir (Lake Kir) is often filled with visitors from a host of countries. It's a short bus ride (or a long walk) from the city center, about 1½ km beyond the train station on Road N5. Those staying at the campground should be sure to visit the Well of Moses (Puits de Moïse), hidden away in the grounds of the adjacent psychiatric hospital.

Dijon was named the capital of the duchy of Burgundy in 1015, and from that date on the city has played a major role in this region's politics and cuisine. Lively streets, historic buildings, and outstanding museums make a visit to Dijon a cultural feast. Be sure to visit the Palace of the Dukes of Burgundy with its excellent fine arts museum. Plan a sightseeing stroll through the *vieille ville*. Whatever you do, don't leave Dijon without consuming at least one *baguette* sandwich smeared with the city's namesake spicy mustard.

Your ride from Dijon to Beaune will take you through the vineyards of the Côte d'Or (Golden Hillside) on the signed *route des Grands Crus*. Traffic can be heavy along the way, depending on the time of year. Al-

The tiled roofs of Burgundy are famous throughout France.

though the Burgundian wine harvest in September is a delight to witness, you'll share your viewing with hordes of visitors—better to come to the area in the spring, when new leaves are sprouting on the vines.

Leave Dijon to the **south** with **Road D122**. The thoroughfare begins as the **rue Chenôve** and is signed for **Chenôve** and **Nuits–St. Georges**. Enjoy quiet, effortless cycling through a handful of wine villages as you parallel the busy Road N74 toward Beaune. Vineyards cover every inch of ground as you cruise through Chenôve, **Marsannay-la-Côte, Couchey**, and **Fixin**. Feast your eyes on vines and wine châteaux whose names read like a famous-label lineup on your supermarket shelf.

From **Gevrey-Chambertin**, pedal on to **Morey–St. Denis** and **Vougeot**, then **join N74** toward **Nuits–St. Georges**. Less-than-idyllic cycling follows as you fly down N74 with fleets of trucks and tourists. Escape the hubbub for a stroll through the pedestrianized center of Nuits–St. Georges, a town with one of the most famous wine names in Burgundy. Then rejoin N74 once more.

If you don't mind a bit of fussing around with small roads and junctions, you can forsake N74 for a quiet ride through the vineyards to the east. Veer **left** off N74 in **Comblanchie**, and follow the **rue d'Église** past the city **church**. Angle **right** before the **train tracks** to gain **Road D20F** toward **Corgoloin** and **Serrigny**. Silent, hill-less cycling leads on to **Chorey**, then you'll begin picking up signs for **Beaune**. Wander back to N74 to cruise into the city.

You'll pass signs for Beaune's **campground** before you reach the downtown core. The deluxe but expensive facility is just off the main road and offers convenient access to the city. One note of warning—if you're visiting Beaune between July 1 and mid-November, you may not find an open site without advance reservations. Hotels in the city are often filled and undeniably expensive. The nearest **youth hostel** is in Chalon-sur-Saône, 28 km south.

Undisputed capital of the Burgundy wine trade, Beaune is an attractive midsize city with more than its share of thirsty tourists. Stop in at the remarkable Hôtel-Dieu (hospital) for an inside look at medieval medical care. Chances are, you won't see a pamphlet or guidebook on Burgundy that doesn't picture the Hôtel-Dieu's fantastic tiled roof. Every bit as famous as the building's roof, the Hôtel-Dieu's wine cellars host an annual wine auction each November. Billed as the largest charity sale in the world, proceeds from the auction are directed toward the advancement of modern medicine.

Beaune to Tournus: 60 kilometers

Leave Beaune with **Road D18** toward the south, signed for **Bligny-lès-Beaune** and **Demigny**. You'll have relatively quiet riding on this level secondary road, passing farms and vineyards en route to Demigny. Road D18 becomes **Road D19** in Demigny, as you continue south toward **Chalon-sur-Saône**. Pedal through the pleasant Forêt de Beauregard and pick up increasing hills and traffic before you enter Chalon's industrialized suburbs.

You may want to try to time your ride through Chalon for a lunch-hour lull or a weekend, as the city is very big and very busy. Stay with the **avenue de Paris** leading south through Chalon. In the center, angle right with the flow of traffic and continue past the **tourist of-**

fice as you make your way to **Road N6** out of town. Since N6 is nothing short of awful, it's worth the extra time and effort it takes to avoid it.

Endure the terrifying roadway a short distance, then exit toward the **east** in the suburb of **Lux**. You'll need more than a little patience and all of your route-finding skills to trace the small roads that lead through **St. Loup-de-Varennes**, **Varrennes-le-Grand**, and **St. Cyr**. Trust us—it's worth it! **Rejoin N6** in **Sennecey-le-Grand**, an interesting town with a fortified château and a fine view of the hillside church of St. Martin-de-Laives. (You can stay off N6 even longer by continuing south via Jugy and Boyer, but you'll add to the hefty hill that precedes Tournus.)

Grit it out to Tournus with the main road or wander in with smaller ones. You'll see signs for the **tourist office** and the *centre* as you enter town. Tournus is a delight, especially after the tourist-packed cities of Dijon and Beaune. Pleasant pedestrian streets and the wonderful Abbey of St. Philibert will combine to make your visit memorable. Be sure to allow sufficient time for a visit to St. Philibert, the 10th-century church that was the heart of one of France's most ancient abbeys.

If you're camping, you'll find Tournus's simple municipal **campground** on the south side of the city, tucked between the Saône River and a soccer field. Ask at the tourist office for a listing of hotels, if you need a bed. On our first visit to France, Tournus introduced us to what has since become one of our favorite French treats—"pudding." This most humble offering of local *pâtisseries*, assembled from leftovers and whatnots of dubious origins, often looks like nothing more than a wedge of overdone pumpkin pie. Dribbled with chocolate frosting and wonderfully moist inside, it's tasty and cheap—try it!

Tournus to Cluny: 40 kilometers

Today you'll cycle from the site of one of France's oldest abbeys to the location of one of France's most powerful—Cluny. Along the way, you can stop at the 20th-century religious community known as Taizé. This is quite a blend for one day.

Depart Tournus with **Road D14** signed for **Taizé**, and **climb steadily** with the quiet roadway. Pause for a fine view back to Tournus and the Saône Valley, then descend into **Ozenay**, just one of many delightful villages along the route. Ozenay has a picturesque château and a Romanesque church to tempt you from your bicycle. Another steady climb leads to the turnoff for **Brancion**, an exquisite little settlement on a hilltop. A fortified château dating to the 10th century and a 12th-century church make the brief side trip to Brancion worthwhile.

Return to **D14** and savor a **long descent** through the Forêt de

Chapaize. Be sure to stop in **Chapaize**, where a wonderful medieval church boasts pillars so fat, you'll swear they've been eating pudding for centuries. Then pedal on to **Cormatin**, where you'll join the much busier **Road D981**. Continue south to reach the signed turnoff for **Taizé**. The old village of Taizé is probably only worth a look if you're also interested in the town's modern-day Christian community and wish to acquaint yourself with its religious settlement.

The community known as Taizé was begun in 1940 as a nondenominational blend of various Christian groups. Young people from all over Europe and the world gather here for study, fellowship, and prayer, and the little settlement offers inexpensive hospitality (food and tents) to those who wish to participate in communal life for a few days or weeks.

Return to **D981** and finish with a flat and easy ride to **Cluny**. The midsize town of Cluny is dwarfed by the ruins of its abbey, once the most powerful in Europe. At one time, the abbey ruled 10,000 monks, scattered across a host of countries. Vast riches led to increasing decadence, and the abbey declined steadily from the 14th century on. The French Revolution brought physical destruction to the abbey buildings, and today the abbey complex is but a shadow (albeit a majestic one) of its former self.

Modern Cluny offers several hotels, a large **hostel**, and a convenient municipal **campground**. Stow your bicycle and gear, then pay for the tour of the abbey complex. Stroll among Cluny's crumbling stones and dream of the untold power and wealth that once pulsed through this sleepy French town, surrounded by the emerald hills of the Mâconnais.

Cluny to Paray-le-Monial: 57 kilometers

Leave Cluny with **Road D980** toward **Mâcon**. Heavy traffic will make you wish for a quick escape, and you'll grab your chance as you veer **right** onto **Road D22** for **Charolles** about 4 km from Cluny's center. Rejoin the main road (now **Road N79**) very briefly, then dive **right** again to ride through **Ste. Cécile**. Angle **left** with **Road D987**, then stay on the **north side** of the main road, enjoying lovely scenery as you pedal **Road D121** past **Brandon** and **la Chapelle**.

Merge with **Road D41** after la Chapelle, and cross **under the main road** to ride through **Chandon**. Return to the **north side** of N79, and climb past trees and farms as you ascend the **Col des Vaux**. A breezy descent leads to an unwelcome reunion with the main road, and you'll endure heavy traffic for about 3 km. Seek some sanity by veering **right** onto **Road D121** signed for **la Fourche**, then take the **first left** to ride under the main road and continue with a **tiny, unsigned roadway**.

Ascend through trees, pedaling past **Vendenesse-lès-Charolles** and on to **Collanges**. You'll swing **left** onto **N79** here, and endure a roller-coaster ride toward **Charolles**. Keep to the **left** when the main road branches, and descend into Charolles's **center**. The city has a pleasant old core ruled by medieval towers (there's a **campground**, too, if you need to stop). Unfortunately, we were so disgusted with the cycling on N79, we found it difficult to appreciate the city astride it.

Leave Charolles on **Road D10** signed for **Lugny**, and watch for a charming little fortified château (on the left) as you continue. Just past Lugny's **church**, find your lowest gear and turn **right** to **climb very steeply** on **Road D270**. Veer **left** immediately after onto an **unsigned side road**, and treat yourself to a wonderful stretch of riding through farm- and forestland as you head northwest toward Paray-le-Monial. Pedal straight through **Hautefond**, then make a grudging return to **N79** and finish off the final few kilometers into **Paray-le-Monial**.

Signs for the **basilica**, the *centre*, and **camping** lead to the **right** and into the heart of town. Paray's **campground** is outstanding, set on the banks of the Bourbince River, just a short stroll from the city's beautiful basilica. A handful of hotels offer beds to tentless travelers, as well.

You'll long remember your first look at Paray-le-Monial's Basilica of the Sacred Heart, especially if you see it as we did, glowing golden in the light of a setting sun, its simple façade mirrored in the gray-green waters of the Bourbince River. The church's chevet is outstanding, a delightful expression of Romanesque exuberance, and the interior is dark and vast, sheltering a 14th-century fresco.

Paray-le-Monial to Decize: 82 kilometers

Your ride today will be flat and pleasant, *if* you're fortunate enough to escape the persistent head wind that plagued us when we pedaled this section of the route. If not, shift down a notch or two, savor the scenery at a slower pace, and try to make the best of it. Leave Paray on the road signed for **St. Léger** (**Road D248**), and enjoy quiet riding to **Neuzy**, paralleling the Boubince past farms and fields sprinkled with white cows. In Neuzy, veer **left** onto **Road D994** toward **Digoin**, and cycle a **bike path** along the main road. Ride through Digoin, a busy town overrun with mega-stores, then keep to the **right** on **Road D979** when the main route branches. You'll join company with the Loire River here, and stay with D979 along the **right bank** while most of the truck traffic takes Road N79 to the south.

Effortless cycling follows, and you'll **cross the Loire** just after **Gilly-sur-Loire** to enter **Diou**. **Join N79** very briefly to pedal toward **Dompierre-sur-Besbre**, then veer **right** onto **Road D15** for **Decize**.

What a treat! This is a wonderful French roadway, slicing through flat, pastoral surroundings. If you're not fighting the wind, you'll simply fly.

Pass the sprawling abbey complex of Sept-Fons about 4 km beyond Diou, and keep to the **right** to stay with D15 toward the north. Pedal through the towns of **Beaulon**, **Garnat-sur-Engièvre**, and **Gannay-sur-Loire**. Road D15 becomes **Road D116** near **Lamenay-sur-Loire**, and you'll have views of the Loire River on the right and a placid canal on the left as you push onward.

Stay with D116 to **Decize**, a midsize city with a medieval church that hides a 7th-century crypt. Decize is a gathering point for a handful of important waterways—the Loire River, the Nivernais Canal, and the Loire Lateral Canal. As such, it's an attractive and bustling city. Shopping, hotels, and a **campground** should provide all your needs during your visit.

Decize to Nevers: 40 kilometers

Leave Decize with **D116** toward **Avril-sur-Loire**, and pedal along the **left bank** of the river and its paralleling canal. Watch for the ruined Château de Rozemont beyond **Fleury-sur-Loire**, then stay with **Road D13** to the **right** to continue toward **Chevenon**. Climb steadily to cross a forested ridge before Chevenon, then descend past the little city ruled by its massive pink castle. Road D13 leads on for **Nevers**, and a **steep climb** will make you feel your legs before you're finished.

Glide through a scenic finale, as you cruise into Nevers on a narrow, tree-lined roadway, enjoying pleasing views of the riverside city. Hit the growling **Road N7** and veer **right** to cross the **Loire River** and gain the city center. Nevers's wonderfully situated municipal **campground** hugs the left bank of the river here. If you're camping, you're in luck. Claim a site and aim your tent doorway at a vista of the city's cathedral and ducal palace that could put a four-star hotel to shame.

Those in need of a bed can pedal on across the Loire to find Nevers's **tourist office** at the place Carnot. A handful of hotels and a low profile as a tourist town should make your lodging hunt a breeze. Settle in and set off to see Nevers's captivating cathedral, a gigantic mix of architectural contributions ranging from the 5th to the 20th centuries. Grab a *baguette* at a streetside *pâtisserie* and head for one of Nevers's host of parks to spread a picnic, then stroll the busy city's lively avenues, delighting in hidden shops and aging churches.

Nevers to la Charité-sur-Loire: 40 kilometers

Depart Nevers on the tiny **Road D504** along the **right bank** of the Loire River (it's unsigned). You'll have peaceful pedaling as you leave

Nevers's affluent suburbs behind, keeping **straight** with D504 through several junctions. Shortly beyond the confluence of the Loire and Allier rivers, swing **right** with D504 and signs for **Marzy** (the road continuing straight turns to gravel).

Climb steadily toward Marzy, and pick up a delightful view of the church's handsome belfry. Swing **left** at a junction with **Road D131** just before the city, riding on for **Fourchambault**. Descend to pedal through **Corcelles** and **Folie**, then go **left** on **Road D40** signed for **Cours-lès-Barres**. You'll **cross the Loire** and keep to the **right** for Cours-lès-Barres, then join **Road D45** toward **Marseilles-lès-Aubigny** and **la Charité-sur-Loire**.

Pedal onward beside the Loire canal, with views of factory towns and scattered châteaux. Riding is flat and easy through **Beffes** and **St. Léger**, then stay with signs for **la Charité** to cross the Loire into the city. If you're hoping to camp, la Charité's municipal **campground** is on an island in the river, set beside the city swimming pool. Pleasant surroundings and a great view of the 12th-century Church of Notre Dame make the spot a winner.

Look for la Charité's **tourist office** across from the *Hôtel de Ville* if you want help with lodgings or information on the city. La Charité's abbey was founded in the 11th century by monks from Cluny, and it grew to a position of tremendous wealth and power. The city's name is a tribute to the monks' kindness and generosity, bestowed on the medieval pilgrims and travelers who passed this way. Spend a happy afternoon admiring la Charité's impressive church from a host of angles, and climb to the grassy hilltop ramparts for a delightful vista of the city set beside the river.

La Charité-sur-Loire to Gien: 74 kilometers

Cross to the **left bank** of the Loire and get on **Road D7** toward **Herry** and **Sancerre** as you leave la Charité. Join **Road D45** soon after, ride through Herry, and continue with **Road D920** for **Sancerre**. Quiet cycling through gentle hills leads past **St. Bouize** and on to the banks of the **Loire Lateral Canal**. Stay with D920 through **Ménétréol**, and pedal on beside the water. Vineyards flow down steep hillsides to the river, and the ridgetop city of Sancerre, famous for its wines, may tempt you upward.

If you're not feeling terribly energetic, you could simply admire Sancerre's magnificent château from water level, and stay with the low route through **St. Satur**. Get on **Road D955** signed for **Cosne-sur-Loire**, and endure a 9-km stretch of main-road riding. The suffering ends as you shun the turnoff for Cosne and continue **straight** for **Léré** instead. Regain a pleasant canalside passage on **Road D751**. Léré hides a wonderful fortified church where a significantly aged

Saint Martin cuts his coat with a weatherworn sword.

Stay beside the canal to **Belleville-sur-Loire**. The nearby nuclear plant is unappealing, but the little city boasts a charming canalside park with free hot showers. **Beaulieu** shelters another ancient church, then continue with **Road D951** signed for **Gien**. Leave the canal to climb before **Châtillon-sur-Loire**, then revel in a breezy descent through the city, casting a blurred look at its lofty Gothic church along the way.

Regain water level and ride on with **D951** between the canal and the Loire. **Briare** is the site of a unique "canal bridge" across the river—a "must" stop for engineers. Cross **under the canal** and continue with D951 along the Loire's **left bank** to arrive in Gien. Although the midsize city was devastated by bombing raids during World War II, careful restoration has reclaimed its beauty, and a riverside setting adds to Gien's charms. Yet another wonderfully situated French **campground** (on the Loire's left bank, just beyond the bridge) will add to your enjoyment, if you're tenting.

Cross the river into the city center, and look for Gien's **tourist office** at the base of the city's massive château. Hotels and shopping opportunities are plentiful here, and Gien's medieval château houses an international hunting museum. For those interested in more peaceful pursuits—perhaps fine dining—Gien is famous for its porcelain manufacture, as well. The city's faience factory contains a porcelain museum.

Gien to Orléans: 78 kilometers

You'll be riding into the vast city of Orléans today, and if you don't already possess a map of the metropolis, it might be a good idea to pick one up in Gien before you leave. Pedal out of town on **D951** along the **left bank** of the Loire. If the day is hot, you'll be thankful for the French fondness for London plane trees. Leafy branches shade the busy roadway, and traffic eases after **Poilly-lez-Gien**, adding to the pleasantness of the ride.

Continue with D951 through **St. Gondon**. Just before **Lion-en-Sullias** (the town will be in view) swing **right** onto an **unsigned road** toward the river, and pick up a stretch of wonderfully secluded cycling atop the levee. Views of the river on your right and small farm complexes on the left, glimpses of herons splashing in the water, and the song of carless silence will add to your delight. The pavement gets a little knobby in spots, but any extra effort is well worthwhile.

Stay atop the levee road, shunning the side roads that dive off, and watch for the turrets of Sully-sur-Loire's enchanting château in the distance. There's a nice **campground** on the river, adjacent to the château. Even if you don't plan to go inside the château, at least duck into the park surrounding this lovely building. Green lawns, glowing

The sprawling city of Orléans is dominated by its majestic cathedral.

stone, and a dark moat—it's a postcard-perfect scene.

From Sully-sur-Loire, **cross the river** to enter **St. Père-sur-Loire**, then veer **left** onto **Road D60** for **St. Benoît-sur-Loire**. Enjoy easy cycling to St. Benoît, where a wonderful old basilica harbors carved capitals and a unique belfry porch. A Benedictine abbey was established here in the 7th century, and Charlemagne contributed to the abbey's immense prestige. The existing structure dates from 1067 and is renowned as one of the finest Romanesque churches in France.

Continue with **D60** to **Germigny-des-Prés**, where a small church (one of the oldest in France) will thrill you with an ancient mosaic. Hidden for centuries, the mosaic was discovered by chance in the mid-1800s. Today, thousands come to admire it in the summer season. Road D60 leads on to **Châteauneuf-sur-Loire**, set on a low bluff above the river. A hilltop park/museum complex at the far end of the city center will probably lure you into a picnic. The rhododendrons here are fabulous in spring.

Return to the junction with **Road D11** for **Sigloy**, and descend to **cross the river**. Take the **first right** to get on a small road with an even smaller sign for **les Vallées**, and keep **right** to gain more lovely levee riding. Pedal through **la Bourdonnière** and **la Fontaine**, then enter **Jargeau** (a swiftly growing suburb of Orléans). Go **right** in Jargeau for the **Pont sur la Loire** (the Loire bridge), and stay with the signed bridge route through town. Continue **straight across the bridge road** (don't cross the Loire), and continue cycling the **left bank** with the paved levee route.

Pass unappealing gravel pits and secluded farms as you work your way toward Orléans. You'll gain glimpses of the soaring towers of Orléans's cathedral as you press onward. Pass a large swimming complex (to the right on the river), and stay to the **right** when the road branches. Cross under a **train bridge**, then ride under a busy **auto bridge**. Ascend to the **Pont Royale** and swing **right** to cross the **Loire River** into the heart of Orléans. You'll have an incredible vista of the cathedral, the city, and the river as you pedal across the bridge.

Continue straight ahead (north) through the teeming city, cycling cautiously to reach Orléans's well-signed central train station (*gare*) and the main **tourist office**. Hotels abound in this vast city, and a pleasant **hostel** and a somewhat inconvenient municipal **campground** (to the south in Olivet) round out accommodations options.

Invest an afternoon in Orléans's magnificent cathedral—it's lovely both inside and out. A vision of the floodlit building beneath a velvet evening sky is nothing short of heavenly. While in Orléans, you'll see a host of reminders of the city's loving relationship with its most famous daughter, Joan of Arc. Visit the Centre Jeanne d'Arc to gain a better understanding of this French heroine.

If you're cycling onward from Orléans, consider hooking up with our Tour No. 5. You can pick it up in Meung-sur-Loire, just downriver. Pedal on to Angers, then loop back toward Paris; or swing south toward Bordeaux with Tour No. 6. Those who simply must finish their ride in Orléans will find excellent train connections to Paris (and other points in France) from the city's central station. Pack up bike and baggage, then set out on foot for a final stroll among Orléans's host of delightful bakeries, cafés, and assorted goody shops, savoring just one last taste.

SPLASHING THROUGH BURGUNDY
Dijon to Dijon

Distance: 584 kilometers (363 miles)
Estimated time: 9 riding days
Best time to go: June through September
Terrain: Challenging hills and pastoral scenery
Maps: Michelin Nos. 61 and 65
Connecting tours: Tour Nos. 4, 12, and 14

This loop ride from Dijon to Dijon explores the lovely slice of Burgundy just southeast of Paris. You'll fight some tough hills along the route, but wonderful scenery and silent roadways will recompense you richly for your labors. Ancient walled cities, charming city cores, and exquisite churches all await you as you ride. You can fuel your muscles with the wonderful cuisine of Burgundy and probably never even gain an ounce!

CONNECTIONS. The large city of Dijon is the starting point for this tour. If you arrive by train from Paris, there's an **information desk** at the main station on the west side of town. Several trains per day connect Dijon with Paris, and the ride takes about 2½ hours. Be sure to obtain a city map before heading out into the busy city streets.

You can also pedal into Dijon via a hookup with our Tour No. 4 from Brussels to Versailles, hopping on in Troyes or Sens, then continuing past Dijon to close the loop again. Possibilities for other routes out of Dijon include Tour No. 12 to Orléans and Tour No. 14 to Strasbourg. Both of these cities offer excellent train connections to Paris.

INFORMATION. The Michelin *Green Guide* for *Burgundy* and the one for *Île-de-France* are relevant to this tour. Prentice-Hall's *Insight Guide Burgundy* is a beautifully illustrated guide to the region, less oriented to specific sites than to a general understanding of the area's culture, cuisine, and history. Please refer to our Burgundy paragraphs in the preceding tour (Tour No. 12) for more information on the region.

Dijon to Pouilly-en-Auxois: 56 kilometers

Please read the first few paragraphs of the Dijon-to-Beaune section of Tour No. 12 for information on sights and accommodations in Dijon.

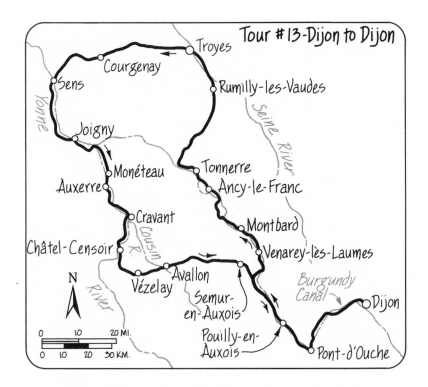

Tour #13-Dijon to Dijon

Troyes

Courgenay

Sens

Rumilly-les-Vaudes

Yonne

Joigny

Seine River

Monéteau

Tonnerre

Auxerre

Ancy-le-Franc

Cravant

Cousin R.

Montbard

Châtel-Censoir

Venarey-lès-Laumes

N

Avallon

Vézelay

Burgundy Canal

Dijon

River

Semur-en-Auxois

Pouilly-en-Auxois

Pont-d'Ouche

0   10   20 MI.

0   10   20   30 KM.

You'll be following the course of the 242-km-long Burgundy Canal as you trace a meandering route to Pouilly-en-Auxois. The riding is scenic and serene, once you free yourself from Dijon's big-city embrace. Leave Dijon with the busy road toward **Plombières**. Traffic is hectic for a time, but things ease as you pass **Lake Kir**, Dijon's **campground**, and the junction with the **A38 freeway**.

Cycle through the center of Plombières and continue with **Road D10** for **Velars-sur-Ouche**. Turn back for a farewell look at the vast city of Dijon, bidding good riddance to its traffic. Pedal through Velars, then cross the **Ouche River** and the **Burgundy Canal**. Go **right** to cycle between the **A38 freeway** and the river with **Road D905** toward **Pont-de-Pany**. Follow this small road beside the freeway for 9 km of noisy, rotten riding. Things improve from here.

Recross the **Burgundy Canal** and get on **Road D33** toward **Pont-d'Ouche**, swinging south beside the river and its companion waterway. Savor the scenic Ouche Valley as you ride, sneaking a breather here and there as you pause to watch busy lockkeepers shepherding the scores of tourist boats toward Dijon. Arrive at the **Pont-d'Ouche**, where an amazing feat of engineering allows the Burgundy Canal to cross the Ouche River on a man-made bridge. Then leave D33 to swing north with the canal and the road toward **Crugey.**

Road D18 leads on across the **A6 freeway**, with increasingly wonderful views of the hilltop town of **Châteauneuf.** You may be tempted to visit this picturesque fortified village, but be forewarned that a detour to Châteauneuf will cost you a monster climb of 2 to 3 km. However you choose to experience the little city, it is a joy to behold in any season, framed by green fields dotted with grazing cows, and hovering above the placid waters of the Burgundy Canal.

Push on to **Vandenesse-en-Auxois**, veer **right** to cross the canal, then go **left** to regain the company of **D18**. Ride through **Créancey** and angle **left** for **Pouilly-en-Auxois**. Work your way through a knotlike tangle of roads and freeway, and let signs for **Pouilly** lead you on with **Road D970**. Pouilly-en-Auxois offers a handful of hotels, ample shopping, and a pleasant municipal **campground** (well signed from the main road). The Burgundy Canal dives into a long tunnel here, as it crosses from the Rhône watershed to that of the Seine. You can view the tunnel entrance, just to the west off D970.

Pouilly-en-Auxois to Montbard: 60 kilometers

Leave Pouilly with **D970** toward **St. Thibault.** You'll have about 5 km of gently rolling riding, then things flatten out and St. Thibault's unique village church comes into view. Pause for a peek at the exquisite main doorway, then duck inside to admire the church's five-sided choir. St. Thibault is an unanticipated treat. Continue north with D970, and veer **left** onto **Road D70** 4 km later. Endure a brief but all-too-busy ride on D70 before diving **right** toward **Semur-en-Auxois** (on D970 once more).

Pedal on to **Villeneuve**, then veer **right** onto **Road D10** toward **Marigny-le-Cahouët** to stay beside the meandering canal. Keep with D10 to **Pouillenay**, and turn **left** onto **Road D9** here. Cross the **Burgundy Canal** and dive **right** onto **Road D119** for **Venarey-lès-Laumes.** Pedal on past **les Granges** (still on D119) and stay within shouting distance of the canal all the way to **Montbard.**

Montbard is a busy but surprisingly pleasant city, strategically situated for a visit to the Cistercian **Abbey of Fontenay** (11 km roundtrip). You'll find a well-equipped and well-signed **campground** in Montbard, as well as a sprinkling of hotels. The old city core is nice for strolling—unspoiled by tourist crowds, it offers an unassuming picture of day-to-day life in France. Join the locals in their early-morning quest for the perfect *baguette*, then slather thick slices with Nutella (a decadent chocolate-hazelnut spread). Sip a cup of steamy *café au lait*, and consider applying for French citizenship.

Tanlay's château invites a leisurely look.

Montbard to Tonnerre: 52 kilometers

You'll enjoy scenic cycling along the valley of the Armançon River as you begin today, leaving Montbard with **Road D905** toward **Ancy-le-Franc**. It's likely you'll have steady traffic to contend with on this main road, although it was quite pleasant on the May day we followed it. Ride through **St. Rémy** and on to **Rougemont**, savoring views of the river and the houseboat-sprinkled canal. Long-poled fishermen complete the scene, strung out along the shoreline in companionable silence.

Stay with D905 to **Nuits**, then swing **right** onto **Road D953** for **Ravières**. Cross the river and canal, and veer **left** in Ravières onto the road for **Ancy-le-Franc**. Follow a rolling route through windblown fields to arrive in Ancy, where a handsome Renaissance château rules the heart of the city. Take the tour of the château's interior, if you wish. There's a **campground** nearby.

A **stiff climb** leads out of Ancy with **Road D12** toward **Pimelles**. Veer **left** shortly afterward, and ascend through patchwork fields of brilliant yellow rape. Reach the crest of your climb and revel in an exhilarating downhill glide to **Ancy-le-Libre**, then cruise on through **Argentenay** and **St. Vinnemer** en route to **Tanlay**. Tanlay's château is a beauty, adorned with glowing turrets and water-lapped bridges, and surrounded by a murky moat where vigilant swans perform their gliding guard duty. Pause for a long look and/or a tour.

Leave Tanlay with the small road signed for **Commissey**, and take **Road D56** to its junction with **Road D952**. Go **left** here to cycle into **Tonnerre**, a hopping little tourist town with plenty of attractions. If you see nothing else in Tonnerre, see the Fosse Dionne, a lovely old wash basin hidden within the city. It's easy to imagine the townswomen gathering here each morning, sharing conversations as they beat their husbands' shirts against the smooth gray washing stones.

Tonnerre's hillside Church of St. Peter and the former hospital (*Ancien Hôpital*) are also well worth a visit. Settle in at Tonnerre's excellent little **campground** beside the Burgundy Canal, or claim a hotel room in the city proper, then enjoy the town at leisure.

Tonnerre to Troyes: 70 kilometers

You'll struggle through some exhausting hills this morning, but don't despair—the terrain mellows as the day wears on (or as you wear out!). Leave Tonnerre with **Road D944** toward **Coussegrey**, and endure a **long climb** to start your day. Swing **right** for **Chesley** onto the quiet **Road D3**, with plenty more hills in store. Grueling ups and downs lead past Chesley and a score of family farms, then push on to **Maisons-lès-Chaource** and **Pargues**. Leave Pargues with **Road D28** toward **Praslin**, **Lantages**, and **Rumilly-lès-Vaudes**.

Enjoy easier cycling from here, as you follow the valley of the Hozain River all the way to **Rumilly**. Rumilly's château is small and studded with towers (you'll get the best photo angle as you draw away from town). Stop in at the little city's 16th-century church. Wonderful portal carvings illustrate the story of Saint Martin, grinning gargoyles guard the eaves, and a light interior and carved rood screen await.

Continue with **D28** to **St. Parres-lès-Vaudes**, and swing **left** for a mercifully short stretch of cycling on **Road N71**. Dive **right** just after to cross the **Seine River** into **Villemoyenne**, and keep **left** through Villemoyenne/**Courbeton** to gain **Road D49** along the Seine. Pedal through **Clérey** and **Verrières** (a neat little village with fine carvings on its church), then push on with D49 past **St. Julien-lès-Villas** and into the heart of **Troyes**.

Follow signs for the **center** and arrive at the Cathédrale St. Pierre et St. Paul. Enter the church's cool interior and watch the lines of stone pillars unfold before you, dappled with colored sunlight and stained by windows of brilliant glass. Check in at the **tourist office** near the train station for accommodations listings and information on the city. The **youth hostel** is 5 km south of the city core in Rosières, and Troyes's municipal **campground** is on the north end of town, beside the Seine. (It's crowded and mediocre, but it provides excellent access to the city.) There are plenty of inexpensive hotels to choose from, too.

Troyes is a wonderful city for strolling. Visit the old town to walk along the rue des Chats—lined by half-timbered houses—explore the city's wealth of churches, or simply pull up a chair in a cozy *crêperie* and fill your hungry cyclist's stomach with a taste of France.

Troyes to Sens: 70 kilometers

This day of riding traces the same route followed in our Tour No. 4 from Brussels to Versailles, offering a potential hookup with that cycle trip. Please refer to the Troyes-to-Sens section of Tour No. 4 for the route description for this section.

Sens to Auxerre: 72 kilometers

If you have the time and patience to meander with our route toward Auxerre, you can avoid the main road into the city and gain much more pleasant cycling in the process. You'll need to keep a close eye on your map and refer to this text frequently, however, as dozens of turns and junctions lie ahead. Leave Sens from the **west bank of the Yonne River**, following the busy road (**Road N60**) signed for **Paron**. The cycling is gruesome through Paron and you'll angle **left** onto **Road D72** through **Gron**.

Grunt through Gron, then savor a marked decrease in traffic as you pedal on with D72 toward **Villeneuve-sur-Yonne**. Be sure to swing **left** across the Yonne for a peek at Villeneuve, a pretty town ruled by a formidable church. Ancient gateways guard both ends of the city, and there's a nice **campground** beside the river here. Recross the Yonne and continue south (now with **Road D3**) to **St. Julien-du-Sault**. Although not quite as wonderful as Villeneuve, St. Julien has an attractive center, too. Make the detour if you have the time.

Continue with **D3** toward **Joigny** (becomes **Road D182** as you proceed), and enjoy easy cycling to your intersection with **Road D943**. A vast construction project was underway when we pedaled through here in 1991, so road changes may confuse things just a bit. Continue **straight** across the main road and ride toward **Chamvres** on **D182**. Cycle through a shade-rich glen between Chamvres and **Paroy-sur-Tholon**, and go **straight** across **Road D955** to continue with a silent (unsigned) road into the fields.

Rejoin **D182** before **Champlay**, and swing **left** in town at a small sign for **Vers RN6**. Take the subsequent **right turn** to pedal through lovely countryside en route to **Epineau-lès-Voves**. You'll cross the dreaded **Road N6** here, and cycle a small road toward **Migennes**. Stay with signs for Migennes until you cross the **Yonne River**, then veer **right** and go **left** immediately afterward for **Cheny**. You'll be struggling through an unpleasant industrial suburb of Migennes through here. Avoid the city center at all costs, taking **Road D91** through **Cheny**.

As you depart Cheny, angle **right** off D91 with signs for **Beaumont**, and gain more pastoral cycling on **Road D380**. Pedal to **Chemilly-sur-Yonne** and yet another junction. Go **right** and then veer **left** immediately after to descend with **Road D80** away from town. Continue straight, with **train tracks** on your right, riding through quiet fields and farms. You'll hit **Road D84** before **Monéteau**. Turn **right** to cycle into the city, then go **right** again to **cross the Yonne** once more.

Just across the river, dive **left** and follow a quiet riverside road all the way into **Auxerre**. You'll love your first view of Auxerre, gained as you gaze upward from the banks of the Yonne River. The city's joyous Gothic churches fly their buttresses from the crest of the steep hillside, luring you upward with their sheer exuberance. Signs for the **center** and the **cathedral** will lead you on. (Be sure to stop in at Auxerre's riverside **tourist office** before you make the climb.)

Auxerre is a delightful city, filled with half-timbered buildings and sprinkled with attractive squares. Get a hotel room or set up a tent at the **campground** just south of town. There's a **youth hostel** in Auxerre as well. Spend an enjoyable afternoon simply wandering the city, exploring the pedestrian streets around the Tour de l'Horloge (a 15th-century clock tower) and ducking into the Cathedral of St. Stephen and the Abbey Church of Saint Germain.

Auxerre to Vézelay: 58 kilometers

Leave Auxerre with **Road D163** signed for **Vaux** (**campground signs** lead this way, too). Pedal through parklike suburbs on your way out of the city, passing soccer fields, a velodrome, and the city campground. Beyond Vaux, wonderful cycling commences, as you swing **left** to cross the **Yonne River**, then veer **right** for **Champs-sur-Yonne**. Do a slow dance with the river as you wind toward the south, waltzing along on tiny, traffic-free roadways in the shade of leafy trees.

Stay with **Road D362** past **Champs** and on to **Bailly**, a pretty village with signs for wine tasting (*dégustation*). You'll **climb** away from the river for a brief time after **Vincelottes**, cruising onward to **Cravant**. Old fortifications and a neat clock tower make Cravant worth a pause. Join **Road N6** here to **cross the Yonne**. Just across the river, escape to the **left** and cycle **Road D139** toward **Bazarnes**.

The hilltop basilica at Vézelay is visible for many kilometers.

A stout church overlooks the river here, and old men in black berets toss *boule* balls in the plaza.

Pedal on with **Road D100** to **Trucy-sur-Yonne** and **Mailly-la-Ville**. Stay on the **west bank** of the Yonne, but keep to the **left** when the road branches (Road D950 climbs to upper Mailly) and stay with the **low route** (**Road D39**) beside the river instead. Cycle the silent D39 to the ancient bridge below **Mailly-le-Château**, a picturesque village named for the sleek château that clings to the ridgetop here. **Cross the Yonne** on the bridge, then cross the **Nivernais Canal**.

Cycle **Road D130** toward **Chatel-Censoir**, and arrive at an intersection with **Road D100**. Go **right** here and continue south beside the Yonne. Lovely, peaceful pedaling leads beneath the **Rochers du Saussois**, a popular haunt for rock climbers, then cruise on to **Chatel-Censoir**. This busy little tourist town is a launching spot for visitors to the area, and a well-signed route leads on for **Vézelay** from here.

Follow **D100** on through open fields to **Asnières**, then get on **Road D36** signed for **Vézelay**. The gentle uphill grade turns brutal after Asnières, and you'll **climb steadily** from here. Try to forget your muscles' agony and concentrate on the views instead, as the road ascends the rolling green hills of the Parc Naturel de Morvan. You'll get your first look at Vézelay's incredible hilltop basilica from about 2½ km away. A joyous descent deposits you at the foot of a final **excruciating climb** as you **join Road D951** toward the city atop the hill.

Push your bicycle up Vézelay's steep and often crowded streets to reach the Romanesque wonder known as the Basilique de la Madeleine. Built in the 12th century as a resting place for Mary Magdalene, this hauntingly beautiful church has attracted hordes of pilgrims and tourists for the past 800 years. Although rival cities' claims to possess the holy relics eventually slowed the pilgrim flood, the beauty of the basilica still draws rivers of religious and architectural pilgrims today.

Vézelay's basilica holds a collection of stone carvings you'll never forget, beginning with the amazingly preserved tympanum above the main portal, and moving on to the scores of intricately carved pillars that grace the vast interior. If you're fortunate enough to visit Vézelay's beautiful basilica in the off-season, when ribbons of mist hang on the hilltop and heavenly silence pervades the chilly interior of the church, the time you spend here will be divine.

Hotels in Vézelay are hard to come by in the summer months, but there are two **hostel** options in town. Ask at the **tourist office** on the rue St. Pierre for information and/or directions to the nearby **campground** (down the hill in St. Père).

Vézelay to Semur-en-Auxois: 57 kilometers

Follow signs for **Avallon** as you draw away from Vézelay with **Road D957**. A **steep descent** leads to **St. Père**, then you'll climb to the ridgetop cross at **Fontette**. Enjoy pleasant pedaling to **Pontaubert**, and swing **right** onto a small roadway, just after the **bridge** across the **Cousin River** (it's signed for **Vallée du Cousin**). Scenic cycling along the shaded waterway will bring you in below the hilltop city of Avallon.

Veer **left** for the **center**, then take the **sharp right** that follows, and **ascend very steeply** beneath Avallon's watching ramparts. You'll enter the little city via the **Petite Porte**. From here, a cobblestone street will take you (and your loose fillings) to Avallon's Church of St. Lazare, where two wonderfully carved portals await.

The city **tourist office** is nearby, and the impressive Tour de l'Horloge serves as a gateway to the busy center of Avallon. Thanks to lots of cobblestones, this city is best appreciated without a bicycle. Push it or lock it, take along your valuables, and head out for a stroll. A walk along Avallon's lofty ramparts is especially worthwhile. If you decide to linger overnight, pick up a listing of hotels at the tourist office, or seek out the **campground** a few kilometers away.

To continue your ride toward Semur-en-Auxois, find your way to the main road (**Road N6**) toward the **east**. Veer **left** (still in Avallon) with signs for **Road D957** and **Sauvigny**. Pedal onward to Sauvigny, then turn **right** onto **Road D105** toward **la Cerce**. Avoid a reunion with the harrowing N6 by diving **left** in la Cerce. You can follow **Road D50** all the way to **Guillon** from here, savoring easy cycling through windblown fields, with only occasional cars to break your reverie.

Climb away from Guillon on **Road D11** signed for **Toutry**, a pleasant riverside town with a humble **campground**. Push on to **Epoisses** and pause to admire the city's attractive moated château and its 12th-century church. There's a municipal **campground** here, as well. Continue east from Epoisses, following **Road D954** toward **Semur-en-Auxois**. The cycling is mellow to **Pouligny**, then you'll have rolling hills to contend with for the final 7½ km to Semur's center.

Savor spectacular views of the walled city as you approach, its picturesque skyline studded with towers and the profile of a lofty Gothic church. Cross the looping **Armançon River** on the Pont Joly. This is the place for your photo of Semur! Catch your breath while you snap your pictures, then endure a **stiff climb** toward the city center on quaint (but extremely annoying) cobblestones.

Semur's Church of Notre Dame is a beautiful twin-towered sanctuary covered with cavorting stone creatures and made awesome by a narrow, soaring nave. The **tourist office** is not far from the church, on the place Gustav Gaveau. Ask about hotels, seek directions to the convenient **hostel**, or head for the **campground** 3 km south of town. If you're interested in horse racing, you may want to time your visit to Semur for the final week of May. On May 31, Semur hosts the oldest horse race in France, and a festival-like atmosphere pervades the town for weeks.

Semur-en-Auxois to Dijon: 89 kilometers

The ride from Semur to Dijon is essentially a reversal of the first day (and part of the second day) of this tour route. Leave the city with **Road D970** and pedal to **Villeneuve**. You'll be on familiar ground from here. If you want to venture into some new territory en route to Dijon, use a small-scale map, refer to a good tourist guide, and simply go for it!

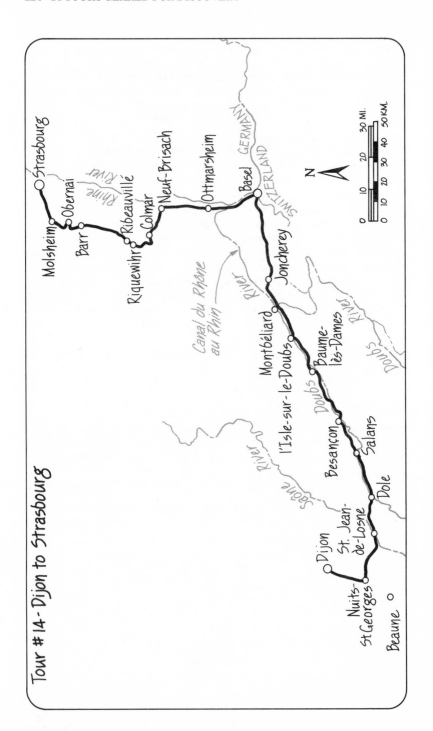

Tour #14 - Dijon to Strasbourg

TOUR NO. 14

A BLEND OF WINES AND CULTURES
Dijon to Strasbourg

Distance: 480 kilometers (298 miles)
Estimated time: 7 riding days
Best time to go: June through September
Terrain: A riverside roll into a hill-heavy finish
Maps: Michelin Nos. 66, 70, and 87
Connecting tour: Tour No. 13

This tour from Dijon to Strasbourg offers an enticing blend of Burgundy and Alsace, two much-loved regions of France. You'll follow the Doubs River beyond Besançon, then ride on toward Basel and a glimpse of Switzerland. As you turn north along the Rhine River, following along the German–French border, you'll exchange French culture for a unique Alsatian blend that displays both German and French influences.

CONNECTIONS. The large city of Dijon is the starting point for this tour. If you arrive by train from Paris, there's an **information desk** at the main station on the west side of town. Several trains per day connect Dijon with Paris, and the ride takes about 2½ hours. Be sure to obtain a city map before heading out into the busy city streets.

You can pedal into Dijon with our Tour No. 13, an attraction-packed loop tucked between Dijon and Paris. Hop onto the loop in Troyes or Sens, then cycle onward to Dijon. The large but infinitely lovely city of Strasbourg marks the route's delightful finish. Be sure to allow yourself enough time to explore this beautiful city of canals and soaring churches, set beside the Rhine River. Those planning to explore a bit of Germany will find Strasbourg an excellent starting point.

INFORMATION. There is a *Green Guide* for *Burgundy* (in English) and one for *Alsace-Lorraine* (in French and German), and they cover much of this tour. Two Prentice-Hall *Insight Guides* also apply to this ride, one for *Burgundy* and one for *Alsace*. Please check our paragraphs on Burgundy in Tour No. 12.

Alsace is a hill-studded land of hiking trails and vineyards, perched on the border between Germany and France. If you know France at all, you'll know right away that Alsace is very different. Despite the people's fierce loyalty to France, their culture is undeniably influenced by their German history.

Campgrounds are as plentiful as wine cellars here, owing to the region's enormous popularity with tourists. And, if you're afraid you might be spoiled after pedaling through delicious Burgundy, don't worry—Alsace is equally famous for its table. Feast on regional specialties like *choucroute garnie* (sauerkraut cooked in wine and studded with chunks of ham) or *tarte à l'oignon* (an onion and cream tart). If you have any room left after consuming these filling dishes (and you must *always* have room for *fromage* in France), sample a chunk of the Münster or Emmenthal cheeses that are so common in this region.

Of course, Alsace is known for its wine, as well. Sip one of the sweet white Gewürtztraminer vintages at the finish of a challenging day of cycling and sightseeing. You may feel there are simply too many good things to taste here—and too many things to see. Perhaps in Alsace more than anywhere, you should ignore our directions whenever you feel inclined—choose a tempting village and spend the afternoon, stretch a one-day ride into two or three. Take things slowly here. You'll be glad you took the time to simply settle back and enjoy.

Dijon to Dole: 70 kilometers

Please refer to the first several paragraphs of the Dijon-to-Beaune section of Tour No. 12 to get you started on your ride today. You'll find background information on Dijon there as well. Our route to Dole deviates from the ride to Beaune, beginning in **Vougeot**. (Those with a particular interest in the wines and architecture of Burgundy may want to continue to Beaune with Tour No. 12, then backtrack about 20 km to regain this route.)

In Vougeot, **cross Road N74** and cycle through **Gilly-lès-Cîteaux**. Keep **right** through Gilly's center, sneaking a look at the village's four-star hotel/château as you pass. Signs for **St. Bernard** lead over the **A31 freeway**, then continue for **Villebichot** with **Road D109C**. Enjoy pleasant cycling past fields and forest as you follow signs for **Cîteaux** to **Road D996**. Turn **right** here to pass the Abbey of Cîteaux, ancient cradle of the Cistercian order. Not much remains of the settlement founded by Saint Bernard in 1114, but the present-day religious community is once again composed of Cistercians.

Veer **left** off D996 just beyond the abbey, following signs for **Bonnencontre** onto the idyllic **Road D12A**. Cycle through the Forêt de Cîteaux en route to Bonnencontre, then swing **left** onto **Road D20** for **St. Jean-de-Losne**. Effortless pedaling will take you past a series of small towns. Keep **right** when the road branches after **Esbarres**, and gain the company of the Saône River as you cruise into St. Jean.

A hopping little port for the tourist-filled barges that ply the Saône,

St. Jean is a lovely village. Marvel at the characteristic tiled roof on the city church, then munch a picnic lunch with barges, fishermen, and swans for company. Cross to the **south side** of the river and enter **Losne**. At the intersection beyond town, veer **left** onto **Road D24** for **Dole**.

Pleasant, easy cycling follows, and you'll have glimpses of the Saône River to **St. Seine-en-Bâche**. Angle **right** to gain **Road D31** signed for **Champvans** and **Dole**. Cross the **A36 freeway** and begin a **long, steady climb** through Champvans, an interesting village that's a great excuse for a rest. More climbing leads to the outskirts of **Dole**, and signs for **tourist information** and **camping** will take you to the place Grévy and the city's **information office**.

Ask here for a listing of hotels, or get directions to the youth **hostel** or the somewhat spendy **campground** just across the Canal du Rhône au Rhin. It's tucked in beside the city sports fields and boasts a fine view of Dole's cathedral by night. Dole has no overwhelming tourist sights, but it's an exceedingly pleasant city for strolling, with a long pedestrian avenue lined with shops and packed with people. Be sure to explore the large covered market adjacent to the cathedral, too.

Dole to Besançon: 55 kilometers

You'll be following the winding course of the Doubs River today, savoring serene cycling and encountering gentle hills along the way. From **Dole's center**, take **Road D244** (signed for **Brevans**) away from town, swinging **right** for **Falletans** to cross the **Doubs River** and continue with D244. Those leaving from the **campground** should simply cross the **Canal du Rhône au Rhin** and go **right** immediately after to gain a paved, canalside road.

Pedal D244 through **Falletans** and push on with signs for **Rochefort-sur-Nenon**. Don't descend into Rochefort. Instead, continue **straight** through **Nenon**, then gain **Road D76** to **Eclans**. Road D76 leads past **Our**, **Etrepigney**, and **Rans** (with an attractive château), then you'll arrive in **Fraisans**. Shop here, if you're in need of lunch supplies, and head out with **Road D228** signed for **Salans**.

As you coast through Salans, watch for a small road to the **right** signed for **Rozet** (spelled "Roset" on map). A gentle climb leads into Rozet, a picturesque village with a château overlooking the Doubs River, then you'll dive **steeply downhill** to cross to the **right bank** of the Doubs. (Those with an interest in prehistoric caves may want to make the slight detour to the nearby Grottes d'Osselle.)

Follow **Road D13** beside the river to **Routelle**, then angle **left** onto **Road D106** toward **Grandfontaine**. Climb through scenic farmland to reach the town, then watch for a sign to the **right** for **Montferrand** (still on D106). Go **right** here, then keep **left** when the road branches just afterward. You'll **descend steeply** to pass a handsome church, then stay with the roller-coaster route signed for **la Marne**.

Regain the banks of the **Doubs River**, and swing **left** to cycle through **Avanne**. Stay with the **tiny, riverside road** (which was thronged with cyclists and picnickers on the sunny Sunday we traveled through) all the way to **Velotte**. From Velotte, a small road continues along the **right bank** of the Doubs (most maps don't show it). To find the route, descend through Velotte and grab the **left turn** just before the city's **church**.

Views of Vauban's magnificent fortress unfold as you pedal into **Besançon**, and you'll be awed by the beauty of the setting. The writhing Doubs River cuts a strategic loop into the hills of France's Jura here, and the citadel commands the valley and the city spread below. Seek out Besançon's **tourist office** near the Pont de la République for information on sights and/or help with lodgings. Besançon is big and busy and best seen without a bicycle.

Unfortunately, the **campground** is inconvenient for sightseeing (it's in Chalezeule, northeast of the city), so you'll probably want to get a room. If you visit between July and September, try snagging an inexpensive dorm bed from the university's extensive offerings. Once you're settled in, climb the hill to reach Besançon's cathedral and the base of the citadel. Explore the dark interior of the 18th-century Cathédrale St. Jean, then check out the museums and buildings within the stout walls of the *Citadelle*, built by France's most famous military architect in 1674.

Besançon to l'Isle-sur-le-Doubs: 65 kilometers

Leave Besançon with the uncomfortably busy **Road N57** signed for **Lausanne**. You'll pass through a short **tunnel** on the edge of the city core. Take a road to the **left** immediately after. It's signed for **Chalèze**. Enchanting riverside cycling will color your day from here. If you're pedaling on a sunny weekend afternoon, you may contend with a bit of traffic, but lovely scenery and pastoral surroundings will envelop you as you ride.

Look for the rounded peaks of the French Jura jutting skyward as you work your way northeast. The river valley narrows and the green hillsides gain steepness as you probe deeper into the mounded hills. Savor easy cycling to **Chalèze**, with a brightly tiled church belfry, then push on for **Arcier**, enduring a stretch of steady climbing along the way. In **Vaire-Arcier**, swing **left** for **Besançon**, and descend to cross the **Doubs**.

You'll hit **Road D266** on the other side. Go **right** to ride for **Deluz**, and pedal on along the **right bank** of the river. Wonderful, level cycling leads to Deluz, with another cheerful church belfry. Ride to

Laissey next, then stay with signs for the **tourist route** to **Baume-lès-Dames**. A small, **riverside road** leads through **Douvot** and **Ougney**, then you'll cross the **Doubs** and pick up a few more hills. Climb through the quiet village of **Esnans**, its buildings creaking with age as you puff past.

Pedal onward to reach another **bridge** across the Doubs. You can cross the river to enter **Baume-lès-Dames**, named for a Benedictine abbey founded in 763. You'll find hotels and shopping here, but the river is the big attraction. The little city's **campground** is 1 km out of town, just off Road N83 and clinging to the right bank of the Doubs. It's noisy, crowded, and overrun with kayakers, swimmers, and assorted river rats.

From Baume-lès-Dames, recross to the **left bank** of the Doubs and pedal the roadway signed for **Pont-lès-Moulins.** When this road begins to leave the river, watch for a **paved riverside route** continuing on. Follow this fisherman's/picnicker's route to **Hyevre-Magny**, where a bridge crosses the Doubs from N83. Stay on the **left bank**, and join the tiny **Road D307** to climb along the hillside toward **Roche-lès-Clerval**.

Savor picturesque cycling with plunging vistas to the Doubs, then descend to **Clerval** and its ruined castle. Go **right** on the truck-plagued **N83** to ride toward **l'Isle-sur-le-Doubs**. Effortless, fast, but much-too-busy riding leads to **Rang**, then struggle onward to **l'Isle**. You'll have a **long descent** into this pretty city, where a **campground** and hotels await.

L'Isle-sur-le-Doubs to Basel: 98 kilometers

Afraid we have some bad news for you today—after the lovely dose of cycling between Besançon and l'Isle, there's not much to look forward to on the long ride to Basel. Big towns and heavy traffic plague the route, and the beauty of the French Jura can't work enough magic to make the day a pleasant one. Grit through it and take heart—you have the exquisite Alsace region ahead.

Leave l'Isle with the small road signed for **Blussans,** then angle **left** in Blussans to take **Road D297** through **Colombier-Châtelot**. The road branches just past town. Keep **left** for **Colombier-Fontaine**. Go **left** again in Colombier-Fontaine, then swing **right** for **Etouvans**. Just beyond Etouvans, join **Road D126** toward **Audincourt**.

Traffic is increasingly unpleasant as you enter the snarling development around Montbéliard/Audincourt. Please ride with caution. Pedal to a **roundabout** in **Voujeaucourt**, and go **left** here for **Montbéliard**. Cross the **Doubs River** and stay with the main road (**Road D438**) along the **southeast side** of the **Canal du Rhône au Rhin**.

You'll pass **under a bridge** crossing the canal, then angle **left** to keep the water's company.

Cycle over the **train tracks** and swing **left** for **Exincourt**. Watch for a sprawling Peugeot factory on the left as you cross over the **freeway**, then struggle through Exincourt and on to **Etupes**. Signs for **Fesches-le-Châtel** will lead you to the **left** with **Road D121E** from here. If your knuckles aren't already white against your handlebars, they will be after you've weathered this traffic-heavy secondary road for a while.

The chaos begins to ease after Fesches. Continue on for **Morvillars**, enduring a roller-coaster ride through French suburbia. Yuck! At Morvillars, turn **right** on **Road N19** for **Grandvillars** and **Delle**. If you need a break or it's late in your day, there's a wonderfully secluded **campground** a few kilometers from **Joncherey** (it's well signed from the road). Pedal N19 through Joncherey, then veer **left** onto **Road D463** signed for **Basel** (French signs sometimes spell it **Bâle**).

Pleasant pastoral scenery will cheer you as you press on with D463, encountering rolling hills and lots of fields and forests. Note the changes in architecture as you draw nearer to the Swiss border. Germanic influences begin to show themselves in the half-timbered buildings and the wooden houses decorated with overflowing windowboxes. Work through a **long climb** after **Seppois-le-Haut**, then revel in a quick descent through **Bisel**.

A gemlike Romanesque church will invite you off the road in **Feldbach**, then the hills increase from here, as you ride on with D463. Your secondary route feeds into the growling main road (**Road D473**) at **Folgensbourg**, and you'll continue with signs for **Basel** and **St. Louis** as vistas of the Rhine Valley unfold. A **long, gentle descent** will consume kilometers with ravenous rapidity. The surface is excellent and the traffic is endurable. Join **Road D419** just before **Hésingue**.

Hésingue melts into the sprawling border city of **St. Louis**. You'll reach a junction in St. Louis signed for **Basel (car route)** to the **right** and **Basel (truck route)** going **straight**. If you're bound for Basel's center, go right here. If you plan to camp before entering the city, go straight instead. (To find the **campground**, pedal straight into the center of St. Louis and stay with signs for Huningue. Pedal under the train tracks, then angle left for Lörrach and Allemagne [Germany] when the road branches. Small camping signs lead to a crowded but adequate campground on the banks of the Rhine River. It's a brief bus trip or a 6-km ride into Basel's center from here.)

Although it's big and busy, the Swiss city of Basel is delightfully biker friendly. You'll be amazed by the number of cyclists you'll see in Basel's center. Even so, it's best to stow your bike and view the town on foot. Tidy streets, lovely old buildings, scores of fountains, and a gorgeous red cathedral topped by an exuberant tiled roof all combine to make Basel a treat.

Seek out the **tourist office** at Blumenrain 2, on the river, for help with lodgings (don't forget you'll need to exchange French *francs* for their Swiss counterparts if you're spending any money here). Then walk to the cathedral plaza for an enchanting vista of the Rhine River and its steady flow of ships and barges. Wander the pedestrian streets in the city core, and climb its old stairways to admire wooden buildings from a host of angles. Basel boasts a renowned fine arts museum (Kunstmuseum) and a world-famous zoo (Zoologischer Garten), as well. You won't ever lack for entertainment here. When all your sightseeing has fired up an international appetite, sample Swiss specialties like fondue, sausages, or the delicious *leckerli* (honey spice bread) that's Basel's specialty.

Basel to Colmar: 77 kilometers

Leave Basel with the road signed for **Huningue**, cycling through the city's sprawling port area to reach the French town on the **left bank** of the Rhine. In Huningue, swing **right** for **Lörrach** and **Allemagne**, then arrive at another junction where the road to the right crosses the Rhine River. Continue **straight** instead, pedaling northward toward **Village-Neuf**. (If you're leaving from the campground at Huningue, return to the main road through town, and ride for Lörrach and Allemagne. Continue straight at the subsequent junction to pedal toward Village-Neuf.)

Cycle a peaceful roadway along the **left bank** of the river, stealing glimpses of the water through an almost constant wall of trees and vegetation. Avoid signed lefts for Village-Neuf and Rosenau—simply **parallel the Rhine** through a sprawling nature reserve. Your road branches near a large power plant, with the left branch signed for Kembs. Continue **straight** for **Chalampé** instead, and continue with your quiet riverside route. (A scenic, secluded, but unpaved roadway closer to the Rhine shoreline is an option for those on mountain bikes. It's slow going, however, as it comes and goes.)

The route merges with **Road D468** just before **Niffer**. Despite the increased road size, traffic is surprisingly mellow as you continue north to **Ottmarsheim**, with views across the Rhine to the rounded hills of Germany's Black Forest. Ottmarsheim is a pleasant village, centered around an 11th-century church with a fortified clock tower. Follow signs for **Neuf-Brisach** from here. Cycling is flat and effortless on D468, and the Vosges Mountains begin to pop out of the scenery to the west as you continue.

Reach a junction with the busy **Road N415** just before Neuf-

Brisach. Continue **straight** toward the town **center**, and pierce the city core through a gap in the massive encircling walls. Neuf-Brisach wears the stamp of the prolific French fort builder Vauban. The little city's role as a Rhine-crossing sentinel earned it an octagonal fortification in 1699, and it's a pleasant place to gather a picnic and feast among the peaceful stones.

Leave Neuf-Brisach to the northwest, and join the main road (**Road N415**) toward **Colmar** from here. Traffic is steady and unpleasant, and you'll gladly make your escape on the far side of **Wolfgantzen**, veering **left** onto **Road D1** signed for **Appenwihr** and **Ste. Croix**. Enjoy much quieter cycling to Appenwihr, then swing **right** onto **Road D13** to pedal through **Sundhoffen** and on to **Colmar**. (To find Colmar's convenient **campground**, dive off D13 for Horbourg, then angle left onto N415 to reach the campsites spread beside the Ill River.)

Colmar is a joy to behold. The city escaped extensive damage during World War II (other towns in the region weren't so fortunate), and the old core is a lovely blend of half-timbered buildings, narrow streets, crimson flowers, and camera-toting tourists. Get a free map of town and help with lodgings at the centrally located **tourist office** across from the Unterlinden Museum (there's a **youth hostel** in town), then set out on foot to explore the city.

Besides the obvious delights that spring up everywhere in this tidy, Germanic town, you'll find hidden treasure in the Unterlinden Museum and the Église des Dominicains. But Colmar's byways, canals, and buildings are the real attraction. If you've ever been to Germany, you'll recognize the scene—immaculate streets, brightly painted houses, and overloaded windowboxes. Even the bakeries' offerings taste different. If you visit Colmar during the Alsatian Wine Festival in early August or the Sauerkraut Festival (*Jours Choucroute*) in September, you'll have the opportunity to sample even more of the local "flavor."

Colmar to Barr: 60 kilometers

Load your camera and lose your sense of time in preparation for your ride today. You'll experience a visual overload of lovely towns, beautiful buildings, hilltop castle ruins, and mist-shrouded vineyards. A host of opportunities for wine tasting await you, or you can simply satiate your senses instead. We've selected a breaking point in the small city of Barr, simply because that's where we ran out of time and into a nice campground, but this ride offers an abundance of tempting villages that make great overnight stops for weary cyclists. Divide your Colmar-to-Strasbourg trek however you wish. But no matter what you do, don't hurry through—this route is much too grand for that.

A Dutch tour group pauses in a rain-sprinkled Alsatian square to admire an American toddler in a bike trailer.

Stop in at Colmar's **tourist office** before you leave the city, and pick up the free pamphlet entitled "The Wine Route of Alsace." We've described a suggested cycling itinerary between here and Strasbourg, but you may want to select some side trips of your own. One note of warning—don't try this ride in late August or September, unless you can put up with total tourist mayhem, both on the road and off.

Find Colmar's **Church of St. Joseph** (west side of city center) on your town map, and set out from there. Get on the **rue du Logelbach** to cycle through the suburban community of **Logelbach**. Hit a junction and go **left** for **Colmar**, then swing **right** immediately after to gain **Road D11** signed for **Turckheim**. Cross the **Fecht River** to enter Turckheim, a lovely gate-guarded town renowned for its white wine. You can begin your Alsatian stork vigil here, as Turckheim's skyline is studded with storks' nests.

From Turckheim, stay on the **north bank** of the Fecht River to cycle on to **Ingersheim**, then join **Road N415** toward **Ammerschwihr** and **Kaysersberg**. Steady traffic leads to Kaysersberg, overlooked by a ruined castle. Be sure to pause at the lovely square beside the city church. You'll rattle in and out of most of the villages today, as cobblestones have been left intact to preserve the medieval atmosphere in the town centers. Take **Road D28** to **Kientzheim** as you continue from Kaysersberg. This quiet little town sports a feisty image on its *Untertor* (Lower Gate)—a scowling visage leering at a rival town.

Little-visited Kientzheim offers an opportunity to make a brief escape from the tourist mania that plagues many of the villages in this region. Get a feel for the essence of Alsace by taking the **tiny roadway** leaving from the **old well** in the heart of town, and head into the vine-covered hills that form the fabric of the region's life and character. Pedal a silent road signed by lonely crucifixes (and hard-to-spot signs for **Riquewihr**), and **climb steeply** and steadily for about 1½ km.

Be sure to glance behind you for wonderful views over the valley below. Crest the ridge and descend into Riquewihr. This town is a jewel, albeit a much-polished one. It's easy to see why tourists mob the place. You'll enter via an upper gate, complete with drawbridge, then explore the colorful upper town, ringed by 16th-century walls. Well-kept houses and trinket-packed shops complete the picture. Gather a picnic at a local grocery, then descend toward **Ribeauvillé**. (You'll be following the signed *route du Vin* for portions of the ride today.)

Ribeauvillé is another sparkling little wine village, sprinkled with fine old houses and overlooked by three castles. You might want to make the (uphill) sidetrip to Hunawihr's fortified church from here. Stay with **Road D1Bis** past **Bergheim**, **St. Hippolyte**, and **Kintzheim**, each with attractions of its own. Pedal on to **Châtenois** (now on **Road D35**), and continue **straight** across the main road (Road N59). Signs for **Scherwiller** and **Dambach-la-Ville** lead on.

The walled village of Dambach is a treat. Although not quite as "perfect" as Ribeauvillé and Riquewihr, the town has a more lived-in feel to it, and its charms are much less trampled. There's a **campground** there, if you're running late. Mellow cycling follows, and you'll weave your way through vineyards and gentle hills en route to **Barr.**

Barr boasts a wonderfully situated **campground** (well signed from the center), a handful of hotels, and shopping. Be sure to explore Barr's beautiful town square, sprawled before a somewhat flashy *Hôtel de Ville*. The fountain in the square sparkles with fat goldfish. You'll be fat, too, if you sample an assortment of the sweets from each of the *pâtisseries* in the little town.

Barr to Strasbourg: 55 kilometers

Leave Barr with **Road D35** toward **Heiligenstein**. A brief climb into this tiny wine village yields a pleasant view of vineyards and the

Rhine. Cycle onward toward **Ottrott** (a short detour takes you into this pleasant town), then gain the road leading east for **Obernai.** Cycle into Obernai's busy **center**, and feast your senses on this lovely medieval city. Obernai seems to drip with atmosphere and run with wine. Unfortunately, it literally flows with tourists.

Check out the city's six-bucket well (you'll recognize it from the postcards) and ogle its Kodak-sponsored town square. Fight your way through the countless camera-clicking tour groups to find the city **tourist office** tucked inside its 16th-century tower. There's a fancy **campground** in Obernai, if you're considering a longer visit. Leave the city with the quiet **Road D322** toward **Boersch**, then swing **right** onto **D35** for **Rosheim**.

Rosheim holds an attractive main street flanked by gate towers. Look for the town's serene Romanesque church hiding a bevy of lively stone sculptures. Take D35 to its intersection with the much busier **Road D422**, and go **left** to cycle north to **Molsheim**. Molsheim is a big and busy city, ruled by a grand Jesuit church. Signs for the **center** lead to the sprawling town plaza and a surprisingly serious-looking *Hôtel de Ville*.

Retrace your route away from the center, cross the **Bruche River**, then veer **left** into Molsheim's **industrial zone**. Stay to the **right** at the subsequent **Y intersection**, keeping the large auto manufacturing plant on your left. You'll run into **Road D127** next. Turn **left** here, cross the **train tracks**, then go **right** onto **Road D93**. Hit a **T** and veer **left** for **Ernolsheim**. Cycle a short distance to re-cross the **Bruche**, and go **right** immediately after to gain a **canalside bike route**.

The silent, scenic bike path yields wonderful pedaling as you fly along a flat, smoothly surfaced ribbon of asphalt. Occasional fishermen, no automobiles, and not a (legal) moped to be seen—what more can a cyclist ask? You'll enter the normally hectic suburbs of one of France's largest cities without inhaling a single blast of diesel exhaust. Emerge onto **Road D392**, signed as the **route de Schirmeck**. (If you spot the bus stop marked **Bruche**, you're there.) Go left here to pick up signs for Strasbourg's **campground** and **youth hostel.** Both are excellent accommodations with convenient bus access to the city.

Those cycling directly into Strasbourg in quest of a hotel bed or a train trip back to Paris can stay with the bike path all the way into the city center. Head for the **tourist office** at the main train station for help with lodgings, a map of town, and/or information on Strasbourg's myriad attractions. Even though it's a vast city, Strasbourg is best enjoyed on foot. Stroll beside scenic canals, prowl shop-packed pedestrian avenues, and linger on ancient bridges. When your pegs get weary, simply park them at a streetside café (don't forget to feed the meter).

Strasbourg's cathedral climb boasts a dizzying view of the city.

Perhaps Strasbourg's greatest triumph is its glorious cathedral, soaring heavenward with a sky-piercing spire. Don't miss a climb to the cathedral's heights. The view straight down to the plaza below will suck the air right out of you (if you have any air left after ascending all those stairs). Return to ground level and let the stirring stone sculptures inside the cathedral lift you heavenward again. Then emerge to admire the city's wealth of outstanding architecture, to wander the byways of *la Petite France*, or to seek out one of Strasbourg's handful of noteworthy museums.

If you're cycling on from here, the charms and challenges of Germany's Black Forest are just across the Rhine. Or pedal northwest into the regions of Lorraine and Champagne, hook up with our Tour No. 4 from Brussels to Versailles, and ride back to Paris and its airports with that route. Those of you finishing your cycling in Strasbourg can make train connections to Paris and a host of other major European cities from the infinitely busy central train station on the west side of the city.

INDEX